MW00658720

The Future of the Church

The Future of the Church

HANS SCHWARZ

CASCADE *Books* • Eugene, Oregon

THE FUTURE OF THE CHURCH

Copyright © 2024 Hans Schwarz. All rights reserved. Except for brief quotations in critical publications or reviews, no part of this book may be reproduced in any manner without prior written permission from the publisher. Write: Permissions, Wipf and Stock Publishers, 199 W. 8th Ave., Suite 3, Eugene, OR 97401.

Cascade Books
An Imprint of Wipf and Stock Publishers
199 W. 8th Ave., Suite 3
Eugene, OR 97401

www.wipfandstock.com

PAPERBACK ISBN: 978-1-6667-5870-2
HARDCOVER ISBN: 978-1-6667-5871-9
EBOOK ISBN: 978-1-6667-5872-6

Cataloguing-in-Publication data:

Names: Schwarz, Hans, author.

Title: The future of the church / Hans Schwarz.

Description: Eugene, OR: Cascade Books, 2024 | Includes bibliographical references and index.

Identifiers: ISBN 978-1-6667-5870-2 (paperback) | ISBN 978-1-6667-5871-9 (hardcover) | ISBN 978-1-6667-5872-6 (ebook)

Subjects: LCSH: Church. | Church history. | Church's future.

Classification: BV600.2 S416 2024 (paperback) | BV600.2 (ebook)

01/19/24

Scripture quotations are from the New Revised Standard Version Bible, copyright © 1989 National Council of the Churches of Christ in the United States of America. Used by permission. All rights reserved worldwide.

Contents

Preface

THE FRENCH EMPEROR NAPOLEON (1769–1821) is said to have been in a conversation with Cardinal Ercole Consalvi (1757–1824), the secretary of state of Pope Pius VII. In the course of the conversation the cardinal got more and more on Napoleon's nerves. Finally, the emperor told the cardinal: "Your eminence, don't you know that with a stroke of my pen I could wipe out the church." The cardinal replied: "Your imperial highness, do not overestimate yourself. If we clergy have failed to destroy the church in 1,800 years, do you really think that you will be able to do it?" Yes, the future of the church more than once looked bleak and especially its functionaries did not live up to their tasks. Each time, however, the church renewed itself and continued its mission. It is our fervent hope that this will also be the case in the present. But how should it happen?

When we look at the present scene, things do not look bright for the church. We live in an aging society in which younger people have been brought up with a consumer attitude and this consumer attitude does not stop at the church doors. They ask what is in it for them and if they do not find something worthwhile in the church and its programs, they turn on their heels and leave, and are never seen in the church again. Moreover, the church itself is riddled with scandals, be it sexual abuse or financial misappropriation. This leads to a loss of trust in the church, which is very difficult to regain. We should also not forget that we live in a secular society in which individualism runs contrary to the communal aspect of the church. While religiosity has not vanished, the Christian faith is perceived by many as an "old time religion" whose tenets have lost their luster.

Though the future of the church does not look promising, we should not give up on it too quickly. I am convinced that the church has something to offer which the world needs, which the world does not have. I will emphasize this uniqueness of the church in the following pages and attempt to give some hints as to how the church can face the future with confidence.

This text allowed me to update some items which I wrote forty years ago in my book *The Christian Church* (Minneapolis: Augsburg, 1982), without going too deeply into history since my emphasis in this book is on the present church and its promise.

Again, I thank my wife, Hildegard, for putting up with a husband who, according to her estimate, spends too much time in his study. She has put up with this remarkably well. My thanks also go to Andrea Bauer, the present secretary of my former chair, who helped with various tasks in compiling these pages, and above all, Dr. Terry Dohm, my former doctoral student and now a professor in his own right, who improved both style and contents.

Abbreviations

ABD	*Anchor Bible Dictionary*. Edited by David Noel Freedman. 6 vols. New York: Doubleday, 1992.
ANFa	*The Ante-Nicene Fathers*. Edited by Alexander Roberts and James Donaldson. 1885–87. 10 vols. Repr., Peabody, MA: Hendrickson, 1994.
BC	*The Book of Concord: The Confessions of the Evangelical Lutheran Church*. Edited by Robert Kolb and Timothy J. Wengert. Minneapolis: Fortress, 2000.
CD	Barth, Karl. *Church Dogmatics*. Edited by Geoffrey W. Bromiley and Thomas F. Torrance. Translated by Geoffrey W. Bromiley. Edinburgh: T. & T. Clark, 1936–62.
DC	Denzinger, Heinrich. *Compendium of Creeds, Definitions, and Declarations on Matters of Faith and Morals*. Edited by Peter Hünermann. 43rd ed. San Francisco: Ignatius, 2012.
DVC	*The Documents of Vatican II*. Walter M. Abbott, gen. ed. New York: Guild, 1966.
ELW	*Evangelical Lutheran Worship*. Minneapolis: Augsburg Fortress, 2006.
FaCh	*Fathers of the Church: A New Translation*. Roy Joseph Deferrari, editorial director. 127 vols. Washington, DC: Catholic University of American, 1947–2013.
LW	*Luther's Works* [American ed.]. Jaroslav Pelican et al., gen. ed. 55ff. vols. St. Louis: Concordia; Philadelphia: Fortress, 1955–.
NIB	*The New Interpreter's Bible*. Edited by Leander E. Keck. 12 vols. Nashville: Abingdon, 1994–2004.

NPNFa FS	*The Nicene and Post-Nicene Fathers.* First Series. Edited by Philip Schaff. 14 vols. Grand Rapids: Eerdmans, 1979.
NPNFa SS	*The Nicene and Post-Nicene Fathers.* Second Series. Edited by Philip Schaff and Henry Wace. 14 vols. Grand Rapids: Eerdmans, 1979.
SM	*Sacramentum Mundi.* Edited by Karl Rahner et al. 6 vols. New York: Herder and Herder, 1968–70.
TDOT	*Theological Dictionary of the Old Testament.* 15 vols. Edited by G. Johannes Botterweck, Helmut Ringgren, and Heinz-Josef Fabry. Translated by John T. Willis et al. Grand Rapids: Eerdmans, 1977–2012.
WA	*D. Martin Luthers Werke: Kritische Gesamtausgabe.* 120 vols. Edited by J. K. F. Knaake et al. Weimar: Hermann Böhlaus Nachfolger, 1883–2009.

Introduction

When I was teaching at Trinity Lutheran Seminary in Columbus, Ohio, in the 1970s, Gene Brand, my former colleague there, was working with the Inter-Lutheran Commission on Worship in New York. He was project director for the preparation of the *Lutheran Book of Worship* (1978). At one of our meetings in New York he said, "Within twenty years there will be no congregations left here, because people are so exhausted with their jobs that they do not want to be involved with the church once they return home." As we all know, this prediction has not come true. But it indicated a grave tension between the (work) world and involvement in the church, which has not lessened since then.

Since the church is a worldwide phenomenon, in Africa as well as in Europe, Asia, and in the Americas, it varies greatly in its religiosity and confessional cohesion, depending on the respective region. In the Roman Catholic Church in Germany, for instance, priests are in short supply. Therefore, it draws on India and Africa, where there are still a good number of priests. Just twenty years ago many Roman Catholic priests in Germany came from Poland. But this resource gradually dried up as the Polish population has become increasingly secular. Similarly, while church membership in Europe is steadily decreasing, in Africa the number of Christians is outpacing the increase in the population. New Christian congregations are emerging in the countries in the Mekong Delta in Asia, and a new Lutheran church has been established in Zaire. When I asked a mission expert how this Lutheran church in Zaire came into being, he told me that the influence of Lutheran radio programs had kindled the flame. In the 1960s the Evangelical Lutheran Church of Zaire, now the Evangelical Lutheran Church in Congo, was founded by Congolese laypersons. Several of them received a theological education from the neighboring Evangelical Lutheran Church in Tanzania. In 1980 the church was officially recognized by the government and in 2003 it had five dioceses with more than 100,000 members in almost all provinces of the Congo. With the unstable political situation, however, exact numbers of church membership are difficult to obtain.

Christians outside the Western hemisphere are not timid about mission. When the government in Malaysia forbade Christians to evangelize among the Malay population, the bishop of the Lutheran Church in Malaysia, which is largely of Chinese stock, declared that this was no problem. He told his flock: "There are plenty of unchurched Chinese in our country. So we still have a lot of work ahead of us." This mission-minded mentality is rarely found in Western countries. In the West, mission has the connotation of political and religious imperialism. In many countries in which the Orthodox Church has a distinct majority, such as Russia, Greece, and Armenia, other denominations are often regarded as sects that have no right to intrude. Especially in Russia, there is a strong alliance between the Orthodox Church and the state, from which both benefit. Yet when one compares the official number of the people who belong to the Orthodox Church with the number of people who attend church at high festivals, the numbers differ greatly. Though most people in Russia claim that they belong to the Orthodox Church, only a fraction actually participate in its religious life.

In Western countries, such as Germany and the USA, church membership is steadily declining and so is church attendance. Since situations vary so much from one country to another and from one denomination to another, I will focus in this first situational chapter primarily on the Lutheran Church in the USA and to a lesser extent on the Protestant church(es) in Germany. Yet our focus is not on the demise of the church but on its future, if there is one. Having shown the present situation, I will then focus on the essential elements of the church. It is my conviction that the church can offer something to the world that the world is unable to provide for itself. In the last section I will point out in which direction(s) I believe the activities of the church should be extended so that both the world and the church will have a mutually beneficial future.

PART 1

The Church in Jeopardy

As previously mentioned, the present state of the church is disconcerting. More and more people have little appreciation or respect for the church, especially in the West. In other parts of the world Christians belong to the most persecuted segments of society and their activities are severely restricted. For instance, there are more church-burnings than mosque-burnings, and more Christians are accused by Muslims of blasphemy than vice versa. But here we do not want to deal with interreligious conflict, important as it is; instead, our purpose is to inquire about the future of the church, primarily in its Western context.

1. THE PRESENT STATE OF THE CHURCH

When I started teaching at Trinity Lutheran Seminary in Columbus, Ohio, in 1967, I often heard the comment, "The German church is dead." Coming from Germany, I was surprised about this statement, since especially at that time many young people in Germany decided to study for the ministry. At one time there were more students studying for the Protestant ministry in Germany than there were Protestant pastors. Of course, church attendance had never been a strong point for Protestants in Germany. Since at that time it was still obligatory for Roman Catholics to attend Sunday Mass, many Protestants demonstrated that they were different by not attending Sunday morning worship. But the church was and still is present in the public in a variety of ways and means. Sunday morning church services are broadcast on public radio and on TV. Moreover, the Protestant and Roman Catholic churches taken together are, next to public service agencies such as city halls, internal revenue service, etc., the largest employer in Germany. Approximately 1.3 million people work for the churches in a variety of ways. Hospitals, private schools, kindergartens, and retirement homes are owned and run by the churches. They offer a multitude of services for people in need, for debt reduction, drug addiction, marital problems, etc. Additionally, every church member pays a church tax as a surcharge to the income tax. In this way people are connected to the church even if they enter the church building only three times in their life—for baptism, marriage, and a funeral. Therefore, the claim that the German church is dead is simply not true. Yet times have changed.

The churches in Germany and their service organizations provide jobs for more people than such large companies as BMW or VW. The diaconal engagement of the churches is very much appreciated by the general public and this has not waned over the years. Yet church affiliation has drastically changed. A few years ago, the pastor of the congregation to which I belong told us in a church council meeting that the parents of several youth who were eligible for confirmation class had not responded to the letter asking them to register. When I asked what will happen to these kids, the pastor answered, "They will probably drop out of the church." He continued, "Quite often when young people receive their first paycheck and notice the deduction for church tax, they ask that their name to be taken off of the church register to save that money." Yet pastors and their congregations are not too worried, since the pastors' salaries and most of the congregational budgets are allocated by church headquarters. They receive the church tax that is collected by the government and handed over to the church. The government charges a fee for this service. But for the church it is cheaper and more reliable than setting up its own collection agency. To be sure, allegiance to the church has considerably diminished today. After World War II virtually the whole German population, even in Communist East Germany, belonged either to the Roman Catholic or to the Protestant church. The Protestant church, whether Lutheran, Reformed, or United, was and still is basically mainline. Conservative denominations such as Baptists, Pentecostals, or Mennonites make up only a small minority at less than 5 percent of the population. In the past, being a member of the Protestant church or the Roman Catholic Church was the order of the day. But today this is no longer the case.

Since the late 1960s, things have drastically changed in Germany. Already before that Germany, the *Wirtschaftswunder* or the so-called German economic miracle attracted migrant workers from Italy, Spain, and Greece. While the latter were Orthodox, the Protestant churches cared for them, and those from Italy and Spain were largely Roman Catholic and were helped to adjust to their new host country by the Roman Catholic Church. Then came migrant workers from Turkey, who were exclusively Muslim and outside of the Christian fold. The student unrest connected to the Vietnam War and the rise of the Green party, which was initially strictly antiestablishment, called for a "new society" that was to be nonintegrated and multicultural. Then in 1990 came the reunification of Germany. For the East Germans, the majority of whom were still church members, the church tax was something new. Once they realized that by renouncing church membership they did not have to pay the church tax, they quit the church in large numbers and the church in East Germany soon attained a minority status. In Wittenberg, for example, where Martin Luther (1483–1546) lived and worked for most of his life, only 13 percent of the population claim church membership. In East Germany it was quickly forgotten that during the Communist regime it was only the church which had provided a haven of freedom. It was even forgotten that the church was also the starting point for the first demonstrations that would eventually lead to the fall of the Communist regime in East Germany.

While in 1956 96 percent of the German population claimed church membership, in 2019 it had declined to 52 percent. During the last thirty years more than 300,000 persons annually left the Roman Catholic and the Protestant churches. In 2020 the number of those who left the church was more than 440,000.[1] Since Germany has an aging population, one must also consider that each year more church members have died than young ones were baptized. In 2018 176,000 were baptized into the Protestant church whereas 271,000 church members were buried. Just three years later (2021) 115,00 were baptized and 360,000 were buried, while 280,000 had left the Protestant church.[2] When the German value-added tax was increased in 1968 the number of people who left the church increased immediately. If one has little affiliation with the church, church tax becomes an extra burden that can easily be lifted by rescinding one's church membership. A representative survey showed in 2021 that 28 percent of the Germans who belong to the Protestant or Roman Catholic churches contemplate leaving the church. Of those who are between twenty-five to thirty-four years of age, as many as 40 percent consider leaving.[3] The church, however, is not the only institution which is losing members. Young people are no longer

1. "Der Mitgliederschwund der Kirchen hält an," in *Idea* (July 19, 2021), 6.

2. "EKD-Gliedkirchen: Weniger als 20 Millionen Mitglieder," in *Idea* (March 16, 2022), 6.

3. "Großkirchen: Jedes vierte Mitglied erwägt Austritt," in *Idea* (March 31, 2021), 8.

permanently loyal to social units like older people were. They join and leave sports clubs and political parties depending on their shifting preferences and whether they feel they can gain something from remaining a part of these social units. There is a significant difference between generations.[4] While those above forty often mention that they leave the church because they are annoyed about a concrete issue, for instance a bishop's statement concerning women or a political statement by a church official, it is different with the younger generation. They often do not even care about the church and therefore ask whether the benefits they derive from church membership are commensurate with the church tax they pay. This means there is a decided consumer mentality by which young people especially ask what benefit they receive by showing allegiance to persons and institutions. This is also true in general for the services that the churches offer their members. The rate of baptisms, church weddings, and church funerals is continuously decreasing. For many young couples, if marriage is contemplated at all, they are married at city hall, and for funerals, and also for weddings, they increasingly select secular presiders rather than a minister or priest.

But one should not be too hard on the younger generation and on those who leave the church. People feel that they do not find in the church what makes their lives meaningful. In other words, the church becomes less and less relevant for their own lives. The core message of the Christian faith is no longer proclaimed loudly and clearly. Instead, moral appeals and ethical statements made by the church often duplicate concerns in certain secular movements outside the church.[5]

What does this continuous exodus mean for the church in Germany? In certain regions, especially in the northern part of Germany, which is predominantly Protestant, and in the Roman Catholic Rhineland, church buildings are closed, and several congregations are joined together to form a larger one. This is most often done for financial reasons but also because there are fewer and fewer pastors and priests. Presently, finances in many Protestant and Roman Catholic areas are not yet a severe problem. But at the rate things are going, it can be projected that the churches will be financially hurting within the next twenty years. The Evangelical Lutheran Church in Bavaria, for instance, is making provisions to reduce its budget by 20 percent within the next ten years. In virtually all larger cities the percentage of the population which claims church membership has dropped to below 50 percent. In the inner cities nine out of ten school children are

4. For the following see, Bingener, ". . . Jüngere," 4.

5. Cf. statements from major German newspapers as cited by *Idea* (July 19, 2021), 7.

immigrant children, and virtually all of them are of the Muslim faith. In Germany, Christians are fast becoming a minority.

Yet the churches in Germany are still well off compared to churches in the Netherlands and in Sweden, just to name two neighboring countries. In the Netherlands and in Sweden there are no longer theological faculties at state universities, just departments of theology and religion. Since religion is a regular subject in public schools in Germany, the state maintains theological faculties so that teachers who will teach religious instruction will receive a proper education. Since pastors and priests quite often teach religious instruction in schools, their education profits from this arrangement. For the most part there is a good relationship between the churches and the government, but this is because both realize that each benefits from the other. Yet during the recent COVID-19 pandemic the question was raised in Germany whether the churches are *systemrelevant*, meaning "relevant for the system." During the high point of the pandemic, churches were closed for worship and devotions. The same was true for synagogues and mosques. In contrast to railway stations and hospitals, places of worship were not deemed relevant for the system and therefore could be closed for a certain time. The former presiding bishop of the Protestant Church in Germany, Wolfgang Huber (b. 1942), agreed with this but added that while the church is not relevant for the system, it is *existenzrelevant*, meaning "it is relevant for human existence."[6] While we cannot but agree with Wolfgang Huber, we wonder whether the church is really still relevant for human existence since fewer and fewer people attend or are affiliated with the church.

The Protestant Church in Germany (EKD) is predicting that within thirty years it will lose almost half of its membership, with a corresponding decline of church revenues. This would mean that only roughly 13 percent of the German population will belong to a Protestant congregation. Of course, such reduction would severely curtail the impact of the church on society. And yet there is no evidence of a missionary awareness among church members that would stem this decline. To the contrary, when one tries to befriend people of other religions, especially Muslims who claim to belong to the Abrahamic tradition which reveres the God of Abraham, it is more often than not a one-sided affair. For instance, in our department at the university we have a woman student who is a Muslim. Her mother is Christian and her father Muslim, and therefore the daughter must be Muslim. She studies Protestant theology since she wants to know what the Christian faith is all about. While her father condones her studies, he objects to her having a boyfriend who is a Christian. This inability to do mission contributes to

6. Huber, "evangelisch.de."

the decline in church membership. The fact is that this decline of German Protestantism will also have a significant impact on Protestantism around the world. The German churches are the principal financial supporter of the Lutheran World Federation and the World Council of Churches. They also support financially, and to a large extent with personnel, churches in Africa, Asia, and Latin America. They fund humanitarian projects, provide scholarships for theology students and doctoral candidates, and support the building of churches in these parts of the world. These activities would have to be reduced considerably or even halted altogether if church membership in Germany were to face such a drastic decline.

The Roman Catholic Church would not fare much better, especially in the diocese of Cologne, one of the largest in Germany, dates for rescinding one's church membership there are booked up for months in advance at city hall. The reason for the exodus from the church is because of the apparent mishandling of abuse cases by the leaders of the diocese.[7] In a newspaper article from February 2021, the Roman Catholic professor of church history at the Ludwig Maximilian University of Munich, Klaus Unterburger (b. 1971), explained: The faithful expect the clerics to be examples in conduct and to live a life of purity. Yet the image of the Roman Catholic Church today is no longer one of a higher moral institution. Negative news such as the spending of church funds for renovating a castle-like residence of a bishop, including a bathtub for thousands of euros, and the sexual and bodily abuse of children, have left their marks. Even in rural areas more and more faithful Christians are turning away from the church. "The church is collapsing here at a velocity which I could not have imagined," says Unterburger. Even in the conservative Roman Catholic diocese of Regensburg the number of those who are leaving the church is high. According to Unterburger, the system also suffers because of its structure. Demanding celibacy of the priests, which in most cases is not lived out, generates a shortage of priests and increasingly distances the faithful from the church. When congregations are merged, because there are not enough priests, contact with the faithful is lost. The estrangement of the faithful from the church continues to increase. Unterburger surmises that "a time frame of twenty years during which the Catholic Church might fall apart, is unfortunately one that I hold to be realistic."[8] If the Roman Catholic Church in Germany is reduced to half its present size by the middle of this century, its impact on global Catholicism will be drastically diminished. Today the Roman Catholic Church in Germany is still one of the richest Catholic churches in the world and can

7. Pollack, "Wer einmal," 38.

8. Unterburger, "System."

support Catholicism worldwide, including the Vatican. But on its present course this beneficial support will eventually come to an end.

The historian Martin Kaufhold (b. 1963), from the University of Augsburg, who is a member of the Roman Catholic Church, explains that Roman Catholic clerics regard themselves as a special group that lives according to its own rule. Traditionally the clerics are considered to be mediators between God and humanity and are qualified for this task through their consecration as priests. "As members of this group they are primarily subject to the divine law and only in a limited way to civil laws."[9] This self-understanding was developed during the Middle Ages, since the faithful at that time felt like they needed such a group. They needed priests who were closer to God and could guarantee the average penitents that their sins were forgiven. This was a genuine need from which, to a large extent, the image of the priest evolved. Today only very few Roman Catholics attend confession. Therefore, the medieval image of the priest who is so close to God that he can forgive sins is no longer needed. Especially for the younger generation the church has lost its relevancy. "Therefore, nobody gets upset [about the scandals in the church]. This is no longer of interest," concludes Kaufhold.

Church institutions, such as counseling centers and kindergartens, are readily accepted by all segments of society. But they are financed by a smaller and smaller clientele. While it is very difficult to regain lost trust, the wounds will not be healed if there are no concrete steps taken to remedy the situation. Potentially volatile issues such as the priesthood of women and the celibacy of priests must be tackled. The church cannot forever circumvent the issues that are raised by the laity. While on the congregational level the church is largely run by women, they have no influence on structural decisions. The church is still a priestly church of male clerics and not the church of the people of God. How far apart the people are from the church can be seen by the following incident:[10] Protestant Christians in Germany have left the Protestant church because they got annoyed about something the pope of the Catholic Church said, for instance, concerning the blessing of homosexual couples or that there will not be women priests! This shows that for many people the denominational difference between Roman Catholics and Protestants is no longer considered important. They do not even know the difference between Protestantism and Roman Catholicism. For the majority of the faithful in Germany the confessional imprints have largely disappeared. But the Roman Catholic Church still does not allow its

9. Kaufhold, "Heutige Probleme."

10. For the following see the statement by Pollack, "Wer einmal," 39. Pollack is professor of sociology of religion at the University of Münster, Germany.

priests to invite non-Catholics to share the Eucharistic meal with Catholics. Yet at the Third Ecumenical Church Gathering (3. Ökumenischer *Kirchentag*) in Germany ,which took place in Frankfurt in May 2021, during several church worship services the Roman Catholics invited Protestants to take part in the Eucharist, and vice versa. When this happened, there were immediately protests by high-ranking Roman Catholic officials.

When we now look at the USA and there especially at the Evangelical Lutheran Church in America (ELCA), one of the largest Protestant mainline churches, we do not receive a picture that is any more comforting. Superficially speaking, the USA is still a Christian country because in 1990 85 percent of all Americans still called themselves Christians. But in 2019 only 65 percent of American adults identified themselves as Christian. Still, this is a relatively high percentage. Almost half of these belong to a Protestant denomination, while the Roman Catholic Church with 22 percent of all Christians is the largest individual denomination in the US. When the ELCA was born in 1988—resulting from the merger of three Lutheran denominations (the American Lutheran Church, the Lutheran Church of America, and the Association of Evangelical Lutheran Churches)—it had over 5 million members. As of 2019, the ELCA had shrunk to approximately 3.3 million baptized members in 8,972 congregations. Projections are that within twenty years it will lose another 1.5 million members and, according to the ELCA Office of Research and Evaluation, the whole denomination will have fewer than 67,000 members in 2050.[11] This means that according to current trends the ELCA will virtually cease to exist within the next generation.

The ELCA did just lose members by people dropping out of its congregations. In response to some liberal views of the ELCA the association of Lutheran Congregations in Mission for Christ (LCMC) was formed in 2001, which "describes itself as an affiliation of autonomous Lutheran churches and not a denomination."[12] The LCMC is characterized by the stances it takes on Lutheran polity, biblical authority, and human sexuality. The group calls itself "centrist" or "mainstream," noting that it stands between the more liberal ELCA and the more conservative Lutheran Church–Missouri Synod (LCMS) and other Lutheran church bodies in North America. Individual congregations can ordain women as pastors in the LCMC, and in terms of marriage, they strictly understand it as a union between a woman and a man. As of 2021 it consisted of nearly a thousand congregations and more than 300,000 members. Another split from the ELCA occurred with

11. Zscheile, "Will the ELCA?"

12. Lutheran Congregations in Mission for Christ.

the formation of the North American Lutheran Church (NALC). It was founded in 2010 and now has more than four hundred congregations with approximately 140,000 members. It is presided over by a bishop and has its own theological seminary. Theologically conservatives within the ELCA and the Evangelical Lutheran Church in Canada (ELCIC) concluded that their respective denominations were moving away from the authority of the Bible and the Lutheran Confessions and consequently they founded the LCMC and the NALC. The primary issue of concern for them was a 2009 decision by the ELCA, which changed its teaching and policy on sexual ethics, allowing clergy/ministers to be in committed same-sex relationships. These new denominations, or affiliations, stand theologically between the conservative LCMS and the ELCA, emphasizing Scripture as the sole rule of authority by which doctrine and practice are to be judged.

When the churchwide assembly of the ELCA in 2009 decided to allow individual congregations "to recognize, support and hold publicly accountable life-long, monogamous, same-gender relationships" and permitted individuals in such relationships to serve as church leaders, many faithful members turned their heels on the ELCA.[13] The two succeeding years following this decision, the ELCA lost each year more than 200,000 members. Both the NALC and the LCMC explicitly emphasize traditional marriage between one man and one woman. Just a few years ago a pastor of a good-sized ELCA congregation told me: "If I were to touch the issue of homosexuality in the congregation, I would lose members." Along with the sanctioning of homosexuality also came a different interpretation of certain Scripture passages which were traditionally understood to forbid homosexuality. This move also had an effect internationally. Several of the largest and fastest growing Lutheran church bodies in the world cut their ties with the ELCA in favor of the more conservative LCMS. These included the Ethiopian Evangelical Church Mekane Yesus, with its 12 million members.

The ELCA is not alone with its problems concerning sexuality. In the seven years after the United Church of Christ voted to recognize same-sex marriages, it lost 20 percent of its members. The Presbyterian Church (USA) liberalized its stance on sexuality in 2006 and consequently lost 22 percent of its members between 2006 and 2013. Among church members of the mainline churches, sexuality is a very divisive issue. It seems that the more inclusive a denomination wants to be, the more members it loses. A telling example is the Episcopal Church, which lost 18 percent of its members in the decade between 2002 and 2012 on account of its drive towards inclusivity. The question that mainline churches including the ELCA have to

13. Harrod, "Always Declining."

ask themselves is whether sexuality is really such an important topic for the Christian faith. Since two-thirds of the membership favor same-sex marriages while one third oppose them, this continues to be a divisive issue.[14]

Yet another issue is at least as important when it comes to declining membership. The average churchgoer of the ELCA is considerably older than the average American. The youth and young adults are actually missing from congregations. While those between the ages of eighteen and twenty-nine make up 12 percent of the membership, those age sixty-five and beyond make up 31 percent. Moreover, African Americans, Asians, and Latinos are represented by a mere 4 percent, while 96 percent of the congregants are white. The continuous drive of the ELCA for ethnic inclusivity, including teaching Spanish to seminary students, has not met with much success. Moreover, fewer and fewer members attend church services on Sunday morning. "Nearly 30 percent of ELCA churches reported an average worship attendance of fewer than 50 people in 2010. From 2003 to 2011, average weekly worship attendance dropped 26 percent."[15] The reason for this decline is also one of geographic location. The majority of the ELCA congregations are located in rural areas. Most of the young people who were born there move away for college and then never return, since most jobs are in urban areas. It is doubtful whether these young people will look for a Lutheran congregation, or even for any congregation, when they settle in an urban location where they live and work. In contrast to the way their parents and grandparents felt, young adults no longer see the church as relevant for their lives. More than a thousand ELCA churches have closed during the decade between 2003 and 2013, either by locking their doors forever and their members dispersing, or by merging with other congregations. And this trend is continuing. The same is true for the seminaries of the ELCA. As enrollment decreases, they can no longer financially support themselves and they seek alliances either with another seminary, as in the case of Gettysburg and Philadelphia, or by aligning itself with a college, as Trinity Theological Seminary has done with Capital University.

As mentioned, the ELCA is not alone with its steady decline in membership. Even the conservative Southern Baptist Convention is now facing a slight decline after years of spectacular growth. Yet culturally conservative churches such as the Assemblies of God and the Mormon Church are still enjoying strong growth. While religion generally is on a slight decline, nearly 50 million Americans identify themselves as religiously unaffiliated. They are not even looking for a denomination that would be right for them.

14. According to the Pew Research Center, "Members."

15. Radziszewski, "Shrinking Church."

The church does not seem to meet their religious needs. What we are facing is that a large segment of society has left the church behind and is satisfied with mere religiosity.

2. MERE RELIGIOSITY

Since the churches are continuously losing members, does this mean that atheism is on the rise? Or are people simply making up their own religion in some kind of patchwork fashion? Two German studies may shed some light on the situation. The first one, the so-called *Shell Study*, has been conducted since 1954 every few years by the Shell Oil Company. It focuses on the youth in Germany ages twelve to twenty-five, empirically investigating their values, their attitudes, and their social habits. This also includes how they think about religion. The eighteenth study, in 2019, shows that for Roman Catholic and Protestant youth faith has diminished considerably in significance during the last twenty years. In 2019 faith in God was important for barely 40 percent of the youth, while in 2000 it was still significant for 51 percent. On the other hand, faith was considered important for 39 percent of the Roman Catholic youth and 24 percent of the Protestants. According to the study, just 18 percent of the Catholics and 13 percent of the Protestants pray at least once a week. With this considerable decline in religiosity, it is surprising that the institutional church still receives remarkable appreciation. Sixty-nine percent of all the young people find it good that there is a church, of those 75 percent are Roman Catholic, 79 percent are Protestant, and 45 percent are those who do not belong to any denomination.[16] Yet the youths are also critical of the church and demand changes in the church if it is to have a future. Seventy-three percent of the Catholics and 65 percent of the Protestants made this demand, but only 55 percent of those without denominational affiliation see a need for change. Evidently many of those without denominational affiliation do not really care about the church. While the church is still considered relatively important by many, we notice that considerable trust in the church, especially among the Roman Catholics, has been lost. In 2002, 38 percent of all young Catholics still expressed their trust in the church, while in 2019 this was down to 25 percent. This decline may be due to the numerous abuse cases reported in the Roman Catholic Church in the past several years. At the same time, trust in the church by Protestants has stayed relatively the same, from 31 percent in 2002 to 29 percent in 2019.

16. Shell Jugendstudie 2020.

While the above study focuses on the youth, another study, conducted by the Bertelsmann Foundation, worked with 14,000 people ages sixteen and above in thirteen countries, among them Germany and the USA. The survey was conducted between October and December 2012 and included such subjects as their personal religiosity, their values, and their relationship to religion, politics, and society. This empirical investigation was carried out the second time on an interdisciplinary basis, the first being done in 2007. Today it is one of the main resources for quantitative and empirical research in spirituality and religiosity. In Germany there has been considerable discussion about the perception that more and more people are constructing their own patchwork religion by picking and choosing whatever sounds convincing to them, from the plethora of religions and worldviews. Yet research has shown that this perception is wrong. Only a minority of people construct their own syncretistic patchwork religion, 26 percent of those are Catholic and 24 percent are Protestant. A surprising 42 percent of Muslims, however, glean from other traditions.[17] Though the vast majority of Germans are open to other religions, this openness vanishes as soon as one's own religious practice is concerned.[18] They still seem to feel obligated to tradition to the extent that the new religious plurality is not integrated into one's own religious life. While religious plurality is considered as something enriching, it does not affect one's own religion. Most people will not pick and choose from the religions they encounter, rather they stay with the religious tradition in which they were raised, with which they are familiar. If Christianity as the dominant religious tradition grows weak, this does not mean that people will automatically search for new forms of religiosity. This is just one possibility among many. Most likely, with the decline of traditional religiosity, it means that interest in religion is weakening altogether. But experimentation in matters of religion is still a minor issue, even if its significance has recently increased.

With regard to religiosity there is still a strict demarcation between Eastern and Western Germany. In the West the culture is still permeated by a confessional religion. For instance, there is Roman Catholic Bavaria and Protestant Lower Saxony. But in the East the culture is largely secular. Yet in both the East and the West religion has lost its significance in everyday life.[19] In the younger generation a turn to newer forms of spirituality is evident, a so-called patchwork religion. Young people seem to be more open to religious experimentation. This does not compensate, however, for the

17. Pollack and Müller, *Religionsmonitor*, 17.

18. For the following, see Pollack and Müller, *Religionsmonitor*, 42.

19. For the following, see Pollack and Müller, *Religionsmonitor*, 54.

loss of relevancy of traditional forms of religion. While in the East the loss of religiosity can in part be attributed to the consequences of the former Communist regime, in both East and West modernization and urbanization in society has made the religious services of the churches less necessary, for instance in regard to schools, counseling, and social support. What was once the prerogative of the churches has gradually been taken over by communities and the government. There is one baffling phenomenon, however. Church-run schools, though usually small, enjoy good acceptance in the East by parents who have no religious affiliation at all. Perhaps they feel that their children are better cared for and receive a better education in the school of a religious denomination.

The impact of the natural sciences on the enduring validity of religious explanations of the world should also not be forgotten, especially with regard to creation and miracles. Furthermore, an increasing percentage of young people grows up with no relationship to religion. This naturally reduces their openness to religious matters later in life. "The subordinate role of religion in many people's daily lives goes hand in hand with a widespread liberal attitude to ethical and moral ideas such as gay rights and the right to abortion. At this point, the effect of these issues is not primarily a tension between Christians and non-denominational members of the population, but rather differences within the Church itself (in particular, between the 'official' Catholic Church and the laity)."[20]

When we compare Germany with the USA statistically, the USA is much more religious than Germany.[21] While in Germany 18 percent of the population consider themselves highly religious, in the USA it is 62 percent. Only 8 percent of the US population claim not to be religious over against 28 percent of Germans. According to surveys, in Germany 28 percent of the population pray frequently and in the US the number is 68 percent. The religious activities and attitudes of the American people, however, do not indicate whether they are affiliated with a church. Because of the strict separation between church and state in the USA the country is actually decidedly secular. This does not mean that religiosity is slowly disappearing. It is cultivated as private religiosity and issues in a religious pluralism, since there is no unifying main denomination that binds most church members together. In Germany church members usually belong to the Roman Catholic Church or to the Protestant church of the Lutheran, Reformed, or United variety, depending on where one lives. Since Germany is largely a welfare state in which the government takes care of its people, the people do not

20. For the following, see Pollack and Müller, *Religionsmonitor*, 60.

21. For the following see Joas, "Religion heute," 180.

need religion as a means of mastering their lives.[22] This is different in the USA in which self-reliance has been propagated since its founding. This overextends the capabilities of most people, however, and therefore people turn to religion as a helpmate. There is a definite correlation between the improvement of material and social conditions of life and the decline of religiosity.[23] Through technological, economic, and medical progress, human lives in developed industrial societies are less threatened by things that are beyond people's control than was the case in earlier societies. Therefore, people feel that it is no longer necessary to depend on the benevolence of a higher power. They get along well in life and conclude that they do not need God as a transcendental helpmate. Yet the relative inequality of income and the lack of welfare institutions in the USA could be a reason why religion is so significant for Americans, despite the fact that the country is so highly developed economically.

While in the USA religious symbols are not tolerated on government property, the US currency bears the imprint "In God we trust." The military has chaplains being paid by the government who have military rank like all other military personnel. At the presidential inauguration the newly elected president swears the oath using a Bible. The separation of church and state notwithstanding, this indicates that the presence of the divine is deemed important for both the country and the individual. The importance of the divine is also evidenced among the American people since many believe in the presence of spiritual entities, such as angels. Seventy percent of American Protestants believe in the existence and the effect of angels.[24] While in our science-dominated age a divine presence and agency seem implausible for many people, the impact of science on the beliefs of the general population should not be overestimated. We see this especially in the continuous discussions of creation versus evolution. More than a century and a half after Charles Darwin (1809–82) published his groundbreaking thesis on the development of life, evolution remains a contentious topic in the United States. For many religious people, the Darwinian view of the emergence of human life conflicts with both the biblical creation story and the Judeo-Christian concept of an active, loving God who intervenes in human events. According to a Gallup poll from June 2019, "forty percent of U.S. adults subscribe to a strictly creationist view of human origins, believing that God created humans in their present form within roughly the last 10,000 years. However, more Americans continue to think that humans evolved

22. Cf. for the following Höllinger, "Erfahrung," 454–55.

23. So Höllinger, "Erfahrung," 473, with reference to Max Weber.

24 According to Höllinger, "Erfahrung," 469.

over millions of years—either with God's guidance (33%) or, increasingly, without God's involvement at all (22%)."[25] This means that almost 80 percent of Americans believe that God is involved in the affairs of nature and in history. Yet more than half of the general population has no affiliation with any religious denomination. These people find meaning, purpose, identity, and community somewhere else. And that percentage is increasing every year.

Americans without a denominational church affiliation are usually less religious than those who belong to a denomination.[26] According to the Pew Research Center, the unaffiliated are less likely than the general public as a whole to say that religion is very important in their lives. Of course, they are also less likely to attend worship services and pray on a daily basis. While this is to be expected, they are not wholly secular. "Substantial portions of the unaffiliated—particularly among those who describe their religion as 'nothing in particular'—say they believe in God or a universal spirit."[27] Such a description most likely indicates that their belief system is outside the Christian fold. Forty-two percent of those without a church affiliation declare that they are neither a religious nor a spiritual person. Eighteen percent say they are religious, and 37 percent say they are spiritual but not religious. We can conclude that less than one quarter of the American population is truly secular, with no faith in a transcendent power.

I was told by someone not long ago that these so-called "nones" that do not identify with any organized religion have become increasingly fashionable. While in years past a person had to explain why they did not belong to a church, now they must explain why they do belong to one. As Joel Thiessen and Sarah Wilkins-Laflamme relate in the lucid study, *None of the Above: Nonreligious Identity in the US and Canada*: "As organized religion plays a smaller and smaller role in other aspects of social life, such as in education, health and cultural identity, disaffiliation or leaving one's religion becomes a viable option for some individuals in society. In turn, this initial exit from one's religion can generate a snowball effect: as irreligion grows, the stigma that was once attached to it gradually fades and it becomes increasingly socially acceptable to be unaffiliated."[28] It may even be considered as a sign of freedom from convention and from the traditions of one's forebears.

Though a considerable number of people still accept something as being beyond themselves, they are not searching. They have not made up their own religion in some kind of patchwork fashion. They are also not

25. Brenan, "40% of Americans."

26. For the following cf. Pew Research Center, "Religion and the Unaffiliated."

27. Pew Research Center, "Religion and the Unaffiliated."

28. Thiessen and Wilkins-Laflamme, *None of the Above*, 28.

looking for a religion which fits their liking, or they have embraced New Age spirituality, or Eastern religious ideas, or beliefs from some other non-Abrahamic faiths. They are content with their present religious state and show no potential for future church membership. Only about one in ten US adults say they are looking for a religious affiliation. They seem to have still some residue from an earlier church affiliation either by them or their parents and are not interested in religious experimentation. Yet in many ways they are not that different from the general population when it comes to belief in reincarnation, astrology, and the evil eye. And they are only slightly more likely to believe in yoga as a spiritual practice and in spiritual energy located in physical things such as mountains, trees, and crystals. This means that there is a natural religiosity in many people that seems to satisfy their needs. But does religion or faith really need a church?

3. FAITH WITHOUT A CHURCH

The four traditional marks of the church are oneness, holiness, catholicity, and apostolicity. Those without church affiliation, however, contend that belonging to a community of people who share common beliefs and values is not important to them. They are private people whose belief system is not missionary minded. They also do not feel the need to have their belief system strengthened by a community that believes like they do. They may even be afraid that their beliefs might be challenged by others. In other words, they want to be left alone. And they are not ignorant of what the church is and for what it stands. Most of them admit that religious organizations strengthen community bonds and play an important role in helping the poor and needy. Yet they are also critical that these organizations are too concerned with money and power and are too involved in politics. Their view of religious organizations is therefore ambivalent. But does such a private faith really have a future?

In 1974 I was visiting professor at the Gregorian University in Rome, Italy, for one semester. My wife and I had invited some colleagues from the university for a nice evening dinner that my wife prepared in our apartment. The evening went well, but we had hardly finished the main course when the dean stood up and apologized: "I am sorry, I have to leave now, because I still have to finish writing the introduction to my new book." And then he left. Had he been married—all the faculty members were Roman Catholic priests—his wife would have told him in no uncertain terms how inconsiderate and impolite he had been. The hostess, my wife, had spent considerable time preparing a delicious meal and suddenly the dean left in a hurry in the middle of the meal, to do some work which he could have done at some other time. This incident is an example that being too private can cause us to miss out on being affirmed or in this instance of being reproached. The fact is every person needs both correction and affirmation so that life can be balanced and lived to its fullest. Our faith is always lived in a context through which we receive positive or negative input. In his *Smalcald Articles* Martin Luther writes of the "mutual conversation and consolation of brothers and sisters" through which the gospel is instilled in our hearts.[29] A private and solitary faith is always in danger of losing its connection with its original base.

However, the community is not only important for correction and affirmation. When people return from large assemblies, such as youth gatherings and conventions, they feel invigorated. Being together with many others of the same faith, they become aware that they are not alone with their faith conviction. For that reason, the community of the faithful is an important factor in everybody's life. If we remain alone, there is the danger that our faith will wither. The strengthening of our faith often comes from the community of which we are a part. This can be illustrated with Christian baptism. Baptism is never a private affair, so to speak occurring between me and my God—rather, it is a community event. When an infant is baptized, it is brought to the baptismal font, where it is baptized. The adult sponsors pledge that they will help to bring up the child in Christian faith. Then the child is introduced to the congregation, which is encouraged to receive it as a new Christian. In adult baptism the congregation plays a significant role in receiving those baptized as new members. People of faith need the community as the context in which their faith is lived out. The church is therefore often called the whole people of God.

The church is not always an extension of the institutional church. We encounter the church always in its denominational gown, as one of many denominations. But the church is more than all the denominations together. Church father Augustine (354–430) distinguished between the visible and invisible church. While the visible church is the institutional church, the invisible church may be smaller or larger than the institutional one and is known only to God. The faithful are therefore not always synonymous with the church we can see. In more modern times Roman Catholic theologian Karl Rahner (1904–84) talked about "anonymous Christians," whereby he meant non-Christians who conduct themselves in their faith in such a way that, as Rahner said, God is present in them towards salvation.[30]

29. Luther, *Smalcald Articles* (3:4), *BC* 319.

30. Rahner, "Christianity," 131.

While he was criticized for using the term "anonymous Christians," since this sounded like Christian imperialism, Rahner's intention was that God's working towards salvation is not confined to one institutional church or to all of them. Through the power of the Spirit God is present in the whole world. Some people could then be faithful followers of God without their and our explicit knowledge of it. But without the affirming community, the faith of these people is always in danger of veering off of the right path. Of course, being in the church does not automatically make one a blameless and faithful Christian. Augustine therefore talked about the church as a *corpus permixtum*, a mixed bag, consisting both of sinners and saints.[31] Since, however, we encounter in the church both correction and affirmation through the proclamation of law and gospel, it is easier for us to be brought back onto the right track if we are a part of the church than if we try to practice the Christian faith on our own.

But how do we get on the right track? There are so many different denominations and each one seems to claim something different. Indeed, unity has never been a strong point of the Christian church. We already notice in the Luke-Acts that from the very beginning the church had no monolithic structure. The church manifested itself as one church, but in different ways and in different locations (1 Cor 1:2).

Far up into the twentieth century there were almost endless divisions in the church, particularly among Protestants. From the mid-twentieth century on, however, the momentum shifted and began to go in the opposite direction. Disregarding all diversities, members of denominations became more and more cognizant that Christians belong together. For instance, the 1600th anniversary of the Nicene Constantinopolitan Creed (381) was celebrated in 1981 by the churches together. The unilateral change of the Western churches in this creed that the Holy Spirit proceeds "from the Father *and* from the Son" instead of staying with the agreed-on confession that the Holy Spirit proceeds "from the Father," had irritated the Eastern church to the extent that it separated from the West. But now the Roman pontiff relativized this addition by making it an option. This means that the so-called *filioque* (from the Father and from the Son) need no longer be the symbol of separation between East and West. At the Second Vatican Council (1963–65), Protestant and Orthodox faithful who were once called heretics and schismatics, had been invited as official guests and observers. In the *Decree on Ecumenism* the Council even declares: "Promoting the restoration of unity among all Christians is one of the chief concerns of the

31. Augustine, *On Christian Doctrine* (3:32.45), *NPNFa FS* 2:569.

Second Sacred Ecumenical Synod of the Vatican."[32] During the First Vatican Council (1869–70) there was still a mentality of demarcation over against the Protestants. But by the Second Vatican Council this had been for the most part overcome. This shows that one side of the church had learned from the other. While the Roman Catholic Church did not suddenly deny its past, it did put the accent on areas different from what it had done in the past. For instance, concerning the laity it was now said: "They are in their own way made sharers in the priestly, prophetic, and kingly functions of Christ. They carry out their own part in the mission of the whole Christian people with respect to the Church and the world."[33] Or by citing the church father Jerome (347–419) they now stated: "Ignorance of the Scriptures is ignorance of Christ."[34] This almost sounds like the Lutheran emphasis on "Scripture alone." Protestants were also beginning to see some things in a different light. Suddenly, they were no longer allergic to everything Roman Catholic. They realized that Protestants had much more in common with Roman Catholics than they had initially thought.

This readiness to learn from each other is also true for the Protestants themselves. For instance, in Amsterdam, Netherlands, the World Council of Churches with their seat in Geneva, Switzerland, was founded in 1948. At its fifth plenary assembly in Nairobi (1975) the assembly recommended that the churches "provide opportunities for a careful study and evaluation of the concept of conciliar fellowship as a way of describing the unity of the Church."[35] Since then there have been many documents formulated that reveal a growing agreement resulting from bilateral and multilateral discussions between various denominations. The volume that covers only the years 1998–2005 with the complete reports and consensus texts of interconfessional dialogues on a global level contains 640 pages.[36] But it was not only documents that emerged. There were also many mergers of churches, for instance in the Church of South India, and the Church of North India, and the Evangelical Lutheran Church in America. Naturally on the road to unity there were also setbacks. An example is the unfortunate documents *Dominus Iesus* issued by the Vatican in the year 2000. It stated that "the Church of Christ, despite the divisions which exist among Christians, continues to exist fully only in the Catholic church."[37] Then further down it says:

32. *Decree on Ecumenism* (1), *DVC* 341.

33. *Dogmatic Constitution on the Church* (31), *DVC* 57.

34. *Dogmatic Constitution on Divine Revelation* (25), *DVC* 127.

35. *Breaking Barriers*, 69.

36. Gros, Best, and Fuchs, eds., *Growth in Agreement III*.

37. Congregation for the Doctrine of the Faith, *Declaration "Dominus Iesus,"* 16.

"The ecclesial communities which have not preserved the valid Episcopate and the genuine and integral substance of the Eucharistic mystery are not Churches in the proper sense."[38] This means that the only true church is the Roman Catholic Church. Protestant churches are not churches in a true sense of the word because they have no valid episcopacy, meaning that they are not under the jurisdiction of Rome. But such documents cannot stop the journey toward unity. We must mention here the *Joint Declaration on the Doctrine of Justification*, a historic agreement signed by Lutherans and Catholics in 1999 in the city of Augsburg, Germany, effectively resolving one of the key theological conflicts of the Reformation, namely that we are justified and made right in the eyes of God by God's grace alone. Initially a Catholic-Lutheran agreement, it has since been joined and affirmed by three other Christian World Communions, namely the Methodist, Anglican, and Reformed churches. Yet in the same year, 1999, the Roman pontiff announced a special indulgence, carefully circumventing those points in the notion of indulgences which had caused the Reformation.[39]

If churches preach reconciliation and are irreconcilable, they are no longer trustworthy. Moreover, the boundaries no longer coincide with the boundaries between the different denominations, but they cut through the various denominations themselves. For instance, liberal Protestants have more in common with liberal Roman Catholics than with their own conservative brothers and sisters in Christ. Members with differing opinions still participate together in one denomination without having much in common with one another. In addition, many theological differences that allegedly exist between denominations are very difficult for most people to understand. The continued segregation of one group from another in some churches is more the result of institutional inertia than of actual theological differences.

Above all we should not forget that we ourselves cannot create unity. Our unity is pre-given in the one Christ to whom all Christians pledge allegiance. The unity that we already share in Christ is rediscovered in the ecumenical dialogues. The decisive point is not what denomination we belong to, but that we belong to Christ. He is the one who ties us together and who forms our faith. This is also true when we consider the second mark of the church, its holiness.

When we look back at the history of the church or just review the present-day issues of misconduct in sexual and financial matters that rock especially the Roman Catholic Church, the adjective "holy" seems out of

38. Congregation for the Doctrine of the Faith, *Declaration "Dominus Iesus,"* 17.

39. John Paul II, "General Audience."

place. Indeed, the church at large and its individual members have never been holy. But in the Old Testament God enjoins the Israelites: "You shall be holy, for I am holy" (Lev 11:45). In the New Testament Christians are often called "saints" (cf. Rom 16:2). The letters of Paul to the Romans, Corinthians, and Philippians begin and end by addressing the members of Christian communities as holy. Ephesians and Colossians open in this manner too. "At the end of Romans Paul encourages the Church to receive Phoebe the deaconess in a manner 'worthy of the holy ones' (16:2), and to 'greet Philologus [. . .] and all the holy ones' (16:15)."[40] These are members of the community which was established by the sacrifice of Jesus Christ "as God's chosen ones, holy and beloved" (Col 3:12). God chose them for this community. When Paul gathers gifts from the gentiles and brings them to the Christian community in Jerusalem, he brings that offering "for the poor among the saints at Jerusalem" (Rom 15:26). We notice here the general designation of all believers as "holy ones"—or as saints as the NRSV renders the Greek term "*hagioi*"—because they are a new creation. Paul writes in 2 Corinthians 5:17: "So if anyone is in Christ, there is a new creation: everything old has passed away." Holiness is not an innate quality of Christians but is bestowed upon them through their baptism, by which act they are "in Christ." While baptism is administered by the church on account of Christ's death and resurrection, the status of being "in Christ" is not necessarily tied to the church. One does not need the church to claim Christ as one's Savior. Jesus' comment regarding the Roman centurion whose servant Jesus had healed should be remembered here: "Truly I tell you, in no one in Israel have I found such faith" (Matt 8:10). Church membership is not required to have faith in Jesus Christ. We are reminded of Augustine's distinction between the visible and invisible church. There may be very different reasons why one does not have a church membership. Examples might be that a person is simply annoyed about what has been going on in a particular congregation, or someone may feel that the denomination of which they are a part has veered from the teaching of the gospel. And yet without a community that encourages and corrects those who are a part of it, it is difficult to remain in Christ and still be counted among the holy ones.

The next mark of the church is its catholicity. This term has nothing to do with Roman Catholicism, although the Roman Catholic Church often emphasizes its all-encompassing nature, meaning its catholicity. Already Bishop Polycarp of Smyrna (ca. 69—ca. 155) mentions "the whole catholic church throughout the world," meaning by "catholic" simply the global

40. Hodgson, "Holiness (NT)," *ABD* 3:250. In the NRSV, however, the Greek "*hagioi*" is not translated with "holy ones" but with "saints."

extension of the church.[41] Similarly Bishop Irenaeus of Lyons (ca. 135—ca. 200) writes: "The Church, though dispersed throughout the whole world, even to the ends of the earth . . ."[42] Augustine then connects the global extension with the temporal extension when he writes that the house of the Lord "will prevail throughout the whole world" . . . "unto length of days."[43] He even connects dimensionally the church with the kingdom of God, saying: "Therefore the Church even now is the kingdom of Christ, and the kingdom of heaven."[44] This means that the church is really all-encompassing not just in its extensions of space and time but even including the heavenly realm. Where does this leave a person who has no ecclesial or denominational affiliation? Can faith really exist without the church? It seems that initially at least, the church was conceived of as the whole people of God without demanding from the individual an explicit church affiliation. One can be a faithful Christian and affirm the catholicity of the church without belonging to a distinct church or denomination. Yet there is still a fourth mark of the church and that is its apostolicity, meaning that the church stems from and is in continuity with the apostles.

We read in the Acts of the Apostles that the first Christian community in Jerusalem devoted itself "to the apostles' teaching and fellowship, to the breaking of bread and prayers" (Acts 2:42). The first Christian community gathered to listen to the teaching of the apostles. Once the apostles had died their oral teaching was replaced by the written documents that we have in the New Testament. The Roman Catholic Church interprets apostolicity to mean apostolic succession, an unbroken line of tradition from the apostles to the present. Since Protestants cannot meet this unbroken line of succession, the Catholic Church would say that they do not belong to the church in the strict sense. Yet in ecumenical dialogue it has been emphasized more and more that the decisive point is the succession of the truth and not in personal sequence. As many historians have shown, this unbroken line and handing on of the staff from one leader to the next, has never existed. Even in the papacy there have been black sheep. One only has to look at some of the popes during the Renaissance, such as Alexander VI (1431–1503), who most likely was an agnostic. Yet when we go back to Acts 2:42 we read about the teaching of the apostles, the fellowship, the breaking of the bread, and

41. Eusebius, *Church History*, 148, from the *Martyrdom of Polycarp*.

42. Irenaeus, *Against Heresies* (1.10.1), *ANFa* 1:330.

43. Augustine, *Expositions on the Book of Psalms, NPNFa FS* 8:459, in his exposition of Psalm 93.

44. Augustine, *City of God* (20.9), *NPNFa FS* 2:430.

prayers. The breaking of the bread is not just a reference to common meals, but to the Eucharist.

In the *Augsburg Confession* of the Lutheran Church we read "that at all times there must be and remain one holy, Christian church. It is the assembly of all believers among whom the gospel is purely preached and the holy sacraments are administered according to the gospel."[45] In the next article we read, "The Christian church is, properly speaking, nothing else than the assembly of all believers and saints." There is no mention of a certain church structure, of peculiar clerical ranks, or of apostolic succession. All decisive is the gospel according to which the believers structure their lives, and the sacraments in which they participate. In his *Large Catechism* Martin Luther described the church in the following way: "There is on earth a little holy flock and community of pure saints under one head, Christ. It is called together by the Holy Spirit in one faith, mind, and understanding. It possesses a variety of gifts, and yet is united in love without sect or schism."[46] It is not us who gather together to form the church, but we are called together by the Holy Spirit. Being a member of the church is ultimately not an individual decision but is owed to the grace of God.

Yet those who have faith without a church affiliation feel that they do not need the church and can be Christians on their own. The metaphor of the invisible church does not preclude such Christian faith outside the church. But the chances are very slim that such a faith will actually be lived out. First of all, it is a faith without partaking of the sacraments. One may have been baptized as an infant but then left the church as an adult. But what about the Eucharist? The Orthodox Church calls the Eucharist a medicine toward immortality. It is not a memorial meal as some followers of the Swiss reformer Huldrych Zwingli (1484–1531) might still tell us, but is the intimate communion with Jesus Christ as our Lord and Savior. As Luther explains in his *Small Catechism*, the eating and drinking at the Eucharist is not the important event but rather the words which are addressed to us—"given for you" and "shed for you for the forgiveness of sins."[47] We are in a visible way connected was Christ's salvific sacrifice through which the gulf between God and us has been bridged. We are told that in this meal God accepts us on account of our Lord Jesus Christ. A solitary faith without access to the Lord's table can never have this kind of assurance. In the long run people delude themselves when they claim that they can be Christians without being

45. "Augsburg Confession," article 7 and for the following quote article 8, *BC* 42.

46. Luther, *Large Catechism*, *BC* 437–38.

47. Luther, *Small Catechism*, *BC* 363.

a part of a church. There is also another important factor which speaks against the solitary faith without the church, namely apostolicity.

As we have seen, decisive is not the apostolic succession in person, but the succession of truth. If we do not stand in succession with that which the apostles and the other New Testament authors proclaimed, we may easily claim that we have our own gospel. The continuity with the apostles' teachings is the difference between heresy and truth, between following our own ideas and those of Christ. Of course, in its long history the church has often proclaimed its own gospel instead of the apostolic truth. Yet it has always found its way back to that which connects it with its origins, the gospel of its Lord. Even today the apostolicity of the church is threatened by modernistic claims that the gospel must be adjusted to the prevailing trends of society. The catchphrase goes like this: "We can no longer . . ." What is forgotten in such considerations is that society can never be the measuring stick for the gospel. It is the other way around. The gospel is the measuring stick for what is proper and improper in society. That is the very reason why Scripture alone was the watchword of the Lutheran Reformation.

While a sermon can always veer from the truth, there are still the lessons of the Old and New Testament, the Creed, and the Lord's Prayer, things which are unalterably given in a church worship service. These parts of the church service always connect us to our foundation, the biblical truth and our Lord Jesus Christ. A solitary faith, however, does not enjoy this continuous connection with the apostolic faith and therefore is much more in danger to go its own way. As surveys indicate, faith without church affiliation is often reduced to a faith in some impersonal higher power who is no longer a personal God and the Father of Jesus Christ. As a Pew Research Survey of 2017 indicated, "Among those who describe themselves as religiously unaffiliated—also known as "nones"—72% say they believe in a higher power of some kind."[48] Only 17 percent of them believe in "God as described in the Bible." For the "nones" faith is largely attenuated, and they believe in some kind of nondescript world spirit, but no longer in the God whom you can trust and who guides your life. It is important for those who left the church for doctrinal reasons that they can still maintain their faith even without church affiliation. Remember, 17 percent of these people claim that they still believe in the God proclaimed by the Bible. But we should not overestimate the truth of this claim. Chances are much greater that they will lose their biblical faith than if they had continued to be active church members. Chances are they had already been inactive church members and their exodus from the church was not such a big step for them. Yet it could

48. Fahmy, "Key Findings."

have been that as conservative church members they were active but could no longer stand the liberal climate in their church. Leaving the church does not really resolve anything. As a conservative friend of mine once remarked: "We do not give them the joy of us leaving the church unless they throw us out." And the church historian Martin Marty (b. 1928) once said: "I love my messy church." While the church is a divine institution it is populated by people who even with their best intentions are sinful. Therefore, we should not expect too much from any denomination. Yet as a minimum requirement we should notice that every denomination attempts to adhere to the apostolic tradition of Word and sacrament.

4. A CHURCH WITHOUT LEADERS

During the latter part of the Vietnam War, which ended in 1975, seminaries in America were bursting at the seams. Many young people wanted to enter the ministry, often to escape the military draft. Whether these young men—there were no women studying for the ministry at that time—were really all draft dodgers is doubtful. There was a similar increase in the number of seminary students in Germany and there was no threat to them of having to serve in Vietnam. As aforementioned, at one time in Germany there were more young people studying for the ministry then there were pastors serving in the churches. In Germany those who had passed their theological exams with low marks were not accepted into the ministry. Others were told that they had to wait another year before they could start their vicarage. In the Lutheran churches in America the attitude was slightly different. I heard the comment: "First we prayed to the Lord that he would send young men for the ministry and now we have more than we need. But we cannot say: 'Lord, we didn't really mean it.'" To adjust to this situation new ministries were created, such as tentmaking ministries in apartment complexes and part-time ministries in small congregations.

Over the years the situation has changed drastically. At first more and more second career people were entering the seminaries. Yet the number of seminarians stayed about the same. At his point someone should have noticed that there was an impending crisis. Second career people are older than those who come right out of college and their tenure in the ministry is much shorter. This accounted for fewer pastors being available to serve in congregations. Soon the number of those entering seminaries also fell drastically. As a consequence, seminaries have tried to make it easier for students, offering online extension courses and evening classes, and requiring only two years of education in the seminary, the last two years being spent serving in a congregation. This would then alleviate having to move, especially if the spouse had employment, which would tie him or her to a certain location. The result of this drastic reduction in seminary graduates is an increasing shortage of pastors. For instance, one synod of the ELCA applied for ten graduates but only received one to fill the vacancies. Even attractive congregations with excellent compensation packages and a vibrant church life conduct long searches until they find a new pastor. What can be done to solve this problem?

We must remember that Martin Luther emphasized the priesthood of all believers. All Christians are priests through their baptism. They are a part of the Christian community and participate in the signs of the community, administering the sacraments and preaching the gospel. In passages such as 1 Peter 2:9—"You are a chosen race, a royal priesthood, a holy nation, God's own people, in order that you may proclaim the mighty acts of him who called you out of darkness into his marvelous light"—Luther finds support for his claim that the proclamation of the Word belongs to all Christians. Their foremost task consists in the proclamation of the gospel. While Luther sees no justification for distinguishing between different classes of the priesthood, the common priesthood of all believers does not lead to anarchy. Luther states very clearly:

> For whatever comes out of the water of baptism can boast that he is already a consecrated priest, bishop, and pope, although of course it is not seemly that just anybody should exercise such office. Because we are all priests of equal standing, no one must push himself forward and take it upon himself, without our consent and election, to do that for which they all have equal authority. For no one dare take upon himself what is common to all without the authority and consent of the community. And should it happen that a person chosen for such office were deposed for abuse of trust, he would then be exactly what he was before. Therefore, a priest in Christendom is nothing else but an office holder. As long as he holds office he takes precedence; where he is deposed, he is a peasant or a townsman like anybody else. Indeed, a priest is never a priest when he is deposed.[49]

Luther perceives the priesthood in purely functional terms and not as an ontological characteristic that would confer upon the priest an indelible status, as the Roman Catholic Church teaches. Once the functional role ceases, the special priesthood also ceases. For Luther, ordination meant

49. Luther, *To the Christian Nobility of the German Nation Concerning the Reform of the Christian Estate* (1520), *LW* 44:129.

being called to and entrusted with the pastoral office. Since there is no distinction in authority among Christians, Luther argued that to have validity the call to service cannot come only from human beings. Ultimately it must come from God and be mediated through human beings since they actually set someone apart for the specific task of proclaiming the gospel. Especially in his dealings with some of the enthusiasts who claimed to be directly called by God, Luther found it important to insist that every call must be mediated. Conversely, to counteract those who only looked at the external, visible church it was important to show that the call must be from God. Proclaiming the gospel and administering the sacraments is done on behalf of the community that one serves but it is not the Word or the sacrament of the community that is administered. Messages and signs are God's and are administered on God's behalf. The rejection of a special priestly class served to further the unity of the church as the true and equal community under the headship of Christ.

One may wonder whether the emphasis on the officeholder as the only one who is called to fulfill the functions of the priestly office does not render ineffective the common priesthood of all believers. The *Augsburg Confession* refutes such a thought when it says that "no one should teach publicly in the church or administer the sacraments unless properly called" (CA 14). While the priesthood of all believers stands firm, the administration of the public office should not be left to the whim of every individual believer. Therefore, the public administration depends on the authorization of the assembly of believers. We also note that the delegation of the priestly function pertains only to the public aspect of the ministry, but not to the private aspect. Luther was very explicit at this point when he stated that the father does well when he teaches his household the Word of God—Luther wrote the *Large Catechism* for fathers to instruct their families—because God has commanded us to educate our children and families in the Word of God. Yet for Luther the same does not pertain to the administration of the sacraments, since they are public signs and confessions.

If there is such a shortage of pastors, it would only be common sense to designate some willing and able members of the congregation to function as predicants, meaning those to whom the public proclamation of the gospel is entrusted. Since however the proclamation of the gospel and the administration of the sacraments belong together one might also consider to entrusting the predicants with the administration of the sacraments. In this way the shortage of pastors could be alleviated in many congregations if there are people willing and able to function in the pastoral office on behalf of the congregation. Yet such measures do not compensate for the actual shortage of pastors. The church must ask itself why this shortage arose. Is our secular mindset the main reason for the small number of seminary students today? Is the goal of the members in our congregations that their young people seek a profession with a high income and a short work week? Are our young people becoming a generation of narcissists? The answer is not that simple.

One thing is sure, the young people today are more skeptical about organized religion than older folks were when they were young. The saying "Don't do as I do, do as I say," is perhaps revealing. Are we really being a good enough example to today's young people so that they will feel prone to emulate our way of doing things? Or are we just pious with our words but not in our actions? Everybody must answer this for him- or herself. The often heard comment, "Those in the church are not any better than those outside the church" is perhaps a good explanation. Of course, we are all sinners and we all fall short of the mark. In his *Small Catechism* Martin Luther explains the significance of baptism with water in the following way: "It signifies that the old creature in us with all sins and evil desires is to be drowned and die through daily contrition and repentance, and on the other hand that daily a new person is to come forth and rise up to live before God in righteousness and purity forever."[50] Luther explains here that being a sinner is no excuse for the way we live. Baptism is not a onetime occurrence but something that must be repeated on a daily basis, namely by the dying of our sinful self and the rising up of a new person who lives in righteousness and purity. As Luther implies here, we always fall back into our old ways. Yet are we trying hard enough to shed the old and to pursue the new way? Evidently quite often the daily renewal is missing. But young people might consider turning away from self-centeredness and looking to something by which a contribution can be made. This is exactly where seminary education comes in to prepare a person for the ministry.

In the ministry no one makes a lot of money unless they are perhaps involved in a megachurch where a prosperity gospel is preached and emphasis is placed on feeling well and being blessed by God with material success. This is hardly the Christian gospel, which is patterned after the life and ministry of Jesus the Christ. As Jesus himself said, he "came not to be served but to serve" (Matt 20:28). This is exactly what ministry is about, to serve others. This ministry of serving others, be it as a nurse in the hospital or in a hospice, or an aid in a retirement home, is demanding and often involves long hours. A pastor who is involved with his or her parishioners in these places is not supervised or admonished to spend as little time as possible with each person, as it is often the case with nurses. A pastor has

50. Luther, *Small Catechism*, *BC* 360.

no supervisor and therefore has the luxury of his or her own time management. Pastors can get involved in their congregations, sharing the joys and sorrows of their people. There is no schedule pastors must keep and they are largely their own decision-makers regarding what is to be done or not to be done. This kind of freedom outweighs by far the long hours they spend in the ministry and the sometimes incommensurate financial compensation. The rewards lie in the people they accompany on their journey through life, during their ups and downs, sharing with them and also growing with them. Without exaggeration it can be said that pastors have the greatest job on earth. They can preach the gospel of Jesus Christ full time, not only with their words but also with their actions in ministering to others. This is the most wonderful message in the world. There is a God who cares for the creation and the people who live in it. Nobody else can beat this because there is no other gospel, and the gospel consists of the "good news of Jesus Christ." If the people in the pews would realize this, then there would be enough young people going into the ministry. But if young people have a low opinion of their pastors and what they do, then it is no surprise that they look for a profession other than the Christian ministry.

Why are there so few seminarians? The answer is not simple. The question is, have we prayed seriously enough to God as Jesus admonished his disciples: "ask the Lord of the harvest to send out laborers into his harvest" (Matt 9:38)? The harvest is indeed plentiful but the laborers are few. Have we shown convincingly enough how rewarding and satisfying the ministerial profession is? Or do we have a very low opinion of the ministry? Granted, there are black sheep in the ministry who spoil it for many others. But the same could be said for virtually every other profession. To sum it up, the ministry is a great profession and it need not be hidden. Therefore, it is the task of all the members of the church to look out for potential candidates, to approach them with the question as to whether the ministry would not be something for them to pursue. And in all seriousness, we must also pose the same question to ourselves. If all the church members would do their part in being the church, a community of believers who are there for each other, then the load on the shoulders of the pastors would be lightened and they would not be easily discouraged. It would be better for them if they would project a positive image as the leader and the encourager, but not the sole provider.

Providing enough pastors is not only the task of congregations but also of the church at large. When I taught at Trinity Seminary in Columbus, Ohio, during my first years there in the late 1960s we discussed as a faculty whether we should raise 5 percent of our seminary budget on our own. Although the faculty was inclined to say yes, our president told us that such action would undercut the obligation of the church at large. At that time 100 percent of the seminary budget was raised by the church. But now this has dwindled to a small percentage. The seminaries in turn were forced to employ more and more staff to raise money. The same was true for recruiting students because their tuition was needed to finance the seminaries. Back then most students entering seminary came from church colleges. But gradually students began to come from all kinds of institutions and, above all, from other vocations. Eventually, seminaries had to employ more staff for recruiting students and raising money than they had faculty members to teach the seminarians. Finally, this became too costly, since seminaries are much smaller than colleges that have recruiting teams for finances and students. As a result, seminaries either merged or they aligned themselves with colleges. But the primary concern of these institutions is not to educate future clergy and to provide continuing education for pastors. The seminaries survived but at the expense of their own identity. And yet the church at large still does not give adequate support to the education of future clergy. As a consequence, in the ELCA one thousand congregations are without a full-time pastor who would care for and nourish the members of these congregations. The situation is no better in other mainline churches. What complicates the situation is that church attendance is shrinking and with it also congregational budgets. At least one in four congregations in the ELCA can no longer afford to pay a full-time pastor. This means that part-time ministers, which were introduced when there was a surplus of pastors, need to be seriously reconsidered.

But should one simply take as an unalterable given the continuous decline in congregational membership? Where are the mission-minded pastors and congregations? Of course, in rural areas demographics often do not allow for expansion. But in towns and cities where many unchurched people live, neither pastors nor congregations should take the situation as a given. Yet denominations are often looking for more diversity, rather than for a more joyful proclamation of the gospel. What is often overlooked is that diversity will be achieved by itself if growth occurs.

5. POLITICS AND THE CHURCH

Church and politics can become a very hot topic in the church. There was a heated discussion when the EKD, the Protestant Church in Germany, bought a ship that is cruising in the Mediterranean to rescue people from drowning who want to cross over from Africa to Europe. Each year thousands of people try to reach the European continent from Africa and are often put on flimsy boats that are not seaworthy and are unfit for travel. These refugees try to escape from persecution in their home country or they simply see no future for themselves there. Hundreds of these refugees who have tried to cross the Mediterranean in these boats end up dying each year. But many people in Germany questioned the wisdom of such rescue missions by the church. The question was, does this actually help to save people's lives, or does it encourage even more refugees to try to cross the sea? What incensed even more people was that this ship hoisted the flag of Antifa, which stands for anti-fascist action, but is actually a loosely knit organization of the extreme left. It is no surprise that Wolfgang Schäuble (b. 1942), the former president of the German Federal Assembly and a confessing Christian, declared several times that the EKD is hardly distinguishable from a coalition of the Green and the Socialist Democratic parties. Many church members disagree with such a course of action for the church and have either withdrawn from active participation or have left the church altogether. But mixing politics and the church is not just a German issue.

During the 1960s, the time of the civil rights movement in the USA, the following slogan was heard: "Pastor, just preach the gospel and leave politics out of the pulpit." Most church members did not like to hear about certain topics even if they were suggested in the sermon text. For instance, that all people are children of God, blacks as well as whites. Or that we should share our abundance with the needy. People refused to have their way of life and their thinking challenged by a sermon. Everything should remain as it is, including economic and societal conditions. Neither the preacher nor the church should challenge the status quo. I remember the time when our pastor told me that some of our members wanted to leave our congregation because blacks were joining. When I asked who these African Americans were and the pastor told me their names, I was really surprised. Their skin was so white that I would have never considered that they were actually African Americans. Some people can be very easily offended. When pastors were too outspoken about the civil rights of black members, they were often asking for trouble in their congregation. Some even had to leave that congregation and look for another church that was more open-minded, both racially and economically. But everybody who goes through life with open eyes and ears knows that one cannot tread water. A Christian either grows or stagnates and digresses.

Often, however, avoiding politics in the pulpit is seen as a sign of tolerating the prevailing situation in society. Two quotations from Germany may exemplify this: "The time of a politicizing church is over. We hold the high mission of the churches and pastors of both denominations [i.e., Roman Catholic and Protestant] in much too high esteem that we should ever admit that besides its high and responsible office it could influence the shaping of political affairs in Germany."[51] And another quotation: "Each Christian must be saved in accordance with his or her own denomination. But we cannot allow the denominations to decide in political life. Here I am not a Catholic or a Protestant but I am just a German!"[52] Both quotations are from the Third Reich in Germany. During the Third Reich the German government did not only restrict the churches to their so-called religious function but at the same time the Nazi government interfered in many ways with the church's own work, including its proclamation. Quite regularly members of the secret police were sitting in the pews taking down every sentence the pastor spoke. Every word he spoke could then be used against him. But does the demand of a totally nonpolitical sermon not border on wishful thinking? The Word of God must always be related to the peculiar situation in which the listeners find themselves. We should heed the comment made by Dietrich Bonhoeffer: "A purely spiritual relationship is not only dangerous but also an altogether abnormal thing."[53] In a sermon as well as in daily life our spiritual relationship with God must turn to the outside unless our faith is only empty piety. We are reminded of Jesus' words: "Just as you did it to one of the least of these who are members of my family, you did it to me" (Matt 25:40). A sermon always impinges on the world in which we live. Since it is preached by a certain person to a certain congregation at a certain time and place it is always personal and contextual. It occurs in a societal context and addresses this context. Therefore, a sermon must be political, addressing the polis, meaning the place where we live with its people and its challenges. Otherwise a sermon is theoretical and lifeless.

Just like everybody else, preachers have been exposed to various influences. They grew up in a family that influenced their outlook even if they rebelled against it. They are either liberal or conservative, from the lower class or middle class and from a rural or urban context. These are some of the influences that shape what they say and how they think about certain issues. Preachers have some influences which are in common with their audience while they have others which may separate them from the members of their congregations. Since preachers are always called to a specific congregation they must try to include the horizon of the members into their proclamation. Therefore, one would preach differently in a rural congregation than in an urban setting. This does not mean that one should proclaim what the people are expecting, but one should look at the people's mouth, as Martin

51. Siebert, "Kirche ist unpolitisch!," 15.

52. Hitler, "Staatsmann," 9.

53. Bonhoeffer, *Life Together*, 38.

Luther said, to pick up their kind of language. One should not proclaim a different gospel but proclaim the same gospel differently.

Yet the listeners are also tied to their regional situation. This situation influences the people who expect from the sermon impulses for how to arrange their lives. Unless we preach a foreign gospel, this situation must be considered in the proclamation. Often situations, whether political, economic, cultural, or ecclesial, are problem laden. Perhaps politicians have pocketed money instead of being concerned about the common welfare or there is a big gap between the rich and the poor. One is tempted here to address these commonly known facts time and time again. But that does not do justice to a sermon. I live in Regensburg, Germany and one of our sister cities is Odessa in Ukraine. In almost every sermon our dean preached he mentioned this city and the situation in Ukraine. I was so relieved when he finally visited Nicaragua and now at least we have heard about this country too. But a sermon should not dwell on generalities even if they might be interesting; it should deal with the specific and the personal concerns of the individual congregants. Moreover, a sermon should not concentrate on negativity but proclaim the joyous message of the gospel.

Even in the face of the gravest human shortcomings and the most dangerous misdemeanors, in the end the word of grace must clearly be proclaimed. While in the Babylonian exile the prophet Isaiah was reminded by the Lord: "Comfort, O comfort my people" (Isa 40:1). But the negative should not be simply eliminated. A sermon that avoids the law and does not name as negative that which opposes God's commandments pronounces cheap grace and leads to indifference. A sermon should arouse our conscience and condemn sin but not the sinner. It should sharpen our judgment and help us to discern God's ways. The sermon, however, cannot leave us distant from God as if the preacher had nothing else to do than to denounce this and that and simply rail against certain things. The listeners should be led back to God, who accepts them just as the Father received the prodigal son.

We should remember that God's Word always meets us in two ways, as law and as gospel. Law and gospel are different in their functions. The law meets us as God's demanding Word that says that something must be done and something else cannot be done. It makes the accusation that we have not fulfilled God's will. The gospel, however, announces that God's will has been fulfilled in Christ. It shows us a God who meets us in Christ and who discloses to us that God is gracious and has forgiven us our sins. The salvational aspect of God's Word becomes most clear in the life and activity of Jesus Christ. But already the law and the prophets point to the gracious God, a fact that the apostle Paul never gets tired of emphasizing.

During the time of Jesus' life on earth many people understood God's Word as a set of rules and that obeying them would guarantee that they were right with God. Jesus corrected this misunderstanding in the Sermon on the Mount and in many other places. But the same misunderstanding is still held today by many people. They assume that an ethically unblemished life will ultimately be rewarded by God. The German poet Johann Wolfgang von Goethe (1749–1832) expressed this in his dramatic poem *Faust* in this way: "Whoe'er aspiring, struggles on, for him there is salvation."[54] Such a misunderstanding of God's guidelines enslaves humans because they think if they literally fulfill God's Word then they are just. This self-righteousness often erects new barriers of injustice and inequality over against other people. One assumes one is better than others and continually pushes ahead to prove to oneself and others that this is true. If the law is separated from the gospel, this can lead to enslavement instead of liberation. One claims that as a Christian one must do this or that. But if Christ is the end of the law, there should be liberation. Christ has fulfilled for us God's will, and has done justice to the law.

But the law has not simply been abolished. It still serves as God's guidelines for our life. It is no longer something that feels like a burden that oppresses us or shows us our sinfulness, but it guides us to a godly life. John Calvin (1509–64), for instance, writes: "The third and principal use, which pertains more closely to the proper purpose of the law, finds its place among believers in whose hearts the Spirit of God already lives and reigns."[55] To support this statement, Calvin refers primarily to Old Testament texts such as Psalm 19:8, where the psalmist writes: "The precepts of the Lord are right, rejoicing the heart." Philipp Melanchthon (1497–1560), Luther's co-worker, pursued a similar line of thinking when he wrote that "the keeping of the law must begin in us and then increase more and more."[56] We must admit that Christians, too, need moral guidelines for their lives. They need to recognize God's will so they can lead their lives properly. When we are confronted with the gospel and understand how gracious God is to us, then our answer to God's grace does not follow from some guidelines, though we orient ourselves to them, but we live in thankfulness according to God's precepts. This means we do not live according to the law because that would be expected from us, but we live out of thankfulness over against God's unmerited love. Our ethics is not oriented towards the law as a dutiful life, but

54. Goethe, *Faust*, 290.

55. Calvin, *Institutes of the Christian Religion* (2.7.12), 1:360.

56. Melanchthon, *Apology of the Augsburg Confession* (IV: Justification, 136), *BC* 142. Cf. also *Epitome of the Formula of Concord* (4), where the third use of the law is defended.

one coming from God's grace as a life of thankful response. For instance, the introduction to the Decalogue does not start with certain admonitions, but with that which God has done for Israel (Exod 20:1). Only then come the Ten Commandments. Our ethical stance is a response of thankfulness for what God has done for us. Therefore, Luther advocates only a twofold use of the law, a theological and a political, while Calvin also teaches the third use of the law in those who are born again. Following Calvin, Karl Barth writes: "*As the doctrine of God's command, ethics interprets the Law as the form of the Gospel.*"[57] The law is embraced here, so to speak, by the gospel and the danger of a new legalism arises as is often evident in Calvinistic and pietistic communities. When I grew up as a member of the YMCA, which in Germany is still pietistic, we were told that as a Christian one does not smoke, dance, and drink beer. In a similar way, many secular people today live under the continuous pressure exerted by society or by themselves to meet the ruling laws and the expectations of society. The proclamation of the gospel should free us from such pressure.

In contrast to the existence oriented by the law that many people pursue, a Christian lives continuously between two poles. As the imperatives in Paul indicate (Rom 6:12–14), the Christian existence is marred over and over again by sin. Therefore, a Christian is often described as sinner and justified at the same time. Justification before God through which God no longer make us accountable for our sins, does not change our essence. We are still the same people with our imperfections. If we succumb to them God's Word encounters us as law, which accuses us that we have transgressed God's commandments and pushes us back to the gospel. This means that both the gospel and the law are pronounced in the Christian community. If we cling to Jesus, we live according to the gospel and are in union with God. But as sinners we live under the law and forget about God's grace. Just like children we do need not only God's love, but also his authority so that we stay on the right track. Luther explained this in a sermon: "The law uncovers the disease, the gospel gives us the medicine."[58]

We not only need the gospel, the word of God's gracious compassion, to regain our health, but also the realization that we are actually not worthy of that compassion. The Lutheran theologian Dietrich Bonhoeffer wrote:

> Grace interpreted as a principle, *pecca fortiter* [sin boldly] as a principle, grace at a low cost, is in the last resort a new law, which brings neither help nor freedom. . . . So they said, thinking that

57. Barth, *CD*, vol. 2/2: *Doctrine of God*, 509 (§36).

58. Luther, "*Sermon von den Heiligtumen*" (Holy Cross) of September 14, 1522, *WA* 10/III: 338.9–10.

> we must vindicate our Lutheran heritage by making this grace available on the cheapest and easiest terms. To be "Lutheran" must mean that we leave the following of Christ to the legalists, Calvinist and enthusiasts—and all this for the sake of grace. We justified the world, and condemned as heretic those who tried to follow Christ.[59]

In the same way as grace became possible because Jesus offered his whole life for us, so grace can only be efficacious when we dedicate our whole life to Jesus. Luther talked in his *Small Catechism* about daily repentance through which the old Adam must be drowned. Where the old Adam and the old Eve are no longer taken seriously, we slide into libertinism and ultimately even sin is justified for the sake of love. Many Christians then erroneously reason that if God is love, we need not be afraid of him regardless how we behave. This casuistic thinking that the God of love as the goal justifies us regardless of how we act has nothing to do with the gospel.

A sermon is directed to the listeners in front of the preacher and not to those outside the church whom one would like to reach but who are not present. For instance, the point goes right over the heads of the audience if politicians are berated on account of their misconduct when there are no public officeholders in the congregation. Moreover, many of the congregants will have heard of these incidents from the media and furthermore the sermon only indirectly addresses the situation of the listeners. Such a "political sermon" totally misses the audience. Even if there are representatives of public office among the listeners one should be careful that the polemic is well-informed. It is the sign of an uneducated preacher or even of libel if one polemicizes against certain matters and is insufficiently or wrongly informed. Wholesale condemnations are not convincing. If ecclesial representatives are tinged by animosity against new technologies or betray political one-sidedness they should carefully check their prejudices and present these matters in an informed and unbiased way. Of course, everybody including a preacher is entitled to his or her opinion or conviction. But the phrase "the way it seems to me" has no place in the pulpit. There the Word of God is to be proclaimed and not the preacher's opinion.

Preachers should not become opportunistic and only say that which is in vogue or only that which people want to hear. While preachers should serve their congregations, they are not servants of their congregation. They are servants of the Word of God and for this they are called to a certain congregation. They have to serve the Word and nothing and no one else. Therefore, we read in the so-called *Barmen Declaration* of 1934: "Jesus Christ,

59. Bonhoeffer, *Cost of Discipleship*, 57–58.

as he is attested for us in holy scripture, is the one Word of God which we have to hear and which we have to trust and obey in life and in death. We reject the false doctrine, as though the church could and would have to acknowledge as a source of its proclamation, apart from and besides this one Word of God, still other events and powers, figures and truths as God's revelation."[60] Preachers are not prophets who can pretend, as the so-called German Christians did during the Third Reich, when they acted as if it was a special expression of the divine will and therefore that God enlisted their service in an exceptional way. If preachers usurp such prophetic gifts, we must ask them how the interpretation of this specific event is legitimized. Does this interpretation result from their own political, social, or ecological interests or can they support it with Scripture? Often political utopians and sectarian movements have been totally wrong with their pronouncements. We too should be very hesitant in accepting prophetic proclamations. Yet in a given situation God's Word may indeed call us to action so that we stay obedient to that Word. We need no great prophetic gifts to recognize that God entrusts us continuously with new tasks and confronts us with decisions which we must make according to God's way. In other words, we must relate our Christian existence to the societal context to which an appropriate sermon speaks. Yet where are the limits of a political sermon?

Under the leadership of Karl Barth dialectic theology pointed again to the task of the preacher to proclaim God's Word during the turbulent times after World War I. "Preaching means to read what is written, a reading that becomes an address to today's people but in such a way that through the sermon of God's church these people of today become students of Holy Scripture."[61] Preaching a text-based sermon means that the text does not become a pretext for confronting us with this or that concern of the preacher but that the text is expounded in its context to confront us in our present situation with the central message of this text. Yet in the 1930s an emergency situation arose with the rise to power of the Nazi party ensuing in the Third Reich. The government attempted to take over the church and its pulpits with the help of the so-called German Christians. Armed with the biblical message, this usurpation by the National Socialists had to be rejected.

Against the totalitarian leadership of the National Socialists Karl Barth emphasized the kingship of Christ, which called for unmitigated allegiance to Jesus. Faith could no longer be restricted to inner feelings and the separation of faith and politics was in principle excluded. While

60. Barmen Declaration.

61. Barth and Thurneysen, *große Barmherzigkeit*, preface.

this made sense against the totalitarian Nazi regime, the situation after World War II in the newly established German democracy was different. With political sermons pastors now participated in the discussion about the rearmament of Germany, the Vietnam War, the peace movement, and nuclear energy. Political conduct and political actions were declared to be decisions of faith. Here Martin Luther's distinction between the two regiments or ways of God's governing of the world points in a different direction. Luther says:

> God has established two kinds of government among men. The one is spiritual; it has no sword, but it has the word, by means of which men are to become good and righteous, so that with this righteousness they may attain eternal life. He administers this righteousness through the word, which he has committed to the preachers. The other kind is worldly government, which works through the sword so that those who do not want to be good and righteous to eternal life may be forced to become good and righteous in the eyes of the world. He administers this righteousness through the sword. And although God will not reward this kind of righteousness with eternal life, nonetheless, he still wishes peace to be maintained among men and rewards them with temporal blessings.[62]

God governs the people through his Word that is entrusted to the preachers. Through the Word people should be guided in this life to enter eternal bliss in the hereafter. Since, however, not all people in this world are Christians, there must be a worldly government for those who do not care about God. They must be directed by the law to do what is right. The resultant worldly virtues, Luther maintained, God does not reward with eternal life. But they are necessary for worldly order. Even if Christians as Christians follow God's commandments, they still live in this world governed by law. As Luther maintained, we "are all caught in it, indeed, born into it, before we have become Christians. Therefore, we must also remain within it as long as we live upon the earth but only according to our external bodily life and existence."[63] According to our worldly needs we are members of this world and according to our spiritual existence we are members of the spiritual realm.

Life in this world is arranged according to the positive law as it is laid down in the legislation of different human communities. Unless we live

62. Luther, *Whether Soldiers, Too, Can Be Saved* (1526), *LW* 46:99–100.

63. Luther, "Sermon on Matthew 5:38–42," *Wochenpredigten über Matth. 5–7* (1530–32), *WA* 32:390,15–18.

under a totalitarian regime, this legislation is not designed arbitrarily but ultimately it is an expression of the divine law formulated in the Ten Commandments and the Golden Rule. To enact this law, governments need no special revelation. God has endowed us with natural reason, which enables us to discern this law and to conduct ourselves accordingly. Luther maintains that worldly affairs are arranged by reason and political and economic decisions are made according to reason and not according to the Bible. Luther also points out that Christ did not preach anything about economic issues but left this area to reason so that reason teaches us how we should distribute goods and conduct commerce. This would also imply that the pulpit is not the right place to preach in the name of God about economic issues or other worldly things. The preacher can and even should appeal here to human reason. Luther writes: "In temporal things and in those which pertain to a human being a person is reasonable enough and needs no other light apart from reason. Thus, God does not teach in Scripture how to build houses, make clothing, marry, go to war, sail ships, or other similar things that humans do, for in these matters the natural light [of reason] suffices."[64] Luther's understanding of reason does not correspond to that of the Enlightenment, a period in which humans thought they were responsible only to themselves in their use of reason. For Luther reason is a gift of God to whom we are responsible for its correct use. This is still true today when we consider humans as God's creatures and not just as products of natural evolution. If we use reason without regard to God, then this leads to *hubris*, the consequences of which we face in our lives.

If the Bible does not say anything about economic or scientific issues since it is not a primer on economics or a biology book, does this mean that preachers should not take a position on issues in these areas? We must remember two points here: (1) These areas belong to reason and therefore we need appropriate knowledge to deal with issues arising from them. Nothing hurts the credibility of preachers more than when they pontificate on issues without correct knowledge. While they must have competency in exegeting the Bible this competency is also presupposed for secular issues they touch on in a sermon. (2) When Luther says that humans are endowed with reason as God's gift, he does not naïvely presuppose that reason is responsibly used. He knows of human corruption and admits realistically, "Since the beginning of the world a wise prince is a mighty rare bird, and an upright prince even rarer."[65] Luther always had a healthy distrust of power exercised

64. Luther, "Sermon on Isaiah 60:1–6," *Weihnachtspostille* (1522), *WA* 10/I/1:531.6–11.

65. Luther, *On Temporal Authority: To What Extent It Should Be Obeyed* (1523), *LW* 45:113.

in the secular arena. Power always contains a demonic temptation to its misuse. Yet Luther neither turned away from the world nor did he simply consider it as the arena of the devil. All his criticism against power brokers notwithstanding, which he uttered in his voluminous correspondence as well has in his publications and sermons, he was always conscious of his responsibility for the common good.

Luther followed no particular "party line," and emphasized that each citizen owes to the governing authority the word of truth, whether as criticism or as assent. "If it is influenced by this, well and good; if not, you are excused, you suffer wrong for God's sake."[66] This also shows how far a political sermon should go. It should not be used to erect a theocracy, a garden of Eden, or the kingdom of God, in contrast to what Calvin had in mind in Geneva where he wanted to establish a theocracy. A sermon, however, should call public injustice an injustice even if, similar to many Old Testament prophets, such calls bear no success. Yet such calls should not be repeated over and over again so that a sermon becomes ideologically abbreviated and the gospel is forgotten. Luther did not do this either, because he was convinced that a ruthless authority cannot continue its injustice forever. Ultimately God is the one who rules and in his time God will topple a disobedient ruler. We can still today learn from Luther and desist from the vain idea of creating an ideal world. We can neither save the world nor root out all evils. God will do this in his proper time.

In conclusion: A sermon is necessarily political as long as we live in this world and the commandment of love and the Sermon on the Mount maintain their validity. Christians must move beyond their inward spirituality and consider the needs and rights of their neighbors. This is what public theology is all about. The limit of a political sermon consists in the fact that the world, whether in economics or in ecology, will always be foreign to a preacher and he or she can never have the same competency in this field as someone who is at home there. Moreover, such an area should never become the preacher's own field of expertise, because then the area entrusted to the preacher, the Word of God, takes second place. Preachers are never politicians and politicians can never become preachers without abandoning their respective fields. A truly political sermon will never follow a "party line" nor become remiss of its own task to proclaim the Word of God to all people.

66. Luther, *On Temporal Authority*, *LW* 45:124–25.

6. Culture and the Church

Culture and the church are intimately connected. The church does not exist in a vacuum but is always situated in a certain culture. The key question, however, is how the church relates to the culture in which it exists. Does it condone the culture or does it even affirm it, or is it in opposition to the respective culture? Since culture is a human phenomenon that changes in space and time, the relationship of the church cannot be the same all the time. We may think here of the church in Communist countries of bygone days or the church in predominantly Muslim countries in our present world.

When we approach the relationship between culture and the church historically, we can discern that this relationship is as old as humans are. The word "culture" is derived from the Latin verb *colere,* which means to till, to cultivate, or to adorn. In Genesis 2:15 we read: "The Lord God took the man and put him into the garden of Eden to till it and keep it." Humans have the God-given task to till or to change the nature in which they find themselves. They have done this since they have existed, from the first tool-making enterprise to the building of skyscrapers and airplanes. At the same time their urge to change nature has received both praise and criticism. The French writer and philosopher Jean-Jacques Rousseau (1712–78) not only paved the way for the French Revolution but was a vehement critic of culture. He claimed that the arts and the sciences did not result in human progress but in pride and vanity. Moreover, material progress had actually undermined the possibility of true friendship by replacing it with jealousy, fear, and suspicion. Therefore, his call was "back to nature" and in his novel *Èmile* or *On Education* he advocated that Émile be raised in the countryside, which, Rousseau believed, is a more natural and healthy environment than the city.

On the theological side Karl Barth and the neo-Reformation theology that Barth inaugurated claimed that the embrace of culture that dominated large parts of the nineteenth-century theology was the wrong move. Barth called proclamation and theology back to the basics, to the Word of God. Our task is not to talk about morality and culture, about religion, worship, and the possible existence of other worlds, because these are things with which people concern themselves already. But "they want to learn more about what is on the farther edge of [the] living *God*. . . . Man as man cries out for God. He cries out not for *a* truth, but for *truth*; not for *something* good, but for *the* good; not for answers but for *the* answer."[67] Therefore we should not settle for anything penultimate, but strive for the ultimate. Only from the ultimate can we address the human need because humans need

67. Barth, "Word of God," 189–90.

salvation and not solutions. The same focus that is important for the pastor is also mandated for the theologian at the university. Because "as a science like other sciences theology has *no* right to its place; for it becomes then a wholly unnecessary duplication of disciplines belonging to the other faculties. Only when a *theological* faculty undertakes to say or at least points out the need for saying, what the others . . . dare not say, or dare not say out loud, . . . only then is there a *reason* for it."[68] This means that a theological faculty should not become a faculty for the study of religion and talk about religious insights but it must be a faculty of theology, speaking of God and of eternity in time. Barth turns against Schleiermacher's emphasis on religion, saying "that one can *not* speak of God simply by speaking of man in a loud voice."[69]

But then there is Paul Tillich (1886–1965), who is often considered a theologian of culture. Before he came to America on account of the Nazi pressure on people like him who were critical of their ideology, Tillich had touched theology in his lectures only on the periphery. He conducted courses mainly on philosophical topics, such as on philosophy of religion, the religious interpretation of history, and religion and the city. But in his new environment at Union Theological Seminary in New York with daily chapel and an explicit theological curriculum he delved into theology proper with his *Systematic Theology*. There he wrote: "Theology, as a function of the church, must serve the needs of the church. A theological system is supposed to satisfy two basic needs: The statement of the truth of the Christian message and the interpretation of this truth for every new generation."[70] This is exactly what Tillich had in mind throughout his long career, to discern what the Christian message is and to interpret it in the context of his own time. To accomplish this, he used two tools: the method of correlation and the concept of symbols. "In using the method of correlation, systematic theology proceeds in the following way: it makes an analysis of the human situation out of which existential questions arise, and it demonstrates that the symbols used in the Christian message are the answers to these questions."[71] For this analysis one employs all materials made available by our creative self-interpretation in culture. This was one of the reasons why Tillich was interested in virtually everything that humanity did and produced, whether drama, poetry, art, philosophy, or science. Tillich claimed that this analysis is actually the task of the philosopher. The Christian message then provides the answers to the questions implied in the

68. Barth, "Word of God," 193–94.

69. Barth, "Word of God," 196.

70. Tillich, *Systematic Theology*, 1:3.

71. Tillich, *Systematic Theology*, 1:62.

human existence, meaning answers to issues like *hubris*, anxiety, estrangement, etc. Tillich was adamant that the answers that theology provides are not derived from human existence, but from the notion of God.

While Tillich correlated culture with the Christian message, Langdon Gilkey (1919–2004) followed culture as it unfolded in his own life and around him.[72] As Gilkey has shown in *Religion and the Scientific Future: Reflections on Myth, Science, and Theology*, there is a paradox in humanity because on the one hand humanity "is seen as an initiating moral and rational *cause* as well as the determined *effect* of natural and historical forces" to solve our problems. However, then this same human being is understood "as the determined *object* of inquiry" as if humanity had no freedom at all.[73] How can a human being be free on the one hand to objectively investigate and on the other hand not be free at all so that it can be objectively examined? Gilkey therefore concluded: "For if man has still great difficulty in controlling himself, even when he means well, then surely we must be much more realistic about ourselves and hence more careful when we embark socially on programs designed to control ourselves and thus our destiny and ourselves through scientific knowledge."[74] He even ventured to say: "Man cannot believe himself to be the sole arbitrator of his own destiny without intellectual contradiction and historical self-destruction."[75] Since we are presently in a volatile situation and since humanity is unable to chart the course toward the future because of humanity's intrinsic finitude, "we need symbols of ultimacy with which these intense reactions and perilous ventures into the unknown can be illumined, channeled, strengthened and tempered."[76]

Gilkey is a theologian of history, yet in contrast to those of the nineteenth century he is no longer one of progress and human perfection, but also not one of the decline of history. Upheld by God's grace, the historic process reflects human triumphs and failures, yet ultimately it will be elevated into God's kingdom through God's grace and all-encompassing love. Gilkey is not a prophet of pessimism, but reminds us of God's never-ending love. With regard to history and the role humans play in it, he perceptively states: "Although the level of knowledge, theoretical and technical, may steadily rise, our ability to use it creatively does not, nor do self-concern and

72. Cf. for his own interpretation, Gilkey, "Retrospective Glance."

73. Gilkey, *Religion and the Scientific Future*, 81–82.

74. Gilkey, *Religion and the Scientific Future*, 95.

75. Gilkey, *Religion and the Scientific Future*, 98.

76. Gilkey, *Reaping the Whirlwind*, 239.

irrationality recede. Thus, civilization remains as ambiguous and precarious a venture as ever."[77]

Relating culture and the church, one dare not forget H. Richard and Reinhold Niebuhr. Similar to Barth, they started out in the liberal camp and then, as Barth had done, Reinhold Niebuhr (1892–1971) arrived at social involvement and an assessment of society that was both realistic and Christ-centered. His brother H. Richard (1894–1962) too traveled from a monotheistic interpretation of the world, betraying the influence of Ernst Troeltsch (1865–1923), to a more and more Christocentric view. To some extent they did for American theology what Barth had done for European theology, bringing Christ to theology and to the world. While for Barth the turning point was the crisis ensuing from World War I, for the Niebuhrs it was the Great Depression and the resulting economic plight and terrible human misery that showed them the fallacy of liberal theology and its optimistic portrayal of humanity and its future.

In Reinhold Niebuhr's two-volume work *Nature and Destiny of Man* (1941/43), which were his Gifford Lectures of 1939–40, gone is the revolutionary optimism of his earlier days. We are confronted with a sober realism that also reflects the unsettling times of World War II. Not by accident we are confronted on the last pages of his two-volume work with the concept of the anti-Christ. Some of this can already be sensed in an earlier writing *Beyond Tragedy*, of 1937, where he stated that "the Christian view of history passes through the sense of the tragic to a hope and an assurance which is 'beyond tragedy.' The cross, which stands at the center of the Christian worldview, reveals both the seriousness of human sin and the purpose and power of God to overcome it."[78]

Throughout his life H. Richard Niebuhr had a passion for the church. This is demonstrated in all of his publications. In *The Meaning of Revelation* he stated in Barthian fashion: "Christian theology must begin today with revelation."[79] But then he continued with a sentence that might lead into relativism, betraying his indebtedness to Ernst Troeltsch: "It [i.e., Christian theology] knows that men cannot think about God save as historic, communal beings and save as believers." Christian theology must begin with revelation and this revelation can only be found in its historic manifestation, namely in the experience of the believers. This is the sphere of the internal history over against the external one, "the story of what happened

77. Gilkey, "Retrospective Glance," 26.

78. Niebuhr, *Beyond Tragedy*, x.

79. Niebuhr, *Meaning of Revelation*, 30.

to us, the living memory of the community."[80] Revelation is not some kind of hypothesis that then must be shown to be true, but through revelation something happens to us "in our history which conditions all our thinking and that through this happening we are enabled to apprehend what we are, what we are suffering and doing and what our potentialities are."[81] Revelation therefore is existential illumination of our own self and in this way puts us in touch with the one from whom and to whom we are. This means there is a transforming power in revelation, which at the same time is the self-disclosure of God.

This transformative power was also brought forth in *Christ and Culture* (1951). Yet before that publication there occurred the agony of World War II, in which Niebuhr suffered under the ambivalence and the nightmare of war.[82] He was critical of both the pacifists and the just war theorists, since neither one of them really understood the suffering that war caused. In *Christ and Culture* Niebuhr addressed the enduring issue of how Christianity and civilization are related to each other. Throughout history he discerns five different possibilities: Christ against culture, the Christ of culture, Christ above culture, Christ and culture in paradox, and Christ the transformer of culture. While he certainly preferred Christ as the transformer of culture, he concluded that there is not one Christian answer. The reason for this is simply that we are in society and not outside of it. Therefore, we cannot determine objectively what to do. We must decide as Christians in the midst of our cultural history. Yet recognizing this relativity does not mean that we are without an absolute, because in all our doing and thinking we are related to the ultimate absolute, God in Christ. This means the question is whether in our dependent freedom "we will choose with reasoning faithlessness or reasoning faith" which direction we will go.[83] The relationship of Christians to God as agents in culture was decisive for Niebuhr. He had learned from Troeltsch that Western culture and Christian faith belong together.

Therefore, he entitled one of his last publications *Radical Monotheism and Western Culture* (1960), in which he claimed that "radical monotheism dethrones all absolutes short of the principle of being itself. At the same time, it reverences every relative existent."[84] He could even accept naturalism and humanism as critiques of both religion and culture, but not as exclusive

80. Niebuhr, *Meaning of Revelation*, 66.

81. Niebuhr, *Meaning of Revelation*, 101.

82. Cf. for details the brief but illuminating biography of H. Richard Niebuhr by William Stacy Johnson, in Niebuhr, *Theology, History, and Culture*, xvii following.

83. Niebuhr, *Christ and Culture*, 251.

84. Niebuhr, *Radical Monotheism and Western Culture*, 37.

systems of closed societies, since, as he rightly recognized, they could only emerge within the freedom provided by a radically monotheistic faith.

As aforementioned our Western culture is deeply shaped by the Judeo-Christian tradition. The context for modern life, at least in the West, and through our global civilization even beyond that, is the Judeo-Christian tradition. As any calendar, sales chart, and bank account statement shows, our modern life and its progressiveness presupposes a linear concept of time, a time arrow that has a definite starting point and a definite goal. This linear understanding of time originated in the Judeo-Christian religion. As far as we know, all other worldviews and religions, with the exception perhaps of Zoroastrianism, a religion not unrelated to the Judeo-Christian tradition, are confined to a cyclical understanding of time.

For instance, in the Canaanite religion of Israel's neighbors, the most important active figure of their pantheon was Baal, a weather and fertility god. The local differentiations of his name and his being notwithstanding, he is *the* Canaanite god "with whom the nomadic tribes of Israel who confessed Yahweh came into contact from their emigration from Egypt till after the exile."[85] We can still discern several festivals in which Baal played a prominent role. The most important was the fall New Year festival where most likely the return of Baal from the underworld and his enthronement on Mount Sapan was celebrated at the Orontes River near Ugarit. In the spring there was the feast of mourning for Baal and finally in June the feast of the destruction of Mot, the god of death. Baal battled with the god of death and ended when Mot (death) conquered him and took him down to the underworld, from which his sister and sometime consort Anath freed him by destroying Mot after a violent struggle. As William F. Albright (1891–1971) writes: "In the Baal epic it is recorded that at the beginning there was a victory of Death over Baal, which was later followed by a triumph of Baal over Death, at the end of which the sad refrain,

> Truly I know that Triumphant Baal is dead,
> That the Lord of the Earth has perished,

is changed to

> Truly I know that Triumphant Baal lives,
> That the Lord of the Earth exists.[86]

The cult of Baal reflected the cyclic events of nature, which had great significance for the agrarian society in Canaan. "The Canaanites could

85. So Mulder, "Baal," *TDOT*, 2:199.

86. Albright, *Yahweh and the Gods of Canaan*, 126.

explain the change from one season to another and the differences between good and bad years only by believing that sometimes Baal was weak, sick, or even dead. This was a basic assumption of their religion. But such ideas were foreign to monotheistic Yahwism."[87] In the beginning of summer, the people lamented the death of Baal and the triumph of the death god Mot, because in the summer drought all vegetation dried out and perished through the merciless rays of the sun and the gusting winds of the desert. Later in the season people rejoiced and celebrated the death of Mot and the "resurrection" of the fertility god Baal, when the fall or winter rains drenched the dry ground and promised a good crop.

Such a seasonal rhythm between "life and death" does not provide much incentive for any long-range planning, because humanity feels itself subjected to the power of nature. The Indian religions of Buddhism and Hinduism provide even less stimulus to engage in any intensive planning for the future. Again, they portray a cyclical worldview and advocate as one of the main goals of this life the negation of all craving for life in order to break out of the fatal *samsara* (wheel of life) of birth, death, and reincarnation. Any interest in the future and any appreciation of life here on earth would only jeopardize the release from this world and its troubles. While there are significant differences between these various traditions, "the dominant trend is towards a belief that the true self (*Atman*) is unborn and never dies, and that the ultimate goal of the human spirit is to escape a continual cycle of birth, death, and rebirth, and attain either absorption into the Absolute or union with God."[88]

One might argue that the Greeks are an exception, because they reached a very high cultural level without a linear concept of time. There may be some truth in this. But when we penetrate through the cultural facade, we realize very quickly that the Greek view of life, similar to that of Rome, was quite pessimistic. Indicative of this is the fate of the two *kouroi* (i.e., young men), by the name of Cleobis and Biton, whose statues we can admire in the Museum of Delphi, Greece. The ancient historiographer Herodotus (ca.484–ca.425 BC) tells us the myth connected to them. They were two well-liked young men. Their mother was a priestess of Hera and had to be driven on a cart into the Heraeum for the Hera festival at the ancient city of Argos, south of Corinth. When the oxen were late, coming home from the fields, and time was running out, the two sons took the place of the oxen and pulled their mother in the cart to the Heraeum, which was five miles away. They were praised by everyone for this deed and their mother prayed

87. Mulder, "Baal," *TDOT*, 2:200.

88. So Badham and Badham, "Death and Immortality," 3.

to Hera that her sons should receive the best which is available in this world. The reward was that on that day "the two youth fell asleep in the temple. They never woke again, so passed from the earth."[89]

In the Greek understanding this world and the life connected with it have no actual value. Even Aristotle despised manual labor, which he thought should be left to the slaves. Instead, he preferred to concentrate on eternal issues. Plato, too, recognized this world as only a reflection of the eternal and unchanging world. He postulated a release from this earthly prison by which the eternal soul could return to its origin and destiny. The Greeks "were primarily concerned with the *logos* of the *cosmos*, not with the *Lord* and the meaning of history."[90] The *logos* was wisdom and the eternally unchanging; history however was singular and accidental. Only in Christianity did the *logos* become flesh and was understood as the Lord of history (John 1:14). During the classical period of Greek history, however, the gods of Homer (8th c. BC) looked like deified people and were themselves subject to the destiny of the world. In later Hellenism, the mystery religions indicate an unfulfilled yearning for immortality in which the Christian hope of the resurrection of the dead easily found open ears. Friedrich Nietzsche (1844–1900) in his *The Birth of Tragedy* rightly detected a pervasive pessimism through which any optimism eventually "suffers shipwreck."[91]

The British historian Arnold Toynbee (1889–1975) even suggested: the "cyclic view of the process of history was taken so entirely for granted by even the greatest Greek and Indian souls and intellects—by Aristotle, for instance, and by the Buddha—that they simply assumed that it was true without thinking it necessary to prove it."[92] Yet Toynbee himself opted for a "cyclic movement of civilizations round the cycle of birth, death, birth."[93] One civilization emerges, attains its height, and provokes another civilization to originate. The latter conflicts with the former, gains strength while fighting the other, and finally prevails until a third emerges. Like the waves of the sea crashing against the shore and receding, one civilization after the other is doomed to death without any evident progress.

Why is the Judeo-Christian religion so different that it can provide the ground for the modern emphasis on this world and the concern for

89. Herodotus, *History of Herodotus* (1,31), 11.

90. Löwith, *Meaning in History*, 4.

91. Nietzsche, *Birth of Tragedy* (15), 97.

92. Toynbee, *Civilization on Trial*, 14. However, Toynbee conceded the possibility that our present civilization may survive because this cyclic movement is no inescapable fate and leaves room for freedom of choice to give history "some new and unprecedented turn" (39).

93. Toynbee, *Civilization on Trial*, 236.

the future? The reason for this can be found in two basic convictions: (1) the belief in one God; and (2) the identification of this one God as the creator and redeemer of everything that is. Often the people of Israel were attracted to the polytheism of their neighbors, but their religious leaders always brought them back to Yahweh, the only God. Though Yahweh was, in a special sense, regarded as the divine head of the Hebrew community, this theocracy tended to be universalistic. Especially under the influence of the prophetic movement, that is, from about the middle of the eighth century BC onward, the Israelites thought of Yahweh more and more as the divine head of all humanity, while the neighboring nations still worshipped their respective particularistic gods.

Greco-Roman thinking was oriented to the past and was mainly interested in the eternal laws beyond and the history of the spiritual things above, out of which historical events flowed in eternal occurrence and recurrence. Thus the Greeks were not concerned about the Lord of history, but about the regularity and steadiness of the cosmos that they first perceived in the movements of the heavenly bodies. In the Judeo-Christian religion God was perceived as the agent of history, who works in and with history. Though the God of Israel was undoubtedly first understood as the redeemer of Israel, the consequent development of the universalistic view of God led to the understanding of God as the creator of everything that is. One should realize, however, that the gradual understanding of Yahweh as the creator of the world did not evolve to replace other creation stories that might have been prevalent within the Israelite community. As soon as the concept of creation emerged, the Israelites assumed that Yahweh was the creator.

When the Israelites moved into Canaan, they encountered a religion that had much to say about creation. We notice this for instance when Abraham returned from rescuing Lot from the hand of the four kings and met King Melchizedek of Salem, probably the ancient name of Jerusalem.[94] Melchizedek is called a priest of the Most High God (in Hebrew, *El Elyon*). He blessed Abraham and said to him: "Blessed be Abram by God Most High, maker of heaven and earth; and blessed be God Most High, who has delivered your enemies into your hand!" (Gen 14:19–20). In this city a god with the name of *El Elyon* was worshipped, of whom it was said that he had created heaven and earth. When Israel was confronted with such a godhead in the land they had conquered and occupied, the question was inescapable how they should respond to such a claim.

94. For the following cf. Fretheim, *Book of Genesis*, *NIB* 4, in his comments on Genesis 14:17–24.

Was *El Elyon* the creator of heaven and earth and Yahweh only the rescuer from Egypt, meaning the God of history? Such specialization of gods was quite common in the environment of Israel. Fertility statues of Astarte and many other symbols of the worship of gods and goddesses in Israel have been discovered in archaeological excavations. From these discoveries we may conclude that the Israelites were not immune to worshipping other gods. Yet the official line was different. Abraham responded to Melchizedek: "I have sworn to the Lord [Yahweh], God Most High [*El Elyon*], maker of heaven and earth that I would not take a thread or a sandal-thong or anything that is yours" (Gen 14:22–23). Abraham immediately identifies Yahweh with *El Elyon*, the creator of heaven and earth, because it was inconceivable for him that any god but Yahweh could be the creator of heaven and earth.

The understanding of a creator god did not develop as a separate belief system parallel to the notion of Yahweh as the redeemer. The Israelites were practical people, even in their religion. If Yahweh had brought them out of Egypt into the promised land, then he had also provided them with the goods of the promised land. Yahweh was its creator. As the Old Testament scholar Gerhard von Rad (1901–71) said: "From the earliest times this was Israel's view of Yahweh's relationship to the land, and to its way of life. This was the blessed plot given to the nation by the saving activity of Yahweh, the mighty Lord of history, and it still remained Yahweh's land."[95] Yahweh provided the origin of the world, he is active in it and he will provide its redemption. The latter came to its fulfillment in the Christian faith when the history of Jesus of Nazareth was understood as the decisive redemptive act of God. Thus history had a definite beginning (its creation), a definite course (the present acts of God), and a definite goal (redemption in and through Christ). History had a goal worth living for, and the present gained its well-deserved recognition too because it was the arena in which the faithful could prove themselves to be eligible for that final goal.

There was no emphasis on humanity, though. In the Judeo-Christian tradition it was clearly understood that humanity could never reach the final goal without the saving grace of God. This emphasis on the grace of God is already expressed in the concept of covenant. According to Jewish thinking a covenant is always offered by a stronger power (Yahweh) to a weaker power (the Israelite community) and not vice versa. When the Christian church saw itself in continuance with the Old Testament community the church found it impossible to accept the prevailing humanistic

95. von Rad, "Theological Problem of the Old Testament Doctrine of Creation," 132.

anthropology of the Greco-Roman world. In the Greco-Roman world, history was seen as a record of human deeds, purposes, successes, and failures. "The gods have no plan of their own for the development of human affairs; they only grant success or decree failure for the plans of men."[96] Christianity, however, rejected such optimistic ideas of human nature. The inability to achieve clearly planned goals was no longer understood as accidental but as a permanent element in human nature, arising out of the condition of humanity as a fallen creature. It was Augustine especially, with his concept of humanity being corrupted by sin, who influenced the thinking of the Western world for at least a thousand years.

At the same time, this did not mean a rejection of humanity. Admittedly, the historical process is not the working out of humanity's purposes, but of God's, because it is basically salvation history. We do not determine the course of history; God does. But God's purpose is not self-gratifying. It is a purpose intended for us, embodied in human life, and achieved through the activity of human wills. God predetermines the final goal, and he sees to it that everything will eventually move in this direction. But each human being is a historically important and responsible agent. We know what we want, and we pursue it, though often we do not know why we want it. As a result, it may be that we ourselves stand in the way of obtaining what we want.

God still works through us, even when we resist his purpose. We receive ultimate dignity and importance only as vehicles of God's redemptive purpose. All hope is founded and centered in God and not in the belief in progress or in humanity. The acting and active God who provided the beginning, who controls the present, and who will provide the future is the decisive center of all Christian and Jewish hope. Even now Christian churches still emphasize human unworthiness, though sometimes this is done more out of tradition than out of conviction, and it is questionable whether the hope in an active and gracious God still determines the life-orientation of most church members.

During the Middle Ages God-confidence prevailed over self-confidence. The pope ranked higher than the emperor, and everything was done to the glory of God and through God's grace. Gradually, however, humanity became more confident in itself. One of the first documents that shows that self-confidence prevailed over God-confidence is René Descartes' (1596–1650) *Discourse concerning the Method* (1637). He writes that he was in Germany and at the beginning of winter he was put up in a place where he had no conversation partner. "I remained all day near a stove,

96. Collingwood, *Idea of History*, 41.

where I had complete freedom to weigh my thoughts."[97] The result was the introduction of radical doubt into modern philosophy and into Western thought. He realized that it is possible to doubt everything except the fact that he was doubting. If that were denied, too, there would be nothing. Consequently, the starting point for reestablishing reality was "*I think therefore I am*" because "from the very fact that I was thinking of doubting the truth of other things, it followed very evidently and very certainly that I was."[98] Consequently, the "I" of the solitary human being became the foundation of all reality. Though Descartes still needed God to guarantee for him the reality of the world outside of him, the decisive point was made.

One hundred fifty years later Immanuel Kant (1724–1804) went a decisive step further in his essay "What Is Enlightenment?" (1783), by saying:

> Enlightenment is man's leaving his self-caused immaturity. Immaturity is the incapacity to use one's intelligence without guidance of another. Such immaturity is self-caused if it is not caused by lack of intelligence, but by lack of determination and courage to use one's intelligence without being guided by another. *Sapere Aude!* "Have the courage to use your own intelligence!" is therefore the motto of the enlightenment.[99]

Kant is advocating human freedom in political and religious matters and the dominance of human intellect and reason over any outside force. Humanity should no longer be dependent on someone or something else. Kant calls such dependence immaturity. We have become mature and are capable of determining our own destiny. This optimistic attitude prevailed throughout the Enlightenment era.

Gotthold Ephraim Lessing (1729–1781) in *The Education of the Human Race* (1780) draws an important analogy between education and revelation. Education is revelation made to the individual, while revelation is an education that has come and still continues to come to the whole human race. Nevertheless, education does not give a person anything one might not have derived from "within oneself," but one merely obtains it more quickly and easily. By the same token, "revelation gives nothing to the human race which human reason could not arrive at its own; only it has given, and still gives to it, the most important of these things sooner."[100] This would mean that according to Lessing the goal of human progress is no longer found

97. Descartes, *Discourse Concerning the Method* (2:19), 120, where he also refers to the Thirty Years' War during which this treatise was written.

98. Descartes, *Discourse Concerning the Method* (4:40–41), 134–35.

99. Kant, "What Is Enlightenment?," 132.

100. Lessing, *Education of the Human Race*, 83.

beyond humanity, but in humanity itself. But Lessing did not yet realize that his insistence on the rediscovery of "innate ideas" as the goal of progress must necessarily exclude true progress in the sense of creative novelty. Still the optimistic trust in the newly established self-confidence continued.

Charles Darwin's theory of evolution in the nineteenth century made humanity even more optimistic, because now the door seemed to be open for new and unprecedented human progress. The thinking was that if we have evolved so far beyond the animal world, we could evolve much further. While Kant emphasized human autonomy, that we should have enough self-confidence to determine our own views, the next step would be the implicit hope that we would be able to evolve beyond our present state.

Herbert Spencer (1820–1903) shaped the outlook of North America in the second half of the nineteenth century unlike any other writer by converting the theory of evolution into "an instrument of unbridled optimism."[101] Development for him is a cosmic principle that pertains especially to the human species. The universal development has to be made fruitful for humanity to drive it to further progress. Nothing can be excluded from this progress, no knowledge, no value systems, and no feelings. Humanity is in control of its future; humans can determine their own progress and need no longer rely on an active God.

Along with the change from God-confidence to self-confidence, another important shift emerged that contributed to the belief in progress induced by humanity, the secularization of the kingdom of God. The root for this shift lies in the Calvinistic theory of double predestination. In this theory we are predestined by birth either to be received into heaven after life on earth or to be condemned to eternal damnation. Of course, we want to find out as early as possible what our destiny is. In popular understanding the fact of election could be seen in earthly success. Thus, Calvinists worked tirelessly in an ascetic manner to prove to themselves and to others that they were on the right side. The results of this work, of course, could not be enjoyed but had to be added to the constant increase of the employed capital. Max Weber (1864 –1920) and Ernst Troeltsch rightly called Calvinism the forerunner of modern capitalism.[102]

101. Baillie, *Belief in Progress*, 144–45.

102. Cf. Troeltsch, *Protestantism and Progress*, 131–33. Whereas Max Weber sees at this point a close affinity between Calvinism and Judaism, Troeltsch rejects this idea, since the Calvinistic use of Jewish ethical teaching cannot sufficiently explain the phenomenon of modern capitalism (Weber, *Protestant Ethic and the Spirit of Capitalism*, 270–71n58, and Troeltsch, *Protestantism and Progress*, 141–42n1). Though Max Weber's thesis certainly needs modification (cf. Green, ed., *Protestantism and Capitalism*), the stimulus that Pietism and Calvinism provided for the development of modern capitalism and industrialization is undeniable (cf. Benz, *Evolution and Christian Hope*, esp. 129–31).

Pietism played a similar role with its radical orientation toward the other world. Their otherworldliness, by necessity, led pietists to responsible use of time here on earth. Time was not to be spent in worldly joy and amusement but in self-crucifying work. The house-father who presided over devotional meetings is at the same time the forerunner of many industrial endeavors. In the nineteenth century the centers of the pietistic movement in Germany, Rhineland-Westphalia, and Württemberg, became centers of industrial development. The religious convictions of the pietists led to the splendid material success of the grandchildren, most of whom long ago discarded the religious convictions of their forefathers.

In America the development was similar, partly in direct connection with the immigration of German pietists. One of the best-known American steel companies, the Bethlehem Steel Company (1857–2003) in Bethlehem, Pennsylvania, was established by a blacksmith who had immigrated from a community of pietists in Herrnhut, Germany, at the beginning of the eighteenth century.[103] He settled in Bethlehem, a Moravian missionary settlement in the forests of Pennsylvania, and started a small blacksmith shop. Quality and industriousness helped to develop his workshop into a huge enterprise. Though the name Bethlehem still showed the pietistic and pacifist origin of what was once one of the largest steel companies in the United States, it was turned into a huge conglomerate without regard to its religious premise.

In his book *The Kingdom of God in America,* H. Richard Niebuhr pointed to an important factor that caused this loss of the religious premise. He claimed that the spiritualistic and Calvinistic groups favored a heaven of their own design. They considered humanity to be virtuous enough to acquire such a heaven. But the radical transformation of life on earth eventually undermined the expectation of heavenly bliss. Through hard work, conditions on earth became attractive enough to cause them to forget a life in heaven, especially when they felt that humanity was on its way to bringing about the kingdom of God on earth.[104]

This is exactly the point at which the Christian proclamation has to come in: since humans are earthbound, they cannot bring about a new creation by themselves. Wherever this was promulgated, such as in the former Soviet Union and in Mao's China, it failed and brought with it countless victims. Only God can bring about a new creation, since he is creator and perfecter. The church should use this caveat whenever individuals or governments think of themselves as being in charge of this world. This does not

103. Benz, *Evolution and Christian Hope*, 130, provides this striking example.

104. Niebuhr, *Kingdom of God in America*, 150–52.

mean, however, that we can do nothing to improve the present conditions on this earth. The charge expressed in Genesis to till the earth is still valid. It is perhaps even more urgent than ever before, since we have thrown the natural balance in nature out of sync. Not unrelated to this is the second point that we dare not neglect in our proclamation of the Christian message. This is the issue of human sinfulness. Since we have a tendency to not want to make people feel bad, the term "sin" has largely disappeared from our vocabulary, both in the church and in society in general. Though we may be able to avoid the *term* sin, we cannot avoid its facticity. If everybody is living right, why are there so many inmates in our penitentiaries and why are court cases abounding, not to mention the crimes in homes and in the streets?

Encounters with phenomena that are perceived as negative belong to the most fundamental human experiences. While experiences that are judged to be positive are generally and understandably accepted without further reflection, negative experiences, especially in the form of evil or sin, pose for many people a seemingly inexplicable problem. What do we actually mean by saying that something is "evil" or "sinful"? Designations such as "evil," "bad luck," or "sin" are often used interchangeably. We frequently speak of something being "bad," when it does not exhibit the characteristics that we prefer. In other instances we often actually mean to say that a particular act or situation is evil or sinful, though still calling it just "bad." When we pronounce a person guilty of some crime we may tend to speak of sinful structures when what we really have in mind are inadequate social structures.

Underlying this semantic confusion is the fact that the theological concept of "sin" has largely disappeared from our everyday vocabulary. We do not want to offend anybody by calling something or someone sinful, since in our secular society we tend to shy away from a more penetrating religious evaluation and remain instead with a superficial religiously neutral point of view. Sin, as a fundamentally religious concept, usually designates an offense against a religious taboo or cultic law. If one violates, for instance, one of the Ten Commandments, then one has sinned. Moral "evil" overlaps considerably with that which is generally called sin. As a rule, however, evil is understood as the opposite of that which we hold to be good. Thus, evil has a patently ethical character since it is at variance with an intended or expected behavior. The word "evil" can also signify that which has been maliciously brought about. Yet it describes just as easily a negative event that virtually assumes the character of an impersonal fate. Finally, "guilt" designates one's own entanglement in that which is negative. It is through guilt that one bears the burden of what others experience as negative.

Although one may view that which is negative simply as the opposite of that which is experienced as positive, the initial identification of that which is negative or evil is far from simple. We categorize a thing or event as negative, evaluating it as having a "not good" character. In this way that which is contrary to our perceived needs, interests, or wishes is often labeled as negative. This can be seen most poignantly in those instances in which images of an enemy are erected that deny that which is good to the "other," portraying them at the same time as the incarnation of all that is evil. Such subjective defamation, often called a "shitstorm," can be found in both private and public life, and all too often in the realm of international politics as well. Hence other human beings are made to appear satanic and their right to existence denied. Nevertheless, it would be short-sighted to speak only of a subjective characterization of negative experiences as if objective evidence of the perversion of positive experiences was lacking.

Of course, that which we portray as evil, similar to that which we portray as good, is subjugated to a multitude of transformations. Despite all of this semantic maneuvering, the undisputed phenomenon of that which is concretely negative looms before us. Every human society testifies at least indirectly to the existence of this phenomenon. Each has developed a system of laws and regulations based upon the insight that people do not always conduct themselves in a manner that society at large deems appropriate. Similarly, all religious worship, whether monotheistic, polytheistic, or of some other form, witnesses to the fact that people have become alienated from their own essence. Therefore, the spirits or gods are to be appeased for human misbehavior through various religious practices. Even the very concept of redemption implies the acceptance of the fact that we are entangled in something that does not belong to our essential nature. Consequently, we encounter everywhere the idea of a basic evil that contradicts our fundamental orientation and our true self. That which is negative certainly has a subjective aspect, yet it also transcends the merely subjective.

The experience of the negative necessarily gives rise to the question, "Why?" Why is life on this earth characterized by the fact that humans make life miserable for each other? Why are even the "best" people, apart from any human interference, visited by serious diseases and other evils? Is there a force within and yet transcending humanity which functions, as it were, as a "diabolos," as a "distorter," continually detracting from the experience of the good in our lives and turning it instead into something negative? It is precisely this problem of evil, a problem that daily affects us and others, confronting us through newspaper, television, and drama, which has occupied the human mind through the ages. Christian preaching dare not shy away from calling a sin a sin, nor from proclaiming a gospel that can set us free. While a generation ago it was a matter of fact that the church's proclamation consists of law and gospel, it has now been abbreviated to mean the gospel alone and is often just portrayed as a dispensing of cheap grace. But such action misleads humanity because of its intrinsic ambiguity. It needs the law in its convicting way, convicting humans of their wrongdoings, and its guiding way to show them the right path, but also the gospel which frees them from condemnation and shows them God's enduring love.

PART 2

The Singular Elements of the Church

In order to win the world the church has often been tempted to associate itself so closely with the world that it becomes indistinguishable from the world. As a result, the church had nothing to offer that the world could not give too. As we all know, if we have nothing special to offer we are not attractive for people. The first exceptional characteristic of the church is its inclusivity. While secular organizations look for potential members or customers who have special gifts or needs, the church welcomes everybody. Jesus made this clear with his parable of the Great Dinner when he said: "Go out at once into the streets and lanes of the town and bring in the poor, the crippled, the blind, and the lame" (Luke 14:21). Even those for whom nobody else cares are welcome in the church. In talking about the church as the whole people of God we must avoid the twin dangers of inclusivity and exclusivity.

1. EVERYBODY IS INVITED

When we consider who belongs to the church we should not draw the borders too narrowly so that the church becomes an elitist group. Yet we also should not make the borders too wide so that the church becomes indistinguishable from the world. We remember here the distinction which Augustine made between the visible and the invisible church. The visible church is the institutional church, which usually has distinct criteria for church membership. When the church was formed in the first centuries one became a member by baptism and one remained a member as long as one did not deviate from the marks of being a Christian. When one denounced one's loyalty to Christ during persecutions or when one violated the Ten Commandments through crimes such as murder or theft, one was excluded from the Christian fold. Usually, however, through penitence and other means of sorrow and regret, one was accepted back into the church.

But today church discipline is hardly exercised regardless of how a member behaves. If church discipline were proposed today, some in the church would immediately claim that to discipline members does not jibe with God being a God of love. Only some Anabaptist groups, such as the Amish, still exercise "shunning," which means that if a member does something which is sinful, that person is silently banned, and the other members do not associate with or interact with that person. Also, in Catholicism "excommunication" is still practiced so that divorced members cannot be married again in the church. If they are married a second time by a judge, they are denied access to the Eucharist. How far away this is from actual reality I want to exemplify with the following incident: A good friend of mine who is in the real estate business came to me one day. He shared that his two children from his second marriage are now at the age at which they can take part in the Eucharist. But as a Roman Catholic who is divorced and remarried, he is barred from attending the Eucharist with his children. He asked me if I could I help him, so I referred him to my Roman Catholic colleague at the university. My colleague said that since the man's first marriage had been consummated it therefore could not be annulled. He suggested, however, that the man should attend the Eucharist with a different congregation where no one knew him. My realtor friend, however, resolved the issued by paying the salary of the organist of his congregation and consequently no questions were asked about him participating in the Eucharist. For me as a Lutheran such an incident is rather strange and has nothing to do with true repentance and forgiveness. But can we really do without church discipline? The consequences were outlined very well by H. Richard Niebuhr when he wrote: "A God without wrath brought men without sin into a Kingdom without judgment through the ministrations of a Christ without a Cross."[1] But the God of whom the Bible speaks is not a softy who would simply forgive because that is God's job. God also asks for accountability and at least regret and remorse. Otherwise our mindset will move us further and further away from God and God's ways. Therefore, even our definition of church membership needs serious reconsideration.

1. Niebuhr, *Kingdom of God in America*, 193.

In the German *Volkskirche* (people's church) one is a member of the church unless one has officially renounced church membership at the city hall in the town where one lives. Membership in the *Volkskirche* implies that one pays the church tax. This is an 8 to 10 percent surcharge added to one's income tax. The government collects this tax on behalf of the church for a certain fee, which is paid to the government by the denomination. This church tax is then deductible from one's income tax as a charitable contribution. This means one can be a member of the church "in good standing" without ever setting foot into the church sanctuary. In contrast, most American denominations determine active church membership if one communes at least once a year or supports the church financially at least once during the same period. After having been inactive for a certain time one is usually removed from the congregational roster unless the degree of participation improves. Neither one of these kinds of church membership fits the description of the Christians in Acts 2:42–46, where it says that "day by day they attended the temple together and devoted themselves to the apostles' teaching and fellowship."

Moreover, in the Protestant churches in Germany worship attendance on any given Sunday except Christmas is less than 5 percent. In Roman Catholic churches it is at the most around 15 percent and in the US in most mainline congregations less than half of the members attend church services on Sunday. Most denominations remain silent about the lacking communion spirit of their members. They are perhaps grateful that these "members" have not dropped out completely. We also hear nothing about churches trying to bring them back to worship on a regular basis in terms of evangelizing their own members.

Of course, regular attendance at worship and generous giving are not foolproof criteria by which one can determine who belongs to the whole people of God. Often these "positive" attitudes can be the result of either tradition, which we follow without much reflection, or of moralistic self-righteousness. If someone is one of the biggest donors in the congregation, they might feel like they have more influence on what is going on there. It is not without significance that one of the favorite motifs sculptured above the church portals of medieval European churches is the scene of the last judgment. There are always some people among those in the sculpture who are among those being condemned who bear distinctive ecclesiastical attributes, such as the bishop's miter. This indicates that medieval Christendom did not imply that church membership or holding an ecclesiastical office in the church necessarily meant that one belonged to the whole people of God. The boundaries of the institutional, visible church can indeed be larger than the boundaries of the invisible church.

Since the perimeters of the invisible church can, however, at times be larger than that of the visible institutional church, the suggestion has been made that everyone should be included in the invisible church, regardless of their actual religious affiliation, at least the most loyal members of a religion or a pseudo-religion. Living a righteous life is here the main criterion. Thus, the transition between Christians and non-Christians, and between Christians and Christendom itself, is no longer expressed in terms of an absolute either/or, but in a gradual more or less. Though it would be a confusion of terms and a potential act of Christian imperialism to call followers of non-Christian religions "anonymous Christians," as Karl Rahner once did, we should be aware that the whole people of God are not concomitant with active or inactive membership of one denomination, or of all the churches together. The Latin term for church, *ecclesia*, meaning those who are called out of something, reminds us that church members cannot be at the same time a part of something else. Their allegiance has to be within the church.

Luther has a very telling definition of the church when he writes in his *Smalcald Articles*, "God be praised, a seven-year-old child knows what the church is: holy believers and 'the little sheep who hear the voice of their shepherd.'"[2] The important point here is hearing the voice of their shepherd. Christians conduct their lives to the tune of their shepherd who guides them in the right direction. But is this really true? If we ask church members who they are, is their first answer that they are Christians, or will they answer that they are Americans, Democrats, or that they are from Ohio? What is their number one identification? Is it Christian or something else? If as Christians we are called out from the multitude of people in the world, then we must be something different than the others in this multitude. Of course, we can still maintain and rightly so that we are, for instance, Americans, Democrats, or Ohioans. But our number one identification is our affiliation as Christians, which we dare not forget. If this is no longer true, then we need not be surprised that Christians are not much different from other people. They are indeed mainline, following the same paths that everyone else takes in life. But then we lose our prime identification of being set apart by Christ to be his followers.

Being followers of Christ transcends any narrow denominationalism. Of course, most Christians belong to a certain denomination. But their prime identification results from the one who gathers, sanctifies, and enlightens people of all nations and all ethnic and religious origins. Since church members are those who hear the voice of their shepherd, we must

2. Luther, *Smalcald Articles*, *BC* 324. In Luther's time, at age seven a child had learned the Apostles' Creed and knew from this about the church.

first reflect on the nature of the church as it expresses itself in the will of this shepherd, God in Christ, who through the power of the Holy Spirit founded the church. This God-in-Christ centeredness does not make irrelevant the institutional church. It is still the primary institution that treasures the Christian tradition and facilitates a Christian consciousness through its instructional media. Yet it must constantly be measured, criticized, and realigned by the will of its founder, the good shepherd.

The Christian church is not a club that was founded to serve the interests of its members, nor is it a social institution through which a group of people attempts to reform society. As the Apostles' Creed expresses, the church is holy, catholic, and the communion of saints. Similarly, in the Nicene Creed the church is described as holy, catholic, and apostolic. The central determinant that these statements presuppose is Christ. The church is one, not because it is undivided; it is in fact divided, but it is one, because it is founded by one person, Jesus Christ. The unity of the church is given through its origin and promised within its eschatological horizon. The eschaton will not be arranged according to confessional families or denominations. I am reminded of my Greek Orthodox colleague Ioannis Kalogirou, who loved to tell the following story: An Orthodox Christian knocked on the pearly gates. When Peter opened the door he asked: "Are there any Roman Catholics here?" He just wanted to make sure that he was in the right place. When Peter answered with a no, he continued to ask: "Are there any Protestants here?" And again Peter answered with a "no." The Orthodox Christian was sure that neither Roman Catholics not Protestants would enter heaven. So, he continued to ask, "But are there any Orthodox here?" When Peter again responded with a "No," the Orthodox Christian cried out in anguish, "No Orthodox! Who then are in heaven?" "Only children of God," was Peter's reply. Indeed, the church is not divided by Christ into different denominational families and churches. Christ unites us. It is us, the people, who cause divisions and dissensions.

The church is not holy because of its members or its sacral buildings. It is one of the fundamental confessions of its members that they are sinful, and it is commonplace to point out the profane connotations in church architecture. The church, however, is holy because it is sanctified through its founder, who is the source of all holiness. When we talk about the community of saints, we arrive at similar conclusions. The members are not saints because of their conduct. In many ways their unsaintly behavior impedes the mission of the church. But they are saints because their founder has called, accepted, and sanctified them. Similarly, the community aspect of the church is not established through a common concern or a common goal. The concerns and aspirations of its members are as diverse as the membership itself. Through the founder of the church, through Jesus Christ, we find a common orientation and focal point.

It is relatively easy to assess that the central aspects of the church are founded in Christ. But can we as easily assume that Jesus Christ founded the Christian church? While it cannot be established with certainty that Jesus of Nazareth did indeed found the church through Peter (Matt 16:18), there can be no doubt that the followers of Jesus gathered in the name of Jesus Christ upon his marvelous resurrection. We also notice that the Eucharist was celebrated with reference to the express command of Christ: "do this," and we hear that the Christians are baptized into the death of Christ (1 Cor 11:25; Rom 6:4). Similarly, the public proclamation of the apostles is done in the name of Christ and centers around him who was delivered to death by his enemies and who has been raised from the dead and now serves as a point of hope and encouragement (cf. Acts 4: esp. 2 and 18–19). So Christ is the source and the content of the Christian church: it is founded by him, proclaims redemption in his name, and celebrates the sacraments that he instituted.

Traditionally Pentecost is seen as the birthday of the church, when the Holy Spirit was poured out on the followers of Christ. Since the "miracle of Pentecost" is also the instance at which the language barrier separating different nationalities was overcome, the pouring out of the Spirit is often understood as a provision of ecstasy. Yet the Spirit of God should not be understood primarily as providing otherwise inaccessible knowledge or experience, but as the foundation of life. For instance, according to the Old Testament, the Spirit created the cosmos (Gen 1:2) and all life within it (Ps 33:6). The Spirit of God is the active principle that gives physical life and from this Spirit everything living derives its dynamic power. If God withdraws his Spirit, our flesh must die. Thus Job confesses: "The spirit of God has made me, and the breath of the Almighty gives me life" (Job 33:4).

The Spirit is not only the life-giving and sustaining power, but he will bring about the end-time fulfillment. For instance, we hear Yahweh promise to Israel, "I will give them one heart, and put a new spirit within them; I will remove the heart of stone from their flesh and give them a heart of flesh, so that they may follow my statutes and keep my ordinances and obey them. Then they shall be my people, and I will be their God" (Ezek 11:19–20). Similarly, the psalmist prays: "Create in me a clean heart, O God, and put a new and right spirit within me" (Ps 51:10). Of course, the Spirit of God also provides ecstasy, excitement, and a dynamic drive. Its main intention, however, is life-creating, life-preserving, and life-fulfilling.

The miracle of understanding at Pentecost stands in antithesis to the dispersion of humanity (Gen 11:7–8). The state of the church and the outpouring of the Holy Spirit coincide with the rediscovery of human unity that transcends ethnic and national diversity. The power of the Spirit enables humanity to rediscover its original unity. The outpouring of the Spirit and the birthdate of the church are an act of God through which God brings together humanity in unity and community. Since human beings are social beings, unable to exist for long periods in isolation, the Spirit brings to fulfillment the intended communal structure in an exemplary fashion in and with the church. Human community is now possible beyond the arbitrary or intentional confines of political configurations. The church foreshadows the end-time phenomenon of human solidarity and practices it in the midst of today's life. This is at least its mission. Yet the implementation is still wanting. While at Pentecost the creation of the new humanity was begun as an inclusive community of people, almost immediately there were dissensions. Already the apostle Paul was vigorously fighting this spirit of dissension that arose especially in the world-open city of Corinth (cf. 1 Cor 3:4).

In our sinfulness we still attempt to assert our individual selves to the exclusion of others in the face of our common ground and destiny. Only the power of God's Spirit enables the church to be a community. The church owes its unity to its founding in the Spirit, but not to its structure and its practice. This fact is illustrated many times in the New Testament when we are reminded that there is no unity apart from the unity in Christ. For instance, according to the Gospel of John, Jesus tells his disciples: "I am the vine, you are the branches. He who abides in me and I in him, he it is that bears much fruit, for apart from me you can do nothing" (John 15:5). This means that the community is only community as long as it is in communion was its Lord.

Another image for the church, that of the body, is often used by Paul. To free ourselves from the possible misunderstanding of the church as a corporation we must first note that the term "body" is also an integral part of the eucharistic vocabulary. For instance, Paul asks rhetorically: "The bread that we break, is it not a sharing in the body of Christ?" And then he continues: "Because there is one bread, we who are many are one body, for we all partake of the one bread" (1 Cor 10:16–17). The presence of the body of Christ is perceived in two ways: it is the blessing of liberation which frees us from our self-centered selves and it is the power that unites us with Christ. But the community does not simply participate in the body of Christ. The body image shows us our union with Christ and at the same time our union with each other. As Paul writes, as Christians we are "the body of Christ and individually members of it" (1 Cor 12:27). We have gained access to this body in baptism (1 Cor 12:13). The designation as the body of Christ emphasizes our unity as individuals and it reminds us that as members of the same body, we have different functions but are of equal status (cf. 1 Cor 12:14–26).

While the term "people of God" is also used by Paul to connect the church with the history of salvation, the body image is more spatially oriented. Some New Testament writers recognized the danger that could ensue from a narrow identification of the church with Christ and his body. Therefore, the church is related to Christ's cosmic dominion. For instance, in Colossians, Christ is understood as the head of the whole world. Yet only the church is his body and his power permeates it to assure its steadfastness and growth (Col 2:19). While the church is closely related to Christ, we must refrain from the idea that it is identical with him. But this closeness to Christ gives the church a special place in history and it carries an exceptional obligation, to be true to its source of power.

In the Letter to the Ephesians this cosmic aspect of the church receives renewed attention. Christ is designated the head of the church in which the fullness of Christ dwells (Eph 1:23). As Christ's body, the church can even be the bearer of the Christian message to demonic powers (Eph 3:10). We also notice that the writer draws an analogy between the relationship of husband and wife to that of Christ and the church (Eph 5:22–33). Though this passage served primarily as instruction to the married, indirectly we obtain the writer's insight into the relationship between Christ and the church. We hear that "the church is subject to Christ" (Eph 5:24) and is to be obedient to him. But significantly, in comparing husband and wife with Christ and the church, the writer does not reflect upon the copulative act, as could be expected in the context of mystery religions. Rather, the sacrificial love stands in the forefront and reveals itself in Christ's sacrificial death (Eph 5:25). This passage refutes the allegation that Christ preached the coming of the kingdom of God, but then came the church instead of the kingdom. This passage clearly indicates that with the church, God in Christ is also present. The church is the new community made possible through Christ's redemptive act. Of course, this implies the obligation of any church and its members to live according to the kingdom. But does this hold true for our denomination? Here repentance and mending our ways is the call of the day.

In talking about Christ as the head of the church, we must again ask ourselves what we mean by the term "church." Here the New Testament offers valuable help. In the New Testament the term "church" denotes first the local church or congregation, such as the church that is in Cenchreae (Rom 16:1) and the church that is in Corinth (1 Cor 1:2 and 2 Cor 1:1). This might convey the impression that the church is simply the local congregation. But in looking more closely at the Greek text we notice that "the church that is in" really means "the church as it is at." The church is not produced by adding up all the local churches, nor is it the local church by itself. Each Christian community, however small, represents the whole church. Whether there are problems of injustice (1 Cor 6:4) or of tradition (1 Tim 5:16), the issues and problems in the church are never a matter of a strictly local dimensions; they affect the whole church. Especially to those looking at the church from the outside, each church member and each congregation stands for the whole church. For them it is simply "they." Therefore, there are instances of Protestant Christians who leave the church because they are offended by something the pope said to Roman Catholics. They rightly do not differentiate between different Christian denominations.

The church is wherever the Christian community is in union with its founder and head, Jesus Christ. While we do not want to leave the impression that the ecumenical movement serves no useful purpose, even the most vigorous ecumenical movement cannot produce or further the unity of the church by reciting or implementing new plans and models for unity. It can only appeal to the local manifestations of the church, assisting them to live according to the intentions that Jesus Christ has for his church. Through discovering our common ground in Christ the unity is furthered and strengthened. Only a Christocentric emphasis at the very roots of the church, at its local level, can help the cause of unity.

The church is founded by Christ and finds its unity in and through him. But it also represents Christ. It is the visible expression of his Lordship. As Matthew 16:18 clearly indicates, this does not imply any kind of triumphal attitude. Only because of Christ the gates of Hades will not prevail against the church. Only through the wisdom of God in Christ can the church withstand the evil powers and proclaim the good news (Eph 3:10). Therefore, Paul exclaims in joy: "For I am convinced that neither death, nor life, nor angels, nor rulers, nor things present, nor things to come, nor powers, nor height, nor depth, nor anything else in all creation, will be able to separate us from the love of God in Christ Jesus our Lord" (Rom 8:38–39).

Christ has charged the church with the privilege of representing him. This implies that the church is endowed with saving power. The reason for this is that the church is the only agency that treasures and administers Word and sacrament, and it is commanded in the Great Commission to go into all the world to baptize and to preach. But the Great Commission includes the reminder, "teaching them to obey everything that I have commanded you" (Matt 28:20). This means two things: (1) The church is placed under the same Word which it proclaims and (2) The church does not proclaim its own word but the Word of its Lord. The church is the mediator of Christ and of his gospel. This is its privilege and its uniqueness. Small wonder that already in the early church bishop Cyprian of Carthage (ca. 200–258) declared that "there is no salvation out[side] of the Church."[3] That he meant here more than the church as an institution becomes obvious when he states on another occasion, "He can no longer have God for his Father who has not the Church for his mother." In the church and nowhere else is the Word of God present through the proclamation. This then facilitates our awareness of God being our Father as we confess it in the Lord's Prayer. If the church neglects making Christ present through word and deed and prefers to announce its own preferences and actions, it is no longer the church. When we hear from some church members, "this is no longer my church," then we must always ask whether the church has deviated from its task or whether these members are unhappy because they do no longer identify themselves with the church's core message.

Especially the Roman Catholic Church has adhered until recently to the notion of being Christ's representative. Until the Second Vatican Council representation was understood in strictly institutional terms. The church meant the Roman Catholic Church and to be cut off from it through excommunication meant to be cut off from the gospel of Christ. While it is certainly true that the church is the body of Christ and it manifests him in this world, this prerogative is not confined to one or several of its ecclesial manifestations. It is true that Christ can only be known through the body of Christ that treasures his memory, celebrates his presence, and instructs the people in this living tradition. Without the churches the knowledge of Christ would diminish rapidly in the human sphere. Moreover, the Christian faith needs a living context in which to express itself. Even Count Nikolaus von Zinzendorf (1700–60), who reestablished a (separate) Christian community, the Moravian Brethren, claimed emphatically that without community he would not accept one as a Christian.[4]

The church is indeed Christ's representative, mediating his message, issuing the offer of salvation, and providing the content for Christian nurture. But in this context it is presumptuous to confine the notion of the church to a certain denomination or even to the sum total of all established churches. The church is where a community is assembled to direct its life according to the Word of its founder and to spread the good news of Jesus Christ. Without such a church, wherever it may manifest itself, we have at most a religious relationship to God, adhering to some general moral and

3. For this quote and the next see Cyprian, *Epistle* 72 (21) *ANFa* 5:384; and *On the Unity of the Church* (6), *ANFa* 5:423.

4. According to Lewis, *Zinzendorf*, 67. Zinzendorf states in a conversation of 1736: "I acknowledge no Christianity without fellowship."

religious principles. However, in doing so we bypass God's living Word and in the process we also bypass Christ.

2. THE COMMON PRIESTHOOD OF ALL BELIEVERS

One of the rediscoveries of the Reformation was that there is no special priestly class. Or to put it in a different way, all the faithful share in the common priesthood delegated by Christ to his church. Since the term "laity" is derived from the Greek *laos*, meaning the people, we should not be surprised that the grassroots movement of the Reformation was behind this rediscovery. As the Septuagint usage shows, originally *laos* meant the people of God, namely Israel. Besides this, of course, the term could also refer simply to the people, the crowd. This is also true for the New Testament. But soon it denoted the Christian community. For instance, Paul writes in quoting Hosea: "Those who were not my people I will call 'my people,' and he who was not beloved I will call 'beloved'" (Rom 9:25). This usage was also continued into the early church.

In the early church, however, *laos* came to stand more and more for the Christian community in distinction from its leaders, especially for those who conducted the worship. This was not an innovation, because we find this distinction already mentioned in the New Testament with reference to the synagogue practice (Acts 13:15). The laity was now no longer seen as comprising the whole people of God but only the people apart from its leaders. Another significant shift occurred in the transition from Judaism to Christianity, where the opposition between *laos*, meaning the Jewish people, and gentiles was no longer seen as an exclusive one. Now we hear that "God first looked favorably upon the Gentiles, to take from among them a people for his name" (Acts 15:14). The new people of God are no longer confined to an ethnic or national group, but are made up of Jews and gentiles.

Today the laity is seldom regarded as the people of God. In everyday language, the opposite of a layperson is not a leader, but an expert. Whether within the church or in other areas, a layperson is considered inferior and ignorant. We might want to defend this usage of the term "layperson," because in theology, as in other fields, the knowledge has increased to such an extent that it can only be mastered by experts. But the problem of distinguishing in the church between laypersons and non-laypersons becomes evident when we remember that the people of God, i.e., laity, also refers to as the community of saints. Is it really permissible, we must ask, to distinguish between a large body of saints and a few especially equipped super-saints?

If we want to preserve the unity of the people of God, then we should not make a distinction in rank between the laity and the leaders. The fact is, there is no ontological difference between them, contrary to the Roman Catholic understanding of "once a priest, always a priest." Only with regard to their respective functions are there differences.

If we take the priesthood of all believers seriously, the activities in a congregation and the planning for these activities must involve all the members and not just the leaders and some experts. Yet my experience of forty years serving on a church council, first in a congregation in the US and then in one in Germany, unfortunately goes in the opposite direction. In Germany it was very clear that if a pastor did not want something it would not happen regardless of what others thought or said. In the US this kind of leadership is more muted. But if pastors drag their feet it is very difficult to go ahead on a certain issue. In both cases this leads to frustration and often to increasing passivity among laypersons. To counteract this problem, we must take seriously the priesthood of all believers and also that we are one community as the people of God. Being a layperson does not mean one is inferior in rank, nor in expertise and activity. But quite often the means with which laypersons carry out their tasks in the church are very different from the way the leadership functions. The differentiation between clerics and laity, but also their basic unity, is well captured in the Roman Catholic Canon law:

> By divine institution, there are among the Christian faithful in the Church sacred ministers who in law are also called clerics; the other members of the Christian faithful are called lay persons. There are members of the Christian faithful from both these groups who, through the profession of the evangelical counsels by means of vows or other sacred bonds recognized and sanctioned by the Church, are consecrated to God in their own special way and contribute to the salvific mission of the Church; although their state does not belong to the hierarchical structure of the Church, it nevertheless belongs to its life and holiness.[5]

Yet we notice here also a tension between the status of the clergy and that of the laity, since it says here that the distinction between them is divinely instituted.

While the people of God never existed without a special leadership, we wonder what this divinely instituted distinction implies. Vatican II shed some light on the issue when it declared, "though they differ from one

5. Code of Canon Law (can. 207).

another in essence and not only in degree, the common priesthood of the faithful and the ministerial or hierarchical priesthood are nonetheless interrelated. Each of them in its own special way is a participation in the one priesthood of Christ."[6] Again the question is left open of the meaning of a difference "in essence and not only in degree." Should we conclude that the clergy are by nature different from the laity? Perhaps we come closer to an answer when we investigate the Roman Catholic understanding of the ministerial office.

According to Roman Catholic understanding the laity shares uniquely in the one priesthood of Christ. This means two things: (1) The priesthood of Christ is not divided into a priesthood which the clerics hold and an inferior priesthood of the laity. There is only one common priesthood in which all Christians participate. (2) Christ is the only source of the church's apostolate. The lay apostolate is founded in the living union with Christ and not in a special gift of an individual. The documents of Vatican II also affirm that "the laity, too, share in the priestly, prophetic and royal office of Christ, and therefore have their own role to play in the mission of the whole People of God in the Church and in the world."[7] The ministry of the laity is not a truncated or additional ministry of the church. Through their relation to Christ the laity share in their own way fully in the church's ministry.

The ordained ministry cannot be understood or carried out in isolation from the general ministry of the whole people of God. This caution is not only directed against an understanding of the pastoral ministry in which pastors are so elevated that they do not seem to need the laity, but also against a totally people-oriented ministry. In this type of ministry certain individuals become oblivious to their own community, since they perceive themselves as God's direct gift and do not need any other congregants. The ordained ministry needs the laity as its support and as the arena in whose midst the ordained can minister. In turn the laity needs the pastor as leader, enabler, and counselor.

The Roman Catholic Church has rediscovered the necessity of the laity for the carrying out of the mission and the work of the church. Since it clearly distinguishes between laity and clerics, it realizes that the laity occupies a unique position. The laity belongs both to the world and to the church in a way that is true neither of the clergy nor of monks. In this dual position the laity are the proper and irreplaceable agents through whom the mission and the work of the church is fully accomplished in relation to the world. If we would obliterate the distinction between clergy and laity and

6. *Dogmatic Constitution on the Church*, *DVC* 27 (10).

7. *Decree on the Apostolate of the Laity*, *DVC* 491 (2).

assume that the clergy can fulfill the witnessing function as well as the laity, we would endanger the effectiveness of the Christian ministry in the world. The validity of this distinction is shown more and more by the effectiveness of laypeople as they witness to the community in which they live and work. Surveys have shown that in the US laypersons are far more effective in winning new members for a congregation than pastors are. The reason for this is perhaps that outsiders would expect pastors to speak well of their congregations since they are paid by them. But if laypersons rave about their congregations, there seems to be more truth in their witness, since they have no financial gain from their efforts.

The laity are called to be servants, charged to be the light, empowered to be the salt, and encouraged to be soldiers. The laity carries on a full and responsible mission in serving others in the midst of egocentricity; they add flavor in the midst of blandness; they enlighten the darkness of the world with the Word of God; they take a militant stand against all injustice, and a conciliatory posture amidst strife and dissension. Their tasks show paradigmatically that the church exists for the world and not for itself. The church therefore should not bask in the glory of Christ, but, in a missionary move, by dispensing this glory and permeating the world with it. Since the laity live in both dimensions, the church and the world, they remind the church of its essential world-relatedness and of its missionary task. Since the church is related to the world it can only give credible witness if it approaches the world in unity. Thus, the rediscovery of the missionary dimension of the church, the awakening of the ecumenical movement, and the rediscovery of the laity, belong together.

Another factor that led to the rediscovery of the laity was the renewed emphasis on the Bible as it emerged in the ecumenical movement. Suddenly what should have always been clear became evident, namely, that all Christians are of equal status before Christ and God. Paul, for instance, emphasizes that "there is no distinction between Jew and Greek; the same Lord is Lord of all and is generous to all who call on him" (Rom 10:12). This does not just imply that the former distinctions in rank have lost their separating power but that there is an immediacy to Christ involved in the Christian faith. The only one who can and does intercede on our behalf is Jesus Christ, who sits at the right hand of his Father. There are no other mediators needed. Before Christ all are equal and nobody can interfere or intercede on someone else's behalf. No one enjoys a preferred status in acquiring or dispensing salvation.

The equal status with regard to Christ has been conferred to us through baptism. Paul reminds us, "for as many of you as were baptized into Christ have clothed yourselves with Christ. There is no longer Jew or Greek, there is no longer slave or free, there is no longer male or female; for all of you are one in Christ Jesus" (Gal 3:27–28). Baptism is incorporation into Christ and therewith into the Christian community. We are initiated into fellowship with Christ and with our fellow Christians. Baptism is the basic ordination of each Christian, commissioning him or her to be part of the church and of the witnessing community. As a sign and seal of this ordination the minister lays the hand on each one who is baptized and the one baptized receives the Holy Spirit. Incorporation into the church means total devotion and service in and with the community of believers. This does not mean that we have lost our freedom or that we must spend every minute of our spare time in the church, as is often the case in sectarian circles. But there is no excuse for congregational inactivity. Christians are active in their congregations or there is something wrong with the kind of Christian life they are leading.

Ordination for the "ordained clergy" is not an additional or separate rite, but something that must be seen in analogy to the commissioning for special tasks that arise within the Christian community. It is as dangerous to divide Christians into ordained and non-ordained members as it is to assume that there are full-time Christians and part-time Christians or trained and untrained ones. All Christians are ordained to full-time service and must be trained in one way or another. It is relatively unimportant whether this means special instruction prior to adult baptism or instruction following infant baptism that results in confirmation. But one cannot be a Christian in the full sense of the word without the basic knowledge of what this privilege of being a Christian implies in general, and in specific situations.

The laity cannot be defined over against the clergy or vice versa. Paul makes this abundantly clear with his imagery of the body. He states: "For just as the body is one and has many members, and all the members of the body, though many, are one body, so it is with Christ" (1 Cor 12:12). On another occasion he claims:

> For as in one body we have many members, and not all the members have the same function, so we, who are many, are one body in Christ, and individually we are members one of another. We have gifts that differ according to the grace given to us; prophecy, in proportion to faith; ministry, in ministering; the teacher, in teaching; the exhorter, in exhortation; the giver, in generosity; the leader, in diligence; the compassionate, in cheerfulness. (Rom 12:4–8)

Several issues are evident from Paul's statement. Since all Christians are joined together, the individual Christian, a congregation, or even a denomination cannot act in whatever manner it pleases without behaving in a way that could be potentially destructive. An individual member can easily bring discredit to the Christian faith as can an individual congregation, or denomination, and therewith discredit the whole church. Many people on the outside are only waiting for a signal to put the blame for all kinds of evils indiscriminately upon all Christians. When one Lutheran body, for example, is torn by internal strife, this does not only grieve all Lutherans, but many people do not differentiate, so they blame all Christians for this sign of disunity. This is similar with other denominations, as recent history has testified. As aforementioned: In Germany people have left the Protestant church on account of some "offensive" statement made by the pope. We might also guess that some of the unchurched want to be left alone on account of what they perceive is wrong with *the church*. Only in mutual consultation and respect can we take action that is appropriate for those representing Christ. Doing one's own thing is more often the sign of the sectarian than of the righteous. As Paul's body imagery indicates, unity does not mean being synonymous or uniform. Each of us acts according to the individual gifts he or she has been given and according to the action demanded from us in a certain situation. Such coordination requires discipline and sensitivity, but it does not mean relinquishing one's individuality.

In line with the clerics who are commissioned to full-time and exclusive service of furthering the kingdom, lay members are also commissioned for the same purpose to fulfill individual tasks within their competency and the time they have available. The pursuit of a secular profession does not mitigate against their involvement in spreading the gospel, but it will enhance their work in a congregation with their particular secular competency. I am thinking here of a retired journalist who composes the newsletter of our congregation and writes most of the articles which the newsletter contains. Confronted with the world, laypersons will share the general missionary and pastoral functions with their fellow Christians as the situation requires. They will proclaim the gospel in word and deed to non-Christians, they will teach as parents, administer the sacraments if necessary, listen to confessions of their fellow workers, and dispense exhortation and absolution. In their work within the church the laity will contribute the skills they exhibit in the secular world, e.g., teachers as Sunday school teachers, banking personnel as financial secretaries, construction workers in building projects, etc. But they will also continue their general Christian duties within the church as need arises, e.g., evangelism and stewardship projects, adult education, preschool programs, etc. Beyond this there are special needs peculiar to every congregation, such as serving as ushers, acolytes, lectors, and perhaps preachers.

The laity does not compete with the clergy nor is it their backup and support system. Laity and clergy cooperate and support each other. But we dare not forget that laypersons usually pursue secular professions and do not have an extended formal theological education. Therefore, their resources of time and their theological expertise are usually limited. It is unrealistic and ill-advised to burden them with demands that require full-time or even part-time personnel or extensive theological training. The laity are not lesser clerics; they are Christians charged with the responsibility of witnessing in an alien world.

3. THE SPECIAL LEADERS

The ministers or priests are neither at the disposal of a certain congregation for tasks nobody else wants to tackle, nor are they professional Christians who get paid for what they believe. They are the called and chosen leaders and, unless they serve in some specialized non-congregational function, for instance, as bishops or district presidents, they are usually paid by the congregation in whose midst and for whom they serve.

It is questionable whether a totally subsidized ministry should always be the rule. Especially in developing countries, a fully paid clergy, as a rule, does one of two things. It imposes an exorbitant financial strain on the local congregation or it means keeping the salaries on such a low level that the pastor and the pastor's family, though expected to devote full time to the ministry, can hardly exist on the salary provided. As a consequence, there are only a few full-time and theologically trained pastors who supervise fifteen to thirty Bible teachers or evangelists. This means, however, that the least theologically educated persons, the teachers and evangelists, have the primary teaching responsibility, while the better trained theologians perform most of the ritual and administrative functions. Of course, in most churches and denominations only ordained pastors are allowed to administer the sacraments, while everybody is allowed to teach. This is especially prevalent in the American Sunday school system.

By this division the administration of the sacraments is restricted to ordained clergy, while teaching the Christian faith is possible for every Christian. Such a division is not well-founded. For instance, the *Augsburg Confession* states that without being properly called nobody should teach publicly in the church—the public teaching is contrasted here with the teaching in the home which at the time of the Reformation was thought to be the prime duty of the father—or administer the sacraments (CA 14). Properly called is not confined to the call for an ordained priesthood. Amid his temptations whether he was on the right track or not Martin Luther regularly referred to his call as a doctor of theology. This comforted him in his biblical stance both against the enthusiasts and also against the papacy. Luther also argued that those who are baptized are entitled to be priests and bishops, though nobody should execute the functions that accompany these offices unless chosen and certified by the Christian community. This means that one cannot fulfill priestly functions indiscriminately wherever and whenever one wants. This restriction was especially important for the enthusiasts who exercised their "priestly" functions wherever they felt that the Spirit led them.

More and more congregations can no longer support a full-time pastor because of declining membership. If they do not want to join a neighboring congregation or cannot share a pastor, the next best possibility is to call a pastor on a part-time basis. Sometimes such part-time positions are attractive if the spouse of the pastor has a very demanding job. If, however, this part-time call is supplemented by some other employment, the danger is high that the pastoral call occupies second place, since its work can never be exactly spelled out. Divided loyalties are never ideal. But regardless of how small congregations are, they need a dependable leadership with theological acumen. As a result, our creativity is demanded.

It is also significant that the Constitution on the Church of Vatican II declared: "Among the principal duties of bishops, the preaching of the gospel occupies an eminent place. For bishops are preachers of the faith who lead new disciples to Christ. They are authentic teachers, that is, teachers endowed with the authority of Christ."[8] The Roman Catholic Church puts the teaching function first and not the administrative or the ritual functions. Yet Protestant churches usually claim to be the churches of the Word, which means they are teaching and preaching churches. One must wonder, however, why in reality they value the teaching function so little, while the priestly function for which the words and motions are usually fairly well prescribed can be exercised by only those who have the highest theological training. Should it not be the other way around: Teaching and preaching is reserved for the ones with the highest theological education, while administering the sacraments can also be done by those who have less theological expertise?

We should remember the early Christian custom according to which the deacons were allowed to administer communion to shut-ins. This is perhaps appropriate where circumstances do not allow for a sufficient number of well-trained pastors, but the fact is, when there is a large number of enthusiastic and unpaid evangelists, one might at least consider assigning to

8. *Constitution on the Church*, *DVC* 47 (25).

them functions for which fairly well prescribed (liturgical) texts exist. The actual teaching function then should be reserved for pastors with sufficient theological training. This would alleviate the problem of the lack of "qualified" pastors in many developing countries, and even in the US, where some congregations are unable to offer the sacraments on a frequent and regular basis.

Encountering the differentiation between the teaching, administrative, and cultic roles, we have already noticed that there is a gradation among the called leaders. This is true for any denominational organization, regardless how high or low it views the role of the clergy. Whether we talk about the hierarchy of ministers, elders, and moderators, or we mention congregations, societies, conventions, and general councils, or we move in a more traditional fashion between deacons, priests, bishops, and archbishops, we notice a hierarchy of jurisdiction and often also one of ordination. In the Reformed and Roman Catholic traditions, church structure and the corresponding offices and clergy are derived from divine law as given in the biblical tradition. The free churches and the Lutherans, however, claim that the hierarchies are designed to facilitate cooperation among the local churches.

We can certainly claim that the leadership function in the Christian community is divinely instituted, but the New Testament does not present a clear order as to hierarchy and polity. It is not clearly spelled out who should preside over the administration of the sacraments or the proclamation of the Word. Paul as the prime New Testament author reminds us repeatedly to do everything in an orderly fashion and according to the tradition (received from the Lord). Within this directive of freedom, it follows that the called leaders act in a truly leading way for whatever function they were called. Though usually only qualified persons are called to a certain office, the authority is not derived from their qualifications. A leadership position should never result in the glorification of the leader, but the leader is there to glorify Christ. The authority for any ecclesial office ultimately rests in Christ, in whose name the office is administered. An office is never the office of the person but of Christ, whom a person serves in a certain capacity. For instance, we hear that Christ "has given us the ministry of reconciliation" (2 Cor 5:18). We should also remember that the office-bearers are selected from the midst of the community that delegates this office to the office-bearers. In this way they execute their duties on behalf of the community.

Since the office-bearer serves and represents Christ, we could even speak of an identification of the called leader with Christ. According to Luke, Jesus told the disciples: "Whoever listens to you listens to me, and whoever rejects you rejects me, and whoever rejects me rejects the one who sent me" (Luke 10:16). It would be wrong to infer from such a statement a special quality of the office-bearer. Yet if we want to be true to our calling we cannot but identify with that for which we stand. This means that we do not administer our own church or our own proclamation, but Christ's church and his proclamation. This is also the deeper meaning of liturgical vestments and of the habit of monks and nuns. They diminish as much as possible the emphasis on the individuals and make them transparent for Christ in whose service these people function.

The called leaders administer Christ's gospel in his name and foster participation in and spreading of the redemptive news. The material limits of this function are given through the content of the gospel and not through our own desires and opinions or through those to whom we minister. The formal limits are defined by the specific location in which the ministry takes place. Since the call is always extended by a community of believers, one will be sensitive to their needs and desires. They extend the call for Christ's sake and not on their own behalf. Their needs and desires must continuously be judged by the demands of the gospel. Thus, a called leader of a certain Christian community can never let his or her calling be degraded to the point that he or she becomes an employee of the community. Of course, a call can be revoked when a certain situation no longer demands a called leader. A congregation can merge with another congregation and thereby a surplus of called leaders could ensue, or a called person through his or her conduct could act contrary to the exemplary lifestyle demanded in leadership positions. Since pastors should be close to their parishioners, sexual misconduct is an ever present danger. If such misconduct occurs, glossing over it according to the motto "we are all sinners" does not do justice to the situation. The broken trust cannot be so easily regained and therefore the relocation of the pastor should be seriously considered.

But a call cannot be revoked just because the Word of God preached by the leader is offensive to the congregants by its implications. The question, however, must be asked whether it would not be wise for a faithful servant to seek a call from a different congregation if the congregation now being served is no longer receptive to the unbiased proclamation of the Word of God. Perhaps a different leader would encounter less bias and could work more effectively. This does not imply a compromise of the office, but an exchange of the office-bearer to insure the continued effectiveness of the proclamation. The called leaders are interchangeable, but the function of the office in which they serve cannot be changed unless a false gospel is being preached.

The one office and its function: It should be self-evident that the pastoral office should enhance and not detract from that for which the church stands.

If the church is the body of Christ, a metaphor that Paul uses, or the community of saints, or the faithful who listen to the Word of the Lord, as Luther mentioned in the *Smalcald Articles*, then the offices must be designed to enhance these basic characteristics. For instance, the *Augsburg Confession* asserts that to obtain such faith (that lives from the grace of God) God has instituted the office of teaching the gospel and administering the sacraments (CA 5). In the Lutheran tradition, the office is basically considered as one which cannot be divided into an office of preaching and teaching and another one for administering the sacraments. The one office in turn has often been identified by the office and role of the pastor. The notion of the common priesthood of all believers notwithstanding, the laity often feel that they are not participating in this office except to do ministry. That has led to a deplorable inactivity of the laity in the traditionally Lutheran countries of Scandinavia and Germany.

The office finds its unity in Christ who is present in his church through Word and sacrament. Christ's presence cannot be divided by claiming that the teaching aspect should be valued higher than the sacramental aspect or vice versa. Both are manifestations of Christ and of God's grace. But the function of that office, even when it is united in one pastor as office-bearer, does not exhaust itself with the narrowly conceived teaching and sacerdotal functions. One of the frequent observations of a conscious pastor is that the multitude of demands on the office are much greater than the time available to fulfill them properly. This means that the office, though in itself one, entails many different functions, since it represents Christ to the Christian community and to the world. To facilitate the greatest possible effectiveness of the office, certain functions are often specialized and staffed with especially qualified people.

Increasingly popular in larger congregations are multiple staff ministries in which one pastor is mainly responsible for the teaching function, another for worship and preaching, while a third concentrates on the counseling aspect of the ministry. This does not imply that there are three different offices, but the one office is in and of itself differentiated to maximize its proper effectiveness. Whether and how such specialization takes place depends on the local needs and should not be determined in advance. The idea that certain specializations are divinely decreed, for instance the distinction between the priestly office and the diaconate, does not always corroborate with the needs in a given area. For instance, on account of the increasing shortage of priests in the Roman Catholic Church the diaconate assumes more and more functions of the priestly office, while still seen in a subservient role. This results in people being often deprived of the presence of the priest, while the deacon is still not allowed to minister in his place.

Such restrictions are contrary to the notion that all Christians participate in the one office through which faith in God's love is acquired. On the other side, the Protestant emphasis on the full-time ordained ministerial office has quite often eliminated a gradation of service, such as deacons and deaconesses, sub-deacons, etc. To be actively involved in the affairs of the church, one often has no other choice but to aspire to become a part of the ordained ministry. Since, however, there is also a shortage of pastors in the Protestant churches, one should spread out the functions of the one office among the faithful so that the ministry to the congregants and to the world can be carried out more effectively.

It is the special function of laypersons to witness in the name of Christ wherever they live. Through their baptism they are authorized to share Christ with their families and neighbors through word and deed. Yet such witness remains individual and private unless laypersons are properly set apart to full-time or part-time evangelistic witness or a teaching ministry (e.g., Sunday school). Called leaders are not exempt from this private role either as fathers or mothers or simply as neighbors. Yet due to the call to a particular office, the leader assumes a public witnessing function through word, action, and administration of the sacraments. The reason why the administration of the sacraments is, with the exception of emergency cases, reserved for called leaders is not that these are holy functions and can only be performed by "holy" people. Yet such ideas are still advocated, for instance, when in some churches women are not ordained or are excluded from administering the Lord's Supper with the reference to some disputed Scripture passages.

We remember that baptism, the Lord's Supper, and in the Roman Catholic tradition the other sacraments too, have a public aspect. We do not celebrate the Lord's Supper when we witness to our neighbor or when we conduct family devotions. Called leaders are the public representatives of the congregation beyond individual and internal matters. To emphasize the church's oneness, in its corporate nature, and its joint witness to the world, the representative teaching and sacerdotal office dare not be taken lightly. Wherever this priestly office was downplayed, as in American denominationalism and in certain segments of the free church movement, the unity of the church suffered at the expense of sectarian individualism, and often self-serving idiosyncrasies emerged. Yet the teaching and sacerdotal office cannot be divorced from the common priesthood of all believers. If this happened, as for instance in the Roman Catholic Church or in segments of the so-called state churches, the church became synonymous with its leaders and therefore void of active and meaningful lay participation. People feel that they are not needed and after a certain period of inactivity they will leave the church in increasing numbers. In order to clarify the function and the status of the so-called leaders, we will now briefly investigate the call to the office.

Character of the call to the office: The call to the office is always a mediated one, extended on behalf of the Lord of the church, but actualized through representatives of the institutional church. The subjective moment, which the one feels who is called by God, is clearly secondary to the objective fact that one is called by the church on behalf of Christ. Similarly, the laity is called to its apostolate through the visible sign of baptism. Being called by the visible church ensures that one stands in the context of the church and in the living tradition.

Since the called leaders are called on behalf of Christ, the notion of an apostolic succession as maintained by the Roman Catholic Church and the Anglican tradition can be misleading. We remember that the apostles exercised a unique and vital role in the first Christian communities. As apostles they preserved the living memory of the earthly Jesus, a role which could not be handed on. But insofar as they were sharers in the responsibility, next to the congregational leaders, of proclaiming the message of reconciliation, "establishing churches and building them up in the apostolic faith, their ministry had to be continued."[9] Thus our ministry must be seen in succession to the apostolic ministry, and not to the singular status of the apostles. It would therefore be better to talk about a material or doctrinal succession, in the sense of the truthfulness of the church, instead of a formal or historical succession of office-bearers depicting an unbroken line of tradition.

The setting apart of the called leaders was already practiced in the Old Testament times. According to Numbers 11:16–17, Moses is commanded by Yahweh to choose among the elders of Israel seventy people who are to share with him the burden of guiding Israel. Consequently, they received the Lord's Spirit that rested upon Moses and they assumed leadership and prophesied. Similarly, we read in Deuteronomy 34:9 that Joshua "was full of the spirit of wisdom, because Moses had laid his hands on him; and the Israelites obeyed him, doing as the Lord had commanded Moses." Rabbinic Judaism saw in the installation of Joshua by Moses the paradigm for the relationship between teacher and disciple. In Jewish understanding there existed an uninterrupted chain of the spirit of wisdom that had been handed on from Moses to later scribes.

9. World Council of Churches, *One Baptism, One Eucharist, and A Mutually Recognized Ministry* (13), 33.

In pre-Christian Judaism a scribe ordained a disciple publicly to the duties and privileges of a rabbi. Prerequisite was the knowledge of exegesis and the understanding and application of tradition. Ordination was a juridical act, and the handing on of wisdom. It was also a singular act and could not be repeated. Once ordained, the title "rabbi" could be used and binding decisions could be made concerning the teaching of the law. Especially from the end of the second century AD onward the Sanhedrin made the selection from among the candidates and the patriarch conducted the ordination. This move was intended to eliminate unqualified students who might explain the law incorrectly. But in the fifth century ordination ceased completely, perhaps because the practice of ordination had now been adopted by Christianity. The ordained scribes were the bearers of tradition that was handed on from generation to generation.

Though there is no specific Greek equivalent for the term "ordination," we have a few cases of the laying on of hands in the New Testament that are analogous to Jewish ordination. They are different from other cases of laying on of hands in the New Testament, for instance to heal, to bless, or to hand on the Spirit. In Mark 7:32 Jesus was asked to lay his hand upon someone who was deaf and had a speech impediment. In Mark 10:16 we read that Jesus laid his hands upon the children and blessed them. And in Acts 19:6 Paul laid his hands upon the disciples of John and they received the Holy Spirit. When the congregation in Antioch sent out Barnabas and Saul to proclaim God's Word, this sending was preceded by the laying on of hands and can still be understood in analogy to the Jewish custom of sending out apostles (Acts 13:1–13). But it is the appointment of the seven (deacons) in Acts 6:1–6 that resembles an ordination ceremony.

In contrast to Jewish practice, the early Christian ordination is accompanied by prayers (Acts 6:6). It is significant that in Acts 6 the congregation chose the ones to be ordained while the apostles ordained them and laid their hands on them. Another case of ordination is presented in the Pastoral Epistles with reference to Timothy. Though it is not clear whether he is ordained by presbyters or apostles, we read that he is selected through prophetic voices. In front of many witnesses he receives a brief summary of apostolic teaching and is instructed to faithful service under a solemn confession. By the laying on of hands by the apostles or presbyters, or perhaps by both, he is ordained. He is also empowered by God with the gifts commensurate with his task. Timothy's work points in the direction of congregational leadership (1 Tim 1:3), to ordain other leaders (1 Tim 5:22), to guard the truth entrusted to him (2 Tim 1:14), to lead the worship service (1 Tim 4:13), and to enforce discipline in the congregation (1 Tim 5:1–2).

The basic structure of ordination has not changed since New Testament times, nor have the basic demands on the called leadership changed. Ordination is done under the laying on of hands by leaders who were themselves ordained. Scripture readings and prayers assume an important place in the rite. The service is always public, with the participation of the assembled congregation. One is also never ordained per se but one is ordained for specific call and service. Ordination is a liturgical act by which one is incorporated into a certain office and enabled to obtain the juridical and spiritual power that allows one to administer the rites and duties connected with the office. Often there are certain hierarchical levels of ordination, as in the Roman Catholic Church where one is ordained to be a deacon, priest, or a bishop, to name just a few of its hierarchical levels.

The Roman Catholic Church at the Council of Trent (1546–63) even speaks of ordination as having a spiritual and an indelible character. Yet for the Roman Catholic Church this indelible character only pertains to this life and has no eternal significance. The idea behind the elevated status of the priest is the fear that the Reformers had obliterated the distinction between priesthood and laity. At Vatican II the Roman Catholic Church rediscovered that though the ordained person is set apart from the congregation, he is not separated from those who still remain his brothers and sisters. Since ordination is considered a unique event, the ordination to the priesthood cannot be repeated.

A certain openness toward a more functional and role-oriented aspect emerges in Roman Catholic thinking as a result of the Second Vatican Council. We are told by the Belgian theologian Piet Fransen (1913–83) in the six-volume encyclopedia *Sacramentum Mundi*, edited by Karl Rahner (1904–84) to sum up Roman Catholic thinking after Vatican II: "There is nothing to prevent the Church freeing a priest temporarily or permanently from the obligations of his ordination to return him to the condition and life of the laity."[10] The indelible character seems to last only as long as the priest fulfills his priestly position. The priestly character is indelible in the sense that he is a priest not only when he performs a certain ceremony, but also when he is "off duty" or on vacation. This is important when a priest assumes some secular function, for instance becoming a party member or joining a demonstration. Even if he claims that he has done this as a private citizen, for those on the outside it looks like he has done it as a priest. The same even goes for a Protestant pastor.

Once the priestly call is discontinued, the indelible character no longer applies. Thus, we cannot speak of a strictly ontological but rather of a

10. Fransen, "Orders and Ordination," 4:325.

functional view of ordination. This is reinforced by the understanding that ordination to the priesthood is a sacrament. However, that sacramental grace conveyed is identical to the fundamental grace of justification. The grace conveyed through ordination is understood as a

> deepening and a re-orientation of baptismal grace in view of the specific mission and service of the priest. It thus allows for the development of a truly priestly spirituality, fundamentally identical with that of the rest of the faithful in the brotherhood of the same faith. This grace also unites the priest to the other members of his order in the priesthood of their common mission.[11]

One cannot but notice the implicit tension contained in this statement issued after Vatican II. It asserts the fundamental unity of all the faithful but insists on a special "truly priestly spirituality."

We find the same tension in the Lutheran position. On the one hand, the emphasis is on the priesthood of all believers. Yet we hear that in ordination a special blessing, the gift of the Holy Spirit, is imparted to the person being ordained. The Reformed tradition is perhaps the most informal, since it conceives of a plurality of offices that can be bestowed on someone and can also be rescinded. Therefore, the Reformed do not regard ordination as conferring a habitual status—it simply designates someone to a functional role. The Anglican communion surpasses the Lutherans on the other side. Importance is given there to apostolic succession where one is ordained by a bishop who is in that succession. In recent years this formalistic continuity has received more positive attention by the Roman Catholic Church. Most members of the Orthodox community and the Old Catholic Church, which constituted itself upon the decisions of Vatican I, even accept the Anglican ordination and ministry as valid.

The most hopeful sign amid the still existing differences in understanding the ministerial office is not found by comparing different traditions but in returning to the biblical documents that engendered this ministry. We might realize which emphases find support in Scripture and where we have gone astray, inventing a tradition of our own liking. We remember that the New Testament witness is far from being unanimous when it comes to church order and organization. Very little is said in the New Testament too how the leaders were appointed and what was required to preside over the Eucharist. The various lines of succession claimed by the early church are more necessary to combat heretics than to reflect historical realities. Thus there is a growing tendency to interpret the episcopal succession as

11. Fransen, "Orders and Ordination," 4:325.

an effective means, but not a guarantee, of the continuity of the church in apostolic faith and mission.

The continuity in faith, mission, and ministry is being recognized in churches that have not retained the historic episcopacy. Even Roman Catholics have suggested after Vatican II that "treatment of the apostolic succession of the whole community should be given precedence over treatment of hierarchical succession."[12] The Faith and Order Commission of the World Council of Churches in its statement *One Baptism, One Eucharist, and a Mutually Recognized Ministry*, which was formulated in cooperation with the Roman Catholic Church, stated: "Many find it possible today to recognize a continuity in apostolic faith, mission and ministry in churches which have not retained the form of historic episcopacy."[13] The formal matter of a strictly apostolic succession is more and more seen as secondary to the apostolicity of doctrine in a given church. Once the apostolicity of doctrine is established, it makes sense to look at the apostolicity of ministry and not the other way around. This is also the insight of the so-called Porvoo Common Statement of 1996—named after the Porvoo Cathedral in Finland—to which the Anglican churches of the British Isles and most of the Lutheran churches of Scandinavia and the Baltics agreed. It echoed the Munich (1982) and Finland (1988) statements of the Joint International Commission for Theological Dialogue between the Roman Catholic Church and the Orthodox Church and stated that "the continuity signified in the consecration of a bishop to episcopal ministry cannot be divorced from the continuity of life and witness of the diocese to which he is called."[14] This reveals once again that the succession in person alone does not suffice to assure a continuity in content.

Significance of Ordination: When we finally consider the significance of ordination we must remember that, like any other ritual in the church, ordination is an act conducted on behalf of Christ. Since ordination is Christ-centered, there is a unity of call, blessing, and sending. Christ creates readiness for ordination, he calls to ordination through the Spirit, and he blesses the ordained. Since the Holy Spirit is already received through baptism it is redundant to expect that the Spirit is received again at ordination. Yet it is a good custom to reaffirm the presence of the Spirit in the ordained.

12. Remmers, "Apostolic Succession," 34:51.

13. World Council of Churches, *One Baptism, One Eucharist, and a Mutually Recognized Ministry* (35), 39.

14. Porvoo Communion, par. 49.

Since the Spirit is undivided, it is unthinkable that a special spirit of the office would be conveyed. Since Christ places the ordained into a special leadership service, we should rather assume that the grace to meet the demands of this office is asked for at ordination. Since the leadership office is a necessary one, we could expect that Christ gives us this grace. But we meet the demand in free responsibility and not as puppets. The history of the church has repeatedly shown that ordination does not guarantee proper fulfillment of the functions of the office. Occasionally people may be ordained who are unfit, or become unfit, for exercising the ministerial office. To minimize this danger and take ordination seriously, and not to regard it as an automatic qualification ritual, the church has always insisted on adequate preparation of the ordained on a spiritual, intellectual, and practical level. This implies adequate physical and mental health, and a good reputation. The person who is ordained should be of such quality that the church can expect that his or her ordination will further the spreading of the gospel and not impede it or leave it at a standstill.

These considerations are of prime importance for denominations that undertake the ordination of women. With reference to 1 Corinthians 14:34 ("Women should be silent in the churches"), Luther remarked that one should certainly obey this teaching of Paul. "If, however, only women were present and no men, as in nunneries, then one of the women might be authorized to preach."[15] If the New Testament scholar J. Paul Sampley is correct, "in 1 Cor 14:34–36 we are probably faced with a later insertion of a text whose posture is at odds not only with Paul's relationships with women in other churches but also with what Paul has said about women earlier in 1 Corinthians," then the ordination of women need no longer be a theological issue that divides us, but primarily a practical and ethical point of concern.[16] If the ordination of women does not hinder or slow down the spreading of the gospel and the recognition of Christian unity, such a move is certainly in accordance with Scripture. The Roman Catholic theologian Elizabeth A. Johnson reminds us that "the exclusion of women from the public culture of the church has resulted in an official memory that has erased a good part of the history of women's discipleship, giving to the communion of saints a largely male face both in heaven and on earth."[17] This lacuna must certainly be filled.

15. Luther, *Sermons on the First Epistle of St. Peter* (1523), *LW* 30:55, in his comments on 1 Peter 2:5.

16. Sampley, *First Letter* to the Corinthians, *NIB*, vol. 10, in his elaborate exegesis.

17. Johnson, *Friends of God and Prophets*, 220–23, 234–36.

We have noticed that Luther followed the reasoning of Paul, insisting that women should not assume public teaching office (in the church). Yet he allowed for exceptions from this rule, if they would enhance the effectiveness of the pastoral office. Analogous reasoning is appropriate in deliberating the ordination of women. Prime concern should not be given to the sociological shift from a patriarchal to a more egalitarian society, or to the public acceptance of women in a variety of "nontraditional" roles. Also, the arguments from the "natural law" basis that women are not fitting for the pastoral office since Jesus was male, are not convincing. The new creation that Christian baptism promises applies to both men and women, and even to children. The argument in favor of the ordination of women by claiming that the ministerial office needs female ministers to be whole and complete again misses the point that this office must be seen in functional terms, and not as being endowed with an ontological quality. The office is whole and complete by its very institution. Whether the administrators of this office are equally whole and balanced is a different question. Yet we must also remember that the efficacy of the function does not depend on the worthiness of the administrator.

The question that must be addressed here is primarily a functional one: does the ordination of women enhance the effectiveness of the pastoral office? An unbiased answer to this question is difficult to give. As the sexual abuse cases in the Roman Catholic Church show, they are most likely due to celibacy and to an all-male priesthood, but also to plain human sinfulness. A married clergy as in the Orthodox churches might alleviate some of the problems. But we should not just look at sexual issues. There are some areas in which ordained women might provide a decided complement to an all-male ministry, e.g., ministering to women and to single parents, and in certain institutional functions. It is also not without significance that laypersons often criticize celibate priests saying "they have no idea about issues in families." Ordained women would certainly have a different approach to these matters. In virtually all denominations that have ordained women to the ministry it has been a success story that has not hindered the spread of the gospel. In many Protestant denominations the problem of entering the ministry whether for men or for women is compounded by the fact that there are no intermediate ranks (deacon, monastic orders, etc.). If one wants to be significantly involved in the church one has no choice but to seek ordination to the ministry and this, thus far, means entering the full-time ministry. Perhaps the need in smaller congregations for part-time ministry would alleviate the problem for those who for a variety of reasons do not want to engage in full-time ministry.

Ordination is always an act of the worshiping community on behalf of its Lord. This means that ordination cannot occur in secret. It must have the approval of the worshiping community that extends the call. The church stands behind the ordained with its support and encouragement. The ordained is entrusted with the gospel and stands in succession of the Christian tradition as represented by the church. By ordaining someone, the community sets apart that person to the office of acting on behalf of God. It is not an office that includes certain privileges and liberties, but that carries the duty of continuing Christ's mission to relate to and care for his people. While ordination is conditional upon certain prerequisites, it does not depend upon one's own worthiness. It is ultimately the will of God that is expressed in the ordination.

Finally, ordination is closely connected with installation, i.e., the designation to a certain task. In contrast to ordination, the installation is repeated with each new task and is usually of limited duration, occasionally even for a period specified in advance (especially for administrative offices). An installation recognizes the specific place within the ministerial office that is to be served. It presupposes an agreement on the specific function, place, range of duties, and remuneration, if any, that the particular call involves. It is performed publicly with participation of the congregation in whose midst the services will be performed. Installation, however, is not primarily for ordained ministers, but also for lay workers, such as Sunday school teachers, acolytes, ushers, and altar guild, choir members, and for many other officers. By subsuming laity and clergy under the aspect of installation we notice again that the service aspect of the Christian life does not fundamentally differ for the laity from that of the professional leadership. The call to serve is different in range and in authority, but not in quality.

After our brief survey of the new people of God in their community and leadership aspects, we must now turn to that which is of ultimate concern and centrality of the life of the people of God, namely the pronouncement of law and gospel and the administration of the sacraments.

4. PRONOUNCEMENT OF LAW AND GOSPEL

One may wonder why such a Lutheran term as "law and gospel" should be introduced here as being central to the Christian community. The reason for this is actually very simple: God's Word does not always meet us in the same way. This Word that is preserved in the Christian community, and that encounters us in the church's doctrine and proclamation, basically addresses us in three different ways or functions. It either judges and condemns us, or it frees and affirms us, or it guides us. The first of these three functions can easily be classified as law, the second as gospel, and the third can be associated with either one of the two. The distinction between law and gospel is not synonymous with the distinction between the Old Testament law and the gospel of Jesus Christ. The distinction between law and gospel is founded in a diametrically opposed perception and reaction to the Word of God. Therefore, we notice a basic unity in the opposition between law and gospel.

Basic unity and opposition between law and gospel: God uses the law basically in two ways among humans, either in a worldly and secular sense or in a theological sense. According to the worldly way, God preserves God's creation, prevents its decay, and also prevents universal chaos. This implies that the law containing basic rules for humanity is universally known to all people. This view has been held in the natural law tradition and has recently received renewed attention by behavioral scientists who argue that basic norms of moral behavior are common to all societies, human and nonhuman.

For the law to preserve public peace according to its worldly use it must be known by Christians, Jews, and pagans alike. Such common knowledge of the law is presupposed in the New Testament. For instance, Paul writes:

> When Gentiles, who do not possess the law, do instinctively what the law requires, these, though not having the law, are a law to themselves. They show that what the law requires is written on their hearts, to which their own conscience also bears witness; and their conflicting thoughts will accuse or perhaps excuse them on the day when, according to my gospel, God, through Jesus Christ, will judge the secret thoughts of all. (Rom 2:14–15)

Paul does not say here that the pagans know the law that was given to the Jews through Moses. But they have in their inner selves something analogous to the Mosaic law and must be as responsive and responsible to this as the Jews are to the Torah. The pagans do not know the divine will from the Torah, but from that which is inscribed in their hearts.

Luther claims on the basis of Romans 2:15 that if God had never given the written law through Moses, all humans would know that which is contained in the Decalogue since the natural law is inscribed in our hearts.[18] "The Decalogue is not the Mosaic law nor was it first given to Moses, but the Decalogue belongs to the whole world. From the beginning of the world the Decalogue has been inscribed in the mind of humanity," Luther argues in

18. Luther, *Die erste Disputation gegen die Antinomer* (1537), *WA* 39/1:402.15–17.

his disputes with the Antinomians, representatives of a movement who only accepted the worldly use of the law.[19] He writes:

> Therefore, there is one law which runs through all ages, is known to all men, is written in the hearts of all people, and leaves no one from beginning to end with an excuse, although for the Jews ceremonies were added and the other nations had their own laws, which were not binding upon the whole world, but only this one, which the Holy Spirit dictates unceasingly in the hearts of all.[20]

The natural law that is largely concomitant with the law of Moses is distinguished from the positive law of the country and the Jewish ceremonial law. Luther does not admit full equality between the law of Moses and the natural law that prevails in other places. Moses, though not the originator of the natural law, interprets and clarifies it. Luther states therefore that "it is clearly and well contained at Mount Sinai and in a better way than by the philosophers."[21]

According to Luther and his interpretation of the New Testament tradition, the law inscribed in the hearts of all people is not just synonymous with the first, worldly use of the law as we encounter it, for instance, in the courthouse. Since the law is expressive of God's will and since all people in some way or other are religious beings, the presence of the law as attested by Romans 2:15–16, also fulfills a theological function. As the eternal expression of God's will the law is present in the human conscience, and serves as a reminder of God's will. It reminds us of our alienation from God and shows us that we do not live as we ought. This feeling that in our thoughts, words, and actions we have been remiss is a feeling shared by everyone. Through alienation from God this second, theological or convicting use of the law is often not clearly expressed outside the Judeo-Christian tradition. We have immunized ourselves against anything coming from God and are oblivious to his commandments. Most people live according to the maxim: we have done our best. If they consider God at all they are convinced that God will be satisfied with their lives. But there is no excuse for not living up to God's will, the divine law, since everyone can at least in part know God's will.

Paul tells us that the "law came in, with the result that the trespass multiplied" (Rom 5:20). Such an assertion sounds strange to us! Would God give the law in this second (theological) sense in order to evoke sin and to let it develop all its power? There certainly was sin before one was explicitly

19. Luther, *Die erste Disputation gegen die Antinomer*, *WA* 39/1:478.16–18.

20. Luther, *Lectures on Galatians* (1519), *LW* 27:355, in his exegesis of Gal 5:14.

21. Luther, *Predigten des Jahres 1540*, *WA* 49:2.1–2, in a sermon on January 1, 1540.

confronted with the law. But, as Jesus shows in the Sermon on the Mount, quite often transgressions against the law are made unconsciously. Sin lies dormant since we do not recognize sin as sin but think our thoughts or actions are okay. Yet God wants sin exposed through the law and perceived for what it really is, rebellion against God. Only in this sense is sin increased and sharpened. The more conscientiously we attempt to fulfill the will of God, the more we realize our shortcomings and discover our immense sinfulness. That which was originally designed as a sign of God's love and care, God's will, becomes a sign of our despair and of God's wrath. This was, for instance, Luther's experience in the monastery when he consciously wanted to live a righteous life without sin and realized that even with his best efforts there were always some things that went wrong. But Luther did not live according to the maxim that our son said when we wanted to scold him for some mischief: "Nobody's perfect." By studying God's word, Luther had a sharpened conscience. But this almost drove him to despair.

Studying God's Word as it is recorded in the Bible, we too detect the law which sharpens our conscience and shows us that we are in a hopeless predicament. For instance, Paul admits in despair: "For I know that nothing good dwells within me, that is, in my flesh. I can will, what is right, but I cannot do it. For I do not do the good I want, but the evil that I do not want is what I do" (Rom 7:18–19). Luther rightly recognizes that the law constantly accuses us; it delivers us to God's wrath, to judgment, and eternal death. The exclusive emphasis on the law leads to condemnation instead of salvation. Yet Luther also emphasized that whoever does not wish the law to be preached refuses to hear the truth of God. The same law that accuses us also moves us to seek God's grace. Supported by Augustine, and similar to Luther, Calvin argues in his *Institutes* that the accusing law makes us ask for God's grace.[22] Grace encounters us in God's redemptive work in Christ.

Paul continues the statement that law came in to increase the trespass by saying, "but where sin increased, grace abounded all the more, so that, just as sin exercised dominion in death, so grace also might also exercise dominion through justification leading to eternal life through Jesus Christ our Lord" (Rom 5:20–21). In his Letter to the Galatians, Paul even states that "Christ redeemed us from the curse of the law by becoming a curse for us" (Gal 3:13). The law leads and urges us towards Christ. The same is expressed when Paul calls the law "our disciplinarian until Christ came" (Gal 3:24). The law as tutor or governor, as the term "disciplinarian" can also be translated, keep us under the tutelage and the yoke until we are released into freedom through Christ. Through Christ we recognize that the law is not

22. Calvin, *Institutes of the Christian Religion* (2.7.9), 1:357.

God's entire word and not the whole content of the Christian proclamation. The gospel stands alongside the law.

All this is correct according to Paul and also to Luther's interpretation of Paul. But, we must ask, can we still confront people today, whether in the church or outside the church, with a law that supposedly comes from God, and condemns and convicts us as evildoers? A condemning and convicting God is diametrically opposed to a God of love as God is usually characterized today. Moreover, in our present society which moves according to the principle "I'm okay and you're okay," a feeling of sinfulness has largely disappeared. Are we then proclaiming a foreign God, perhaps the evil creator God about whom the Manicheans warned, over against the benevolent redeemer God of the New Testament? No, there is only one God who as creator of the world has a decided interest in God's creation, which includes us. But God is not a blanket God who puts a blanket over everything we do. Since God's creation was not a haphazard accident there are certain innate laws or rules according to which everything moves. The higher one gets in the development of creation, the more freedom there is. But at the same time there comes with this freedom the danger of going in the wrong direction. For instance, if a male dog detects a she-dog when she is in heat, the male dog will chase after her according to his inborn drive, regardless of what the owner of the dog does. Yet if a man sees an attractive woman, his inborn drive to go after her is so subtle that he can freely decide whether to pursue an affair with her or not. In order to help him make the right choice God gave us the sixth commandment, either in the Decalogue or inscribed in our conscience. In the Decalogue, in our conscience, and in traditional orders of conduct God's will for us, God's law, and our own decisions come together. The question is, will we offend God's will, or will we act in accordance with it?

Since our society is becoming more and more secular most people want to be as unfettered as possible from the Decalogue, from their conscience, and from the traditional order of things. They want to be free. At the same time, however, we notice that our prisons are bursting at their seams, lawyers are busier than ever, and counseling centers are booked up. We overestimate ourselves if we think we do not need any guidance and that we can simply go ahead on our own. Perhaps the seemingly old-fashioned convicting use of the law is not as outdated as one might think. Moreover, the law is never alone, since God is not just a vengeful God but a God of grace and hope. There is also the gospel, which tells us of God's love for his whole creation.

But law and gospel have very different functions. The law meets us in God's place, demanding that something be done and forbidding the doing of something else. It accuses and condemns us because we have failed to live up to God's will. The gospel, however, proclaims that God's will has been met in Christ. It shows us the God who meets us in Christ and tells us that God is a gracious God who has forgiven us our sins. Paul expresses this eloquently when he says: "But now, apart from the law, the righteousness of God has been disclosed, and is attested by the law and the prophets" (Rom 3:21). God's righteousness has been manifested through the historical occurrence of Jesus Christ. God can now be perceived as wanting the redemption of God's people and not their destruction.

The gospel of redemption is not confined to the Christ event, though it best comes to expression there. Paul reminds us that "the law and the prophets bear witness to it." This means that the Old Testament already testifies to the gracious love of God that culminates in the life and destiny of Christ. Karl Barth seems to have perceived this insight in his famous 1935 paper "Gospel and Law." Barth assures us that he does not intend to reverse the traditional order of law and gospel, but by changing the sequence to gospel and law, he hoped to demonstrate that "the law is in the Gospel, comes from the Gospel, and is directed to the Gospel."[23] If we are going to find out what the law is, we must first of all know about the gospel, and not vice versa.

According to Barth, God's Word contains both law and gospel. Since the law is God's manifest will, we have access to it only where it comes loudly and audibly to us, in Jesus Christ. "When we see here the will of God being done, when, that is, we see his grace in action, the law is manifested to us."[24] When we perceive God's grace, we realize what the law actually demands. "The law, then, is in the Gospel as the tables of Sinai were in the ark of the covenant."[25] Barth can even say that "the law is nothing else than the necessary form of the Gospel, whose content is grace." This reminds us somewhat of Augustine when he defined evil as both a deficiency of the good and a necessary ingredient that helps us to perceive the good ever more clearly. But Barth reverses the process by suggesting that the goodness of the gospel makes us realize our depravity and sinfulness, so that we cling to the gospel. In the light of God's grace we see how unseemly and inept we are. Barth even defines the law as the form of the gospel, since it bears witness to the gospel. He claims that the sequence of law and then gospel is only legitimate if we first look at Christ who reveals himself through the law as our savior. Knowing that Christ affirms God's valid but misused law, we perceive our shortcomings and flee to God's grace revealed in Christ who

23. Barth, "Gospel and Law," 3.

24. Barth, "Gospel and Law," 8.

25. For this and the following quote see Barth, "Gospel and Law," 10.

fulfills the demands of the law. For Barth the proper order actually is gospel-law-gospel instead of law-gospel.

Barth recognized that we only gain a clear vision of the law if we preach the Word of God as law and gospel that both Old and New Testament contain. But while the order of law-gospel may leave the impression that it is synonymous with the succession of Old and New Testament, the order gospel-law-gospel is even more misleading. It obscures the fact that law and gospel are the same Word of God. One cannot divide God's Word in statements that contain law and others that contain gospel. The law or gospel character of God's Word depends on how it meets us, as condemnation or confirmation. If we would envelop God's demand in his grace, the Word would lose its seriousness and we would be in danger of offering cheap grace. Luther was right when he said: "The law deals with sin only in order to reveal it. . . . The gospel, on the contrary, deals with sin so as to remove it, and thus most beautifully follows the law."[26] Therefore, the proclamation of the law is the indispensable and necessary presupposition for the preaching of the gospel. Without the law we do not recognize our own deficiencies and remain secure and proud of our moral capacity. We could even say that without the law we do not need God since there is nothing wrong with us. The law is God's alien work that opens for us the necessity and appreciation of the gospel as God's proper work. Though certainly opposite in their functions, law and gospel are the same Word of God.

The term "law," as used in the distinction between law and gospel, is not identical with the Law, meaning the Pentateuch, or with the Old Testament. The term "gospel" in the same distinction is also not synonymous with the proclamation of Jesus or the New Testament kerygma. Law and gospel are two different functions of the same Word of God, the accusing and the liberating one.

Significance of the law for Christians: In Jesus' time many people had turned the Word of God into a series of human regulations to assure that they were righteous before God and God's law. This was the situation that Jesus addressed in the Sermon on the Mount and on many other occasions. The same attitude is prevalent today with many people who are only nominally in contact with the Christian gospel. They lead ethically virtuous lives, assuming that this lifestyle, though short of perfection, will ultimately be met with divine approval. The German poet Johann Wolfgang von Goethe summed up well this sentiment when he declared in his dramatic poem, *Faust*: "Who

26. Luther, *Against Latomus* (1521), *LW* 32:223.226.

e'er aspiring, struggles on, for him there is salvation."[27] This understanding of the law portrayed here will ultimately enslave people, since it suggests that they are righteous, though they are not. People become enslaved to ethical principles, such as the greatest good for the greatest number of people, or freedom and equality for the underprivileged, instead of responding to the personal will of God. Often these self-righteous attempts lead to the establishing of new barriers of injustice and inequality. Law divorced from the gospel can easily turn into a self-serving and self-justifying philosophy.

Since people sin by focusing their attention on the law instead of on God himself, should we then follow Barth's advice and call for repentance by referring to Christ, the Son of God incarnate? Here Luther reminds us that repentance can be induced by preaching Christ's cross as well as Moses' Law. We are brought to repentance when God's Word encounters us as God's law and not as our self-designed plan. It leads us to repentance by meeting us as a demand and making us recognize our shortcomings. According to Luther, one of the places where God's demanding Word can meet us is in the Lord's Prayer. Each of the petitions is perceived as a demand that reminds us of our imperfection. But the same Word of God can also encounter us as gospel. For example, Luther ensures us that there is much gospel contained in the first commandment, since there God promises us his faithfulness. We are reminded here that originally the Old Testament law served as gospel, as the pledge of God's faithfulness to which the Israelites were asked to respond.

The same Word of God can meet us as law or gospel, as demand or as promise. There is, however, an irreversible movement from law to gospel. If we grasp the gospel in faith we are convinced of the gracious God and know God's acceptance. The condemnation and the accusing function of the law have vanished. The law is replaced by the gospel and we recognize that God has assumed entirely different features. He is no longer the righteous God who demands compliance with God's will, but a gracious God who for Christ's sake forgives us our noncompliance. God's alien work in the accusing function of the law has been changed to God's proper work, the liberating power of the gospel. Such an understanding, of course, leads to the question whether the law still has any significance for Christians.

If Christ is the end of the law, as Paul claims, then the law is abrogated for the justified insofar as it makes demands on them, or accuses and condemns them. Christ, however did not abolish the law but fulfilled it. Through Christ God's will for us has been accomplished vicariously. But the law has not lost its validity for us as God's will. If it had, we would no longer be sinners but justified only.

27. Goethe, *Faust* (11936–37), 290.

Calvin claims that there is a third use of the law. "The third and principal use, which pertains more closely to the proper purpose of the law, finds its place among believers in whose hearts the Spirit of God already lives and reigns."[28] This was also the line of thinking of Melanchthon in the Lutheran *Book of Concord*, and the theologians of Lutheran Orthodoxy. In backing this third use of the law (for the regenerate) with quotations from the Bible, Calvin adduces primarily texts from the Old Testament. For instance, he quotes the psalmist saying: "Thy word is a lamp to my feet and a light to my path" (Ps 119:105). Or at another place: "The law of the Lord is perfect, reviving the soul" (Ps 19:7).

Certainly, the lives of Christians need moral directives and guidelines; Christians need to hear God's will to order their lives. Yet once we are confronted with the gospel, once we understand the full implications of God's gracious will, our response does not come from pressure and coaxing; instead Christians conform freely to God's will. Ideally their ethics is an ethics of response, a reactive ethics, not a deontological ethics, an ethics of duty. Christians live up to the law, not because it is demanded but because they love God and appreciate God's righteousness. This means that not even the Old Testament law can be labeled appropriately as law. For instance, the Ten Commandments are introduced not by claiming: This is what God demands, but: This is what God has done for you. They begin with the reminder of what God has done for Israel: "I am the Lord your God, who brought you out of the land of Egypt, out of the house of slavery" (Exod 20:2). The commandment to love one's neighbor is introduced in a similar way when we hear: "You shall love your neighbor as yourself: I am the Lord" (Lev 19:18). Because God is so gracious, we are responding by transferring God's love to our neighbor. This shows that even in the Old Testament God's Word was originally intended as gospel. It illustrates what kind of God we have and evokes our response, a response freely given.

People who are justified seek do the will of God. This means we must acknowledge the existence of commandments in the Bible that serve as guiding moral directives. It would be potentially misleading, however, to regard them as law. They do not depict a legal and accusing use of the law, but an evangelical use in the sense of a divine command. They do not get from the demand that "you shall in order to . . . ," but rather "you may because . . ." Therefore, they are guidelines to stay in the will of God and not a set of legal devices to assure a righteous life

In contrast to the law-oriented existence of many people, the Christian life is an oscillating existence. Christians do not suddenly find themselves

28. Calvin, *Institutes* (2.7.12), 1:360.

beyond the possibility of sinning in the state of the redeemed. Paul indicates this too with his frequent use of imperatives, that the redeemed Christian existence remains marked by sin. The Christian existence has often been described as one of being a sinner and justified at the same time. Being a Christian is not a matter of possession, but of continuous struggle. Justification before God does not induce an ontological change. Justification is rather indicative of our relationship to God, which, of course, is subject to change. This does not mean that Christians are sitting on the edge of a sword always in danger of falling off the thin edge. Christians can and do lapse into sin. God's Word then again becomes law, accusing a person of their failure and driving them back to the gospel. This is one of the reasons why even in the Christian community the proclamation of the gospel alone does not suffice. Otherwise Christians are lulled into the sleep of a wrong security that nothing can go wrong with them. Having been justified, Christians live without the law, but as sinners they live under the law. The law drives sinners back to a gracious God who forgives and encourages.

The breaking of our relationship with God is never a bilateral action. God never severs the ties to God's people. We stay and remain Christians, even as lapsed ones. The promise of the gospel does not become void—like the threat of the law—once we turn our back on it. God's gracious Word always stands firm. As Christians we do not live under God's thumb. We are called to freedom as sons and daughters of God. This freedom is not unlimited. However, its limits are not in demands that are beyond fulfillment but rather in orders and guidelines that allow us to live in a "responsive responsibility." The Roman Catholic cardinal Walter Kasper (b. 1933) recaptured well Luther's insistence on the distinction between law and gospel when he said: Law and gospel "is regarded as the distinctive feature of the Christian faith as contrasted not only with Judaism but also with all pagan religions, with philosophy, ethics, and the like."[29]

Pronouncement of absolution: The pronouncement of law and gospel assumes a peculiar form in the office of the keys, also known as confession and absolution. It is also quite often part of the regular worship service. The Roman Catholic tradition considers penance a sacrament that includes the office of the keys and the action of confession and absolution. Lutherans, however, see it closely associated with the sacraments but do not actually consider it as one. For instance, in the *Augsburg Confession*, repentance is located after baptism and Holy Communion. In Luther's *Small Catechism* repentance is placed after baptism and before the Lord's Supper, indicating a

29. Kasper, "Law and Gospel," 3:297.

close connection between it and the two sacraments without admitting that it is an actual sacrament. In the Lutheran Hymnal, the *Evangelical Lutheran Worship*, confession and absolution are also added on to "The Sacrament of Holy Baptism."[30] Melanchthon in his *Apology of the Augsburg Confession* states that "absolution (the sacrament of repentance)" is one of the three sacraments. In the Calvinist tradition, however, confession and absolution are not considered a sacrament.

While we do not want to pursue at this point what constitutes a sacrament, it is evident that confession and absolution are intimately connected with the proclamation of law and gospel as the one Word of God. The main passages of the New Testament that undergird the function and office of the keys are in the Gospel according to Matthew. For instance, in connection with the word to Peter that on this rock Jesus will build his church, we hear: "I will give you the keys of the kingdom of heaven, and whatever you bind on earth will be bound in heaven, and whatever you loose on earth will be loosed in heaven" (Matt 16:19). Binding and loosing on earth means here exclusion from and acceptance into the Christian community. In the Gospel of John this function is no longer restricted to Peter and is also understood more theologically as the remission of sins. We hear Jesus say to his disciples: "Receive the Holy Spirit. If you forgive the sins of any, they are forgiven them; if you retain the sins of any, they are retained" (John 20:22–3). That the Christian community, or at least the Twelve, understood themselves to succeed Peter in the office of the keys is obvious from Matthew 18:18, where the function of the office is extended to a wider circle. Now Jesus is portrayed as saying to his disciples: "Truly, I tell you, whatever you bind on earth will be bound in heaven, and whatever you loose on earth will be loosed in heaven."

The office of the keys is intimately connected with the proclamation of the Word of God. This is indicated by the parallel between the consequences of not listening God's Word and of not receiving forgiveness of sins. When Jesus sent out the disciples he admonished them: "If anyone will not welcome you or listen to your words, shake off the dust from your feet as you leave that house or town. Truly, I tell you, it will be more tolerable for the land of Sodom and Gomorrah on the day of judgment than for that town" (Matt 10:14–15). Thus, the proclamation determines life and death, and those who are charged with the proclamation shall symbolize this by shaking off the dust from their feet as a sign that they have separated themselves from those who rejected God's Word. The proclamation of God's Word has eternal significance and those entrusted with it should make that known to

30. *ELW* 1165.

their listeners. The office of the keys then results from the pronouncement of the one Word of God, law and gospel. Response to God's Word has eternal significance. Those who administer the keys are empowered to make these consequences known, by absolving the listeners or leaving them in their sins. Consequently, God's Word is experienced as condemning or liberating.

Since penance is inextricably connected with the Word of God, those who are entrusted with the public proclamation of the Word should also practice penance. This logic is especially well followed in the Roman Catholic Church. Similar to the hierarchical teaching order in the Roman Catholic Church, we encounter a hierarchical order for administering varying degrees of penance. Yet the office of the keys should never be considered purely a juridical matter but should be exercised on behalf of God who issues the Word that gives life and death. Contrary to past use, the office of the keys is not just a convenient means to enforce ecclesial decisions. It should be handled representatively in the exclusive name and authority of the Lord of the church, but not in the name of the leaders he appointed.

Since proclamation and penitence go hand in hand, the church soon realized that the one-time forgiving of sins at baptism was not sufficient. There was a need seen for a lifelong forgiving of sins. This is most clearly expressed in the explanation of baptism in the *Small Catechism,* where Luther says: "The old creature in us with all sins and evil desires is to be drowned and die through daily contrition and repentance, and on the other hand that daily a new person is to come forth and rise up to live before God in righteousness and purity forever."[31] Confession and absolution must be a daily process, and not confined to special occasions when one has committed especially grave sins. This is apparent from the first of Luther's *Ninety-five Theses*: "When our Lord and Master Jesus Christ said, 'repent' [Matt 4:17], he willed the entire life of believers to be one of repentance."[32] We show this in our daily lives when we say to someone, "I am sorry." Yet often this has become an empty phrase with no consequences to follow.

As with the third use of the law, a similar question emerges with penitence. Is it proper to distinguish four parts in the confessional process—contrition, confession, absolution and satisfaction—as the Roman Catholic tradition teaches or shall we side with the Lutheran tradition that sees contrition, confession, and absolution as sufficient (CA 11 and 12)? It is significant that Luther rejects in his *Ninety-five Theses* only satisfaction imposed on the penitent by the clergy, while he insists that "inner repentance is worthless unless it produces various outward mortifications of the

31. "Sacrament of Holy Baptism," *BC* 360.

32. Luther's *Ninety-five Theses of October 31, 1517, LW* 31:25.

flesh."[33] There is certainly no law that can spell out in each case what kind of restitution must be made. Since we are unable to reverse history, a sinful act can never be completely undone. Only God, who set history into motion and has it under God's control, can affect restitution in the true sense. There is no doubt, however, that the one who receives forgiveness needs ethical guidance, showing how to respond properly to the grace freely received. Satisfaction should never become a law or a demand, but an opportunity to restore that part of God's creation that we willfully impaired in our sinful activities. Where this opportunity is not grasped, Luther is right that even the most convincing "inner repentance is worthless."

Even as a freeing word, God's Word cannot be taken lightly. God's Word asks for our response as new beings, a response expressive of our newly found union with God. That the Word of God is not automatically a liberating word underscores the utmost seriousness of the penitential process. It might even be necessary that so-called church sanctions be imposed on the unrepentant sinner. For example, when I was serving on church council, our pastor one day informed us that at certain council member should be removed from church council. When I asked the reason for such action, our pastor responded: "He has treated his wife in such a shameful way when he abandoned her, that he should no longer be a council member." Yet sanctions, such as exclusion from certain offices or activities in the Christian community, should always be administered for the benefit of the one being punished. The movement from law to grace should be at the core of a sanction. Though they should never be administered too quickly, sanctions dare not be considered relics of medieval authoritarianism. Ultimately, they are an offer of the gospel through the administration of the law. God is a God of grace, who does not let sinners run into their self-inflicted punishment, but God punishes sinners, in order that they may mend their ways and be saved.

5. ADMINISTRATION OF THE SACRAMENTS

Sacraments are an essential part of the church. The *Augsburg Confession*, for instance, states that the church "is the assembly of all believers among whom the gospel is purely preached and the holy sacraments are administered according to the gospel" (CA 7). Yet for many people on the fringes of the church or even on the outside, sacraments are void of any deep significance. Therefore, the party following the administration of the sacraments, for instance after baptism or first communion, is much more important for these people than what takes place in the church. We could

33. *Ninety-five Theses*, *LW* 31:25 (thesis 3).

conclude that the sacraments are relics from a bygone era. Yet we should be careful of making such a statement. In former Communist East Germany, for instance, the Communist regime introduced the *Jugendweihe* (youth dedication) in competition with the Protestant confirmation. Under state pressure most young people went to the *Jugendweihe* at which, similar to what happens at confirmation, the young people received gifts from their relatives and friends and from the state. This means that the Communist regime knew that one could not simply do away with confirmation. Humans need rites of passage in their lives, such as baptism at the beginning of life, confirmation or first communion when they pass from childhood, for most people marriage when they become mature adults, and finally the funeral when they leave this earth. It is interesting that in Germany when church membership began to dwindle, there appeared secular agencies with which you can book speakers for the secular version of baptism, confirmation, marriage, and funeral, including all the festive secular trimmings. While people need and want these rites of passage from one stage of life to another, the decisive question is whether they want to focus only on themselves, or whether they want to connect these points in their lives with a power higher than themselves, with God almighty. This is the point at which the Christian church must reintegrate the desires of the people with the significance of the sacraments. People must realize that the sacraments are not outdated relics. So we must first come to a common understanding of a sacrament.

Nature of the sacraments and their relation to God's Word: Among the churches there seems to be no consensus on what a sacrament is or even to the number of sacraments. The *Heidelberg Catechism* of the Reformed tradition states that sacraments "are visible, holy signs and seals. They are instituted by God so that by their use he might more fully declare and seal to us the promise of the gospel" (question 66).[34] When we ask how many sacraments there are, the commentary to the answer declares: "Two: holy baptism and the holy supper" Christ instituted in the new covenant (question 68). The decisive point from which the two sacraments should be approached is not their institution by God, as question 66 makes us believe, but their institution by Jesus Christ. Similarly, we hear in the Augsburg Confession that "the sacraments are instituted not only to be signs by which people may recognize Christians outwardly, but also as signs and testimonies of God's will toward us in order thereby to awaken and strengthen our

34. https://www.google.com/url?sa=t&rct=j&q=&esrc=s&source=web&cd=&ved=2ahUKEwjW4fXU093xAhU9gfoHHfgwCDAQFjABegQIBRAD&url=http%3A%2F%2Fwww.heidelberg-catechism.com%2Fpdf%2Flords-days%2FHeidelberg-Catechism.pdf&usg=AOvVaw2iDC38lxWuQ5kHfm4w_fiw.

faith" (CA 13). When only two sacraments are introduced, Luther too refers to them as "instituted by Christ."[35] When Melanchthon, however, defines sacraments "as rites, which have the command of God and to which the promise of grace has been added," he thereby arrives at three sacraments, baptism, the Lord's Supper, and absolution.[36]

It is interesting that Vatican II does not provide a strict definition of a sacrament, but instead asserts that "the purpose of the sacraments is to sanctify men, to build up the body of Christ, and finally, to give worship to God."[37] Similarly, we read in *Sacramentum Mundi*, which summed up the decisions of the Second Vatican Council, that the sacraments, "as defined in the theology of the Church, are the seven vital actions of the Church in its liturgy, which are efficacious for salvation."[38] Thus the sacraments are seen more as actions of the church than as actions on behalf of Christ. Karl Rahner may have sensed this shortcoming when he declared that since "the Church is of itself the final, irrevocable, eschatologically permanent word of salvation in the world," it is also "the primary sacrament."[39] Since Christ instituted the church, he also instituted those sacraments even though they are not attested to by any express texts of Scripture. Of course, Christ instituted the sacraments mentioned in Scripture as part of the establishment of the church. While this mediated origin of the sacraments (through the church by Christ) as asserted by Rahner would relieve us from the task of ascertaining that all the sacraments were actually instituted by Jesus (Eucharist) or at least by the risen Christ (baptism), it would leave open the room for more or fewer than the seven sacraments specified at the Council of Trent (1545–63).

Perhaps we get a more tenable approach to the sacraments if we investigate their historical origin. In Latin, the term "sacrament" had initially two meanings that had nothing to do with what we today understand as a sacrament. The word could denote a sum of money that two parties to a legal suit deposit in escrow pending the decision of the court. The sum contributed by the losing party was then used for religious purposes. The word "sacrament" could also mean a military oath of allegiance. The latter use seems to give rise to the Western theological use of the term. The transition from the military to the theological use is clearly seen in Tertullian (ca. 155–ca. 220), a prolific Christian author from Carthage in North Africa who was the first

35. Luther, *Large Catechism* (Baptism), *BC* 456.

36. *Apology of the Augsburg Confession* (article 13), *BC* 219.

37. *Constitution of the Sacred Liturgy* (59), *DVC* 158.

38. Schulte, "Sacraments," 5:378.

39. For this and the following cf. Rahner, "Word and the Eucharist," 274.

to use Latin and not Greek in his writings. He refers to the baptismal vows of the Christians, and states: "We are called to the service in the army of the living God in the very moment when we gave response to the words of the sacramental oath."[40] Tertullian also mentions by name the sacrament of the Eucharist and the sacrament of "water."[41] There is no doubt for Tertullian that in performing these sacraments we follow the command of the Lord. It is God who calls us, asking for our response to God's promise given with the sacrament. Thus God binds Godself in the sacrament to the promise and in turn induces an obligation and response from us.

The Eastern Churches preserved for sacraments the New Testament term "mystery." Their administration of the sacraments (baptism, chrism/confirmation, penance, Eucharist, priesthood, marriage, and anointing of the sick) were declared valid by Vatican II. These mysteries, of which baptism and Eucharist have prime importance, are perceived as having their source in Christ. In the New Testament, however, the term "mystery" is not used to denote the sacraments, but primarily the secret (mystery) of the kingdom of God (Mark 4:11–12) and/or the mystery (secret) of Christ (1 Cor 2:7–8), meaning Christ crucified.

When the Eastern Churches used the term "mystery" to denote a sacrament, they left themselves open to the influence of the pagan mystery cults in their Christian understanding of the sacraments. The sacraments could be understood as cultic rites in which the destiny of the deity was portrayed by sacred action before the devotees in such a way as to give them a part in the destiny of the deity. Mysteries therefore promise salvation and allow their devotees participation in the suffering of the deity. The church fathers were not unaware of these analogies. The early Christian apologist Justin Martyr (ca. 100–165), for instance, claimed that "the wicked devils have imitated in the mysteries of Mithras" in the celebration of the Eucharist, "commanding the same thing to be done."[42] Similarly, Tertullian remarked that the devil "by the mystic rites of his idols, vies even with the essential portions of the sacraments of God."[43] It is understandable that the church in the West avoided the dangerously loaded term "mystery" by using the term "sacrament." In so doing, the West took over the freight of the military

40. Tertullian, *To the Martyrs* (3.1), *FaCh* 40:22.

41. Tertullian, *De Corona* (3) and *On Baptism* (1), *ANFa* 3:94 and 669.

42. Justin Martyr, *First Apology* (66), *ANFa* 1:185.

43. Tertullian, *On Prescription against Heretics* (40), *ANFa* 3:262. It is not without significance that he too refers to the "mystic rites," perhaps implying the threatening nature of these cults for the Christian notion of the sacraments, and the affinity of their rituals.

and juridical connotations, a move that led to a rather one-sided ethical emphasis in response to God's grace.

In the East, the term "mystery" allowed more for perceiving the ontological reality of the life to which the sacraments initiate. This is also underscored by the so-called discipline of the secret (Latin: *disciplina arcani*), especially prevalent in the Eastern church between the end of the second and the end of the fifth century. With this custom the knowledge of the more intimate mysteries of the Christian religion was carefully kept from the heathen and even from those who were undergoing instruction in the Christian faith. The administration of baptism and Eucharist and related doctrines and rites were to be kept secret from all people unless they were baptized and thereby full members of the church. For instance, the eloquent archbishop of Constantinople, John Chrysostom (ca. 347–407), referring to the Eucharist, says: "Those who partake of the mysteries understand what I say."[44] The emphasis on initiation implies not just the response to God's grace, but indicates a different state of being. Since the Eucharist is also considered "the medicine of immortality and the antidote which prevents us from dying," Christians are on the way toward the heavenly reality.[45] The West, less interested in divinization as the goal of salvation, preserved the ontological component of the sacraments only in the insistence on Christ's real presence in the Lord's Supper and through the emphasis on the incorporation of the Christian into the redemptive drama through baptism.

Since the sacraments initiate into the redemptive event encountered in Christ, baptism and Eucharist are central for every Christian. The other five sacraments can at the most assume peripheral standing, since they are certainly not all necessary for salvation (cf. priesthood or matrimony). While it is impossible to admit their truly sacramental character—even Rahner's thoughtful construct is of no help here—the redemptive and preserving activity of God addressed in them should not be taken lightly. At the height of scholastic theology Hugo of St. Victor (1096–1141) stated in his *De sacramentis christianae fidei* (On the sacraments of the Christian faith) that some sacraments are necessary for salvation while others, though not necessary for salvation, advance sanctification. Unintentionally Hugo distinguished thereby between sacraments in the proper sense, baptism and Eucharist, and what the Roman Catholic Church calls sacramentals, namely rites or acts that in imitation of the sacraments attempt to produce certain effects. Augustine's definition, for instance, that sacraments "contain

44. John Chrysostom, *Homily 15 on John 1:18*, *FaCh* 33:150.

45. So Ignatius, *Epistle to the Ephesians* (20), *ANFa* 1:58.

the announcement that He [Christ] has been born, has suffered, has risen" could hardly be used to substantiate all seven sacraments.[46]

Augustine used the term "sacrament" more loosely than we do today. For instance, he talked about the "sacrament of Christ's body . . . the sacrament of Christ's blood" and "the sacrament of faith."[47] But he leaves no doubt that the sacrament is intimately connected with the pronouncement of the gospel of Christ. He even called it the visible word, saying: "The word is added to the element, and there results the sacrament, as if itself also a kind of visible word."[48] Luther declared in his *Small Catechism* concerning the issue whether water can produce such great things in baptism: "Clearly the water does not do it, but the Word of God, which is with and alongside the water, and faith, which trusts the Word of God in the water." He stands here in true continuity with Augustine, who stated a thousand years earlier: "Take away the word, and the water is neither more nor less than water."[49] Sacraments are the visible side of the pronouncement of God's redemptive Word. But the sign that signifies the sacrament should not be taken lightly as Augustine assures us, saying: "For if sacraments had not some points of real resemblance to the things of which they are sacraments, they would be no sacraments at all. In most cases, moreover, they do in virtue of this likeness bear the names of the realities which they resemble."[50] The sacraments are not only visible signs of an invisible grace announced in and with their administration; they also depict that grace that is announced in them, e.g., the effects of Jesus' cross and resurrection.

The efficacy of the sacraments: Since the sacraments are the visible side of God's redemptive Word, their efficacy is analogous to the Word. The *Augsburg Confession* points this out very eloquently: "For through the Word and the sacraments, as through instruments, the Holy Spirit is given, who effects faith, where and when it pleases God in those who hear the gospel" (CA 5). The sacraments are powerful instruments of God's grace and should not be administered casually but "in conformity with the divine Word" (CA 7). Since they are God's instruments their efficacy does not depend on the righteousness of those who administer them. The recipients of the sacraments usually do not even have sufficient knowledge of the

46. Augustine, *Reply to Faustus the Manichaean* (19:16), *NPNFa FS* 4:245.

47. Augustine, *Letters* (98.9), *NPNFa FS* 1:410.

48. Augustine, *On the Gospel of St. John* (80.3), *NPNFa FS* 7:344, in his exegesis of John 15:1–3.

49. Luther's explanation of "The Sacrament of Holy Baptism," *BC* 349, and Augustin, *On the Gospel of St. John* (80.3), *NPNFa FS* 7:344, in his exegesis of John 15:1–3.

50. Augustine, *Letters* (98.9), *NPNFa FS* 1:410.

spiritual life of their ministers to judge their worthiness. Therefore, the effectiveness of the sacraments and the assurance of God's gifts would always be in jeopardy if their efficacy were contingent on the worthiness of the ministers. To alleviate such fears the *Augsburg Confession* rightly declares: "Both the sacraments and the Word are efficacious because of the ordinance and commandment of Christ, even if offered by evil people" (CA 8). Sacraments administered by heretics can be accepted as valid. For instance, a re-baptism is the exception rather than the norm, even in cases where denominations do not mutually recognize each other. Because of their intrinsic significance, the church will always see to it that their ministers are examples of faith and conduct, not only to assure right proclamation and administration of the sacraments, but to inspire the faithful through the example of their leadership. We see in the cases of misconduct how these hinder the effectiveness of the ministry. Lost trust and esteem can bring to naught any effective proclamation of the gospel.

If the sacraments can be effective without being administered by worthy celebrants, the question must also be asked whether there is a precondition on the side of the recipient to assure efficacy. Two assertions of the Council of Trent in particular have caused much dissatisfaction among Protestants. The Council declared that the sacraments confer grace "on those who do not place an obstacle in the way," implying the notion of cooperation toward salvation.[51] Yet the Council then stated that in the sacraments grace is "conferred by the performance of the rite itself," implying in effect that it is not faith that grasps the gift offered in the sacrament but that the gift is automatically conferred through that which has been accomplished. The Roman Catholic apologist Karl Keating (b. 1950) cautioned us not to interpret this statement in a crassly mechanistic way. "It refers to the fact that the sacraments confer grace when the sign is validly effected—not as the result of activity on the part of the recipient but by the power and promise of God."[52] The sacraments do not produce their proper effects in an automatic and mechanical way, or by some sort of magic. By the phrase, "from the work which has been worked [*ex opera operato*]" we should rather be assured that the grace is not mediated in the sacrament by virtue of the personal merits of the minister or the recipient. As Rahner explains: "The *opus operatum* is the eschatologically efficacious word of God."[53] God's Word will not return empty but delivers the promises contained in it.

51. For this and the following quote see *DC* 389 (1606 and 1608).

52. Keating, "What Does the Expression 'Ex Opere Operato' Mean?"

53. Rahner, "Word and the Eucharist," 4:274.

The question still must be asked how the phrase of Trent "those who do not place an obstacle in the way" is to be interpreted. We are assured: "While a proper disposition is necessary to receive grace in the sacraments, it is not the *cause* of that grace."[54] We recall that the *Augsburg Confession* does not totally exclude reflection on the condition of the recipient when it says that the Holy Spirit produces faith "in those who hear the gospel" (CA 5). Luther even seems to go one step further when he states in his *Small Catechism* that "the Word of God, which is with and alongside the water, and faith, which trusts this Word of God in the water" produces these great saving effects.[55] It is, however, another step further when we hear on the Roman Catholic side that the mediation of grace "depends on the faith of the recipient as he lays himself open and surrenders to the sacramental grace, as also on the intention of the recipient."[56] The reflection on the recipients and their disposition is certainly necessary to avoid the idea of a mechanistic and impersonal mediation of grace. A stronger emphasis on the primacy of grace would assure the certainty of salvation. Otherwise we may always be in doubt whether our faith was strong enough.

With his forceful renunciation of infant baptism, Karl Barth seems to embark on an even stronger cooperative emphasis than the Roman Catholic Church. He admits that baptism without the willingness and readiness of the baptized is true, effectual, and effective baptism. While it must and ought not be repeated, it is however, not correct usage. "It is not done in obedience, it is not administered according to proper order, and therefore it is necessarily clouded baptism."[57] Barth sees in the attempts of Luther and Calvin to justify infant baptism unconvincing arguments that cannot suffice without exegetical and practical "artifices and sophisms." He wonders whether the real reason for infant baptism operative in the Reformers and in theologians today is the fear that without infant baptism the Constantinian majority church would collapse. Even Luther, he says, once confessed that "there would not be too many people baptized, if, instead of being brought to baptism, they had to come of their own accord." Barth in turn does not want these politico-practical questions to decide the issue. Since baptism always demands a response on the part of the baptized, he simply wants "instead of the present infant baptism, a baptism which on the part of the baptized is a responsible act."

54. Keating, "What Does the Expression 'Ex Opere Operato' Mean?"

55. *BC* 349, in Luther's explication of "The Sacrament of Holy Baptism."

56. Schulte, "Sacraments," 5:380.

57. For this and the following quotes see Barth, *Teaching of the Church*, 48, 49, 52, 53, and 54.

The Reformers indeed devise all kinds of theories to justify infant baptism, as we can see in Luther's case. Yet none of these sufficed. At the end, it is very clear for Luther that baptism is totally God's gift. It summons us to faith and its reality and validity do not depend on our faith. The same is true for adult baptism. In the early 1960s, two prominent New Testament scholars went head to head over the issue of infant baptism. Joachim Jeremias (1900–79) responded with *The Origins of Infant Baptism: A Further Study in Reply to Kurt Aland* to Kurt Aland's (1915–94) work *Did the Early Church Baptize Infants?* (1962), which had been a refutation of Jeremias's earlier publication *Infant Baptism in the First Four Centuries,* originally published in 1938.[58] This shows that the issue of whether only infant or only adult baptism is scripturally valid cannot be clearly determined.

But Karl Barth has touched on a significant point. Our response to the grace offered in baptism is important. Without this, baptism is incomplete unless we grant a mechanistic view of infusion of grace through infant baptism. It was therefore very thoughtful when Vatican II decreed: "The rite for the baptism of infants is to be revised, and should be adapted to the circumstances that those to be baptized are, in fact, infants. The roles of parents and godparents, and also their duties, should be brought out more sharply in the rite itself."[59] This means that no sacrament, not even infant baptism, should be administered lightly. If there is no reasonable assurance of facilitating a response of faith (through Christian upbringing), it would be frivolous to administer infant baptism. Similarly, adult baptism should never become just a traditional act, but a reasonable assurance of an adequate response should be secured. Even in the case of the Eucharist, an adequate notion and acceptance of grace offered are minimal expectations for admission to the sacrament.

In cases in which these safeguards to ensure proper administration cannot be given, as with the so-called "emergency" infant baptism, we should accept the dictum of Barth that "the power of Jesus Christ . . . is not dependent upon the carrying out of baptism" and we should not insist on baptism.[60] Emergency baptism is much more a pastoral case, for the sake of the good conscience of the next of kin, than a theological case, for the sake of salvation. Yet the argument is ill-founded that (infant) baptism is not necessary for salvation. Since baptism, however, means incorporation into

58. Jeremias, *Origins of Infant Baptism*; Aland, *Did the Early Church Baptize Infants?*; and Jeremias, *Infant Baptism in the First Four Centuries.*

59. *Constitution on the Sacred Liturgy* (67), *DVC* 160.

60. Barth, *Teaching of the Church*, 23.

the visible body of Christ, in the case of emergency baptism this incorporation is of such short duration that it would lose its meaning.

In question 74, the *Heidelberg Catechism* deals explicitly with the issue, "should infants also be baptized?," and affirms this with a simple "yes." Then comes a very thoughtful explanation: "Infants as well as adults are included in God's covenant and people, and they, no less than adults, are promised deliverance from sin through Christ's blood and the Holy Spirit who produces faith. Therefore, by baptism, the sign of the covenant, they too should be incorporated into the Christian church and distinguished from the children of unbelievers."[61] Here the emphasis is on what God does and has done and not, as Barth declared, on our response to God's grace. But New Testament exegesis shows that there is no clear theological preference for infant baptism over adult baptism or vice versa. If adult baptism, however, is exclusively based on the personal response to God's grace of the one who is to be baptized, the danger is evident that God's Word no longer has the primacy, but our own action. The proper place for adult baptism is the mission field and not a confessional situation. This became especially clear when in the former Communist East Germany infant baptism and subsequent confirmation deprived the children of many educational and professional opportunities while adult baptism escaped such "confessional" consequences. In such situations, adult baptism may be the wiser decision to circumvent the desired oppression of believers by an officially atheistic government.

Some years ago the issue of infant communion stirred up controversy in some Lutheran circles and was often treated in a more emotional than theological fashion. Richard John Neuhaus (1936–2009) put the issue in the proper light when he confessed: "I believe the communing of infants is permissible (to deny that would be to hereticate the Eastern churches). I am persuaded it is not mandatory and I am not persuaded it is desirable—for reasons theological, pastoral, liturgical, ecumenical, and psychological."[62] The argument for infant communion is usually advanced that "if Baptism is the full initiation into the Church, then Communion could follow immediately."[63] According to Lutheran understanding this is certainly true. The same can also be argued for other "sacraments," such as ordination, marriage, extreme unction, etc. We remember that Luther insisted that through baptism one is already a priest, a bishop, and a pope. Nevertheless, he demanded proper education, and a call to qualify for

61. *Heidelberg Catechism*, Question and Answer 74.

62. Neuhaus, *Lutheran Forum Letter* (March 21, 1980), 5.

63. Gritsch, "Infant Communion," 6.

exercising the priestly office. The full initiation (by baptism) does not imply that one should also assume immediately all the privileges of full citizenship in the visible church. For instance, one does not allow infants to vote at congregational meetings, though theologically we could hardly bar them from exercising this right.

One might be tempted to argue against infant communion on the basis that this practice was not mentioned until about 251 when Cyprian wrote of it in *De lapsis*.[64] Yet the argument of a fairly late date could then also be used against infant baptism, since this was not explicitly mentioned until about AD 180 when Irenaeus referred to it. The rejection of infant communion as a later innovation could easily necessitate the rejection of infant baptism with the same argument, a move that not many are willing to make who argue against infant communion. Also the rejection of infant communion with the argument that its rise stems from the emergence of the prevalent practice of infant baptism is unconvincing, since the Western church finally abandoned infant communion while maintaining infant baptism.

Infant communion is now being practiced almost exclusively in Eastern Orthodox churches. We might not be wrong to assume that the reason for this is that there communion is understood as a means of divinization, the desired goal of salvation in Eastern piety. Thus one should not wait for communion until adulthood, but should start as soon as possible. As the traditional understanding of justification gained more and more importance in the West, there was less and less need felt for infant communion. It was finally dropped completely in the late Middle Ages. In some ways that may seem regrettable. But the Eastern churches are not very consistent in their practice. If communion is indeed so vital that there should be a natural move from the baptismal font to the Lord's table, why is there not more urgency for adults to commune than there is for infants? While infants are quite often brought to communion, adults rarely commune in most Orthodox churches. Perhaps divinization for infants is more symbolic than real (which many parents would painfully admit).

Though it might be good for the West to balance its exaggerated, law-oriented emphasis on justification by recovering the Eastern notion of divinization, infant communion would be the wrong move in this direction. Even for Christians, as they progress in maturity and age, certain rites of passage, such as the sacraments, are helpful aids toward the goal of sanctification. We should not exclude Christian children on theological principles from communion, ordination, or any other grades of participation among

64. Cyprian, *De Lapsis and De Ecclesiae Catholicae Unitate* (9 and 25), 15, 37–38. For more historical information cf. Beckwith, "Age of Admission to the Lord's Supper," esp. 125–27, and Brand, "Baptism and Communion of Infants," 36–38.

the faithful, but on pedagogical grounds. We had a very disturbing incidence of this many years ago as our family attended a communion service when our children were small. We attended the church service as visitors and when communion was served my wife and I went forward carrying our little girl in our arms. We were expecting the pastor to bless her as was customary in our own congregation. Yet to our total surprise he gave her the communion wafer. She took it in her hands and looked at it in amazement and thought it was quite a nice toy. Without adequate preparation and understanding she was given communion instead of just receiving a blessing as we had expected. This action by the pastor was totally inappropriate. But the introduction of a flexible communion age with careful preparation seems a step in the right direction, removing a barrier and establishing guidelines for Christian life and growth.

Another issue that arises in connection with the efficacy of the sacraments is whether they have only a symbolic also realistic character. The two poles here are the extreme symbolism of Zwingli and the concept of transubstantiation in Roman Catholic teaching, with the Lutheran concept of real presence holding a middle position. As the *Leuenberg Concord* of the European Churches of the Reformation conceded in 1973, many of the old stereotypes no longer hold. This proves to be true as one reconsiders and reinterprets the history of one's own history and the history of other denominations, and as biblical exegesis leads to deeper insight. It further stated that "in the Lord's Supper, Jesus Christ, the risen One, bestows himself in his body, given into death for all, and his blood through his promising Word with bread and wine, in his body and blood given for all."[65] The Reformed tradition emphasizes that "although he [Christ] is in heaven and we are on earth, we are nevertheless flesh of his flesh and bone of his bone. And we forever live on and are governed by one Spirit, as the members of our bodies are governed by one soul."[66] Though this statement allows for a kind of "sacramental realism," we should not forget that according to this statement Christ remains in heaven. This means that communion with him is possible only through the Holy Spirit. This does not mean that Christ is present only symbolically in and with the elements. The *Heidelberg Catechism* says with reference to Paul that in "the cup of blessing" there is "a sharing in the blood of Christ" and in "the bread that we break" there is "a sharing in the body of Christ."[67] The Lutheran side also emphasizes very much Christ's real presence saying, for instance, in the *Augsburg Confession* that "the true body and

65. *The Leuenberg Concord* (15), 35:245

66. *Heidelberg Catechism* in the explanation of question 76.

67. *Heidelberg Catechism*, answer 77.

blood of Christ are truly present under the form of bread and wine in the Lord's Supper and are distributed and received there" (CA 10). Similarly, Luther says in his *Small Catechism* that the Lord's Supper "is the true body and blood of our Lord Jesus Christ, under the bread and wine, instituted by Christ himself for us Christians to eat and to drink."[68]

Unlike the Reformed tradition, the Lutheran emphasis on the real presence is not coupled with an equal emphasis on the circumstances of his presence. There is no reflection on the Holy Spirit as the mediator of the real presence or on the difference between the presence of Christ in heaven and in the Lord's Supper. Lutherans insist that, similar to God, Christ can be present wherever he wants, and that he can be present everywhere, even at the same time. Lutheran official documents, however, show a remarkable restraint in pointing out the mode of the Lord's presence.

Through the centuries the Roman Catholic church became more and more specific about the mode of this real presence. At Trent it picked up the notion of transubstantiation, first declared at the *Fourth Lateran Council* (1215), and finally stated:

> His Body and Blood are truly contained in the sacrament of the altar under the appearance of bread and wine, the bread being transubstantiated into the body by divine power and the wine into the blood . . . no one can perform this sacrament except the priest duly ordained according to (the power of) the keys of the Church, which Jesus Christ himself conceded to the apostles and their successors.[69]

Christ's presence is somehow "produced" by the priest through the words of institution. This, of course, considerably increased the power and prestige of the priest. In ecumenical dialogues the question has been repeatedly raised what such transubstantiation actually means. It is evident that it opposes a strictly symbolic understanding of the Lord's presence. Yet it does not imply the transformation of substance (matter) as we would assume according to today's terminology. Substance would mean here either substance in contrast to outward appearance, or substance in opposition to that which is accidental, or substance as that being which underlies any other feature that is added to it. As the Capuchin Franciscan Regis Scanlon explains: "As a result of transubstantiation, the species of bread and wine undoubtedly take on a new signification and a new finality, for they are no longer ordinary bread and wine but instead a sign of something sacred and a sign of spiritual food; but they take on this new signification, this new

68. Luther's explanation of "The Sacrament of the Altar," *BC* 362.

69. *DC* (802), 267.

finality, precisely because they contain a new 'reality' which we can rightly call *ontological*."[70] One could even conclude that "a symbolism and transignification" that maintains the realism of Christ's presence is within the limits that the doctrine of transubstantiation describes.

Each of these different interpretations shows that transubstantiation emphasizes that God acts in the Eucharist, effecting a change in the elements. But it is not a rationalistic attempt to explain the mystery of Christ's presence in the elements. Similar to the Reformed and the Lutheran assertions concerning the real presence, it shows the limits of our theological efforts to explore the mystery of Christ's presence. The same is true for the Orthodox tradition. There too the terms "change, transubstantiation, and re-creation" indicate that the elements of bread and wine are inseparably united with the body and blood of Christ.[71] It becomes clear that with different conceptual tools the presence of Christ in the sacrament is asserted, similarly as we asserted Christ's presence in God's Word of law and grace.

And yet the Eucharist also has a symbolic function, reminding both us and God of Christ's sacrifice on Good Friday. Since Christ's presence is celebrated, it also foreshadows his parousia, his final coming. Without the real presence, the efficacy would be limited to psychological or group dynamic results. But without the symbolism of cross and parousia the sacrament would be robbed of its dynamic structure of memory and hope.

In exploring the efficacy of the sacraments we must finally mention their unifying character. If God in Christ encounters us in the sacraments, Christ is the prime actor. This has become most evident in baptism. Christ calls, Christ incorporates us into his body, and we respond to the grace extended to us. The unity of the church is established through Christ in baptism. Through the act of baptism we then discover and affirm our unity.

Similarly, Christ meets us in the Eucharist. Christ's presence is experienced by us, and Christ sanctifies us through his presence. The Eucharist always has a cleansing effect, being administered for the forgiveness of sins. However, those who reject God's grace, Christ's sacrifice on our behalf, experience judgment. Since the Eucharist is the most intense and intimate communion with the resurrected Lord, it is the expression and symbol of existing unity of the church as Christ's body. Fellowship at the altar and fellowship in the pulpit—proclaiming the same Word of God—signifies the ultimate union among Christians.

When Paul says about the Eucharist: "Because there is one bread, we who are many are one body, for we all partake of the one bread" (1 Cor

70. Scanlon, "Is Christ 'Really' Among Us Today?"

71. Cf. the theses in *Eucharistie*, 23–24 (esp. thesis 4).

10:17), he does not simply mean that the Eucharist is a confirmation of our unity in Christ. Since Christ is the main actor and the gift, we should also expect something, namely that "the sacramental participation in Christ's body makes us into the body of Christ."[72] Wolfhart Pannenberg (1928–2014) comments very appropriately that the Eucharist is

> the source and root from which the unity of the Christian lives and is continuously renewed. This corresponds with the idea that fellowship in the Lord's Supper need not stand at the end of the process of church union, but it can also be already the present power of Christ on the way towards this goal.[73]

It is as wrong to expect that communion fellowship would magically or automatically create church union and to assume that eucharistic fellowship is only permissible if this union has already been achieved. If there is power in the Eucharist through Christ's presence that implies forgiveness of sins, we should also expect that it can forgive the sins of separating and dividing the body of Christ. Otherwise the efficacy of the sacrament is neglected. It becomes more a symbol of what we do or have done than it is expressive of God's own activity. The expectation of God's power is implied in the understanding that the Eucharist, and analogically baptism, is not simply an act of remembrance, reminding us of Christ's death. It is as powerfully an act of anticipation, foreshadowing the return of the glorified Christ and the celebration of the celestial banquet in union with Christ and all the faithful. The sacraments are not only expressive of the union already existing. Because of Christ's presence in them they have unifying character and can properly be celebrated together on the way towards union. Again let me illustrate this with an example. Some years ago my Roman Catholic colleague from our university, Konrad Baumgartner, celebrated Mass on the eve of All Saints' Day in a neighboring village. He had invited to the Mass me and an Orthodox abbot plus two monks who had been visiting us from Greece. In his sermon the colleague explained the meaning of All Saints' Day with an Orthodox icon he had placed on the altar. When it came to the distribution of the sacrament with bread and wine I was in a quandary. Should I go forward and wonder what the people in the congregation would think of what this Lutheran professor was doing (my colleague had introduced us to the congregation), or should I remain in my seat and wonder what my Roman Catholic colleague would probably think? He had given us a special invitation to attend, and what would he think if I at least didn't participate

72. Conzelmann, *1 Corinthians*, 172, in his exegesis of 1 Corinthians 10:17.

73. Pannenberg, "Abendmahl—Sakrament der Einheit," 287.

in the Eucharist? Moreover, the colleague and the abbot with his monks had been invited to dinner at our house following the Mass. Well, I went forward and participated in the Eucharist. When I returned, the abbot immediately confronted me saying: "Why did you do this?" I responded: "This is not the Eucharist of the Roman Catholic Church. They do not own it. It is the Eucharist of Jesus Christ." His answer was: "I never thought of it this way." Indeed, the Eucharist is never the possession of one single denomination; Jesus Christ offers it to all who desire its benefits with a contrite and thankful heart.

Yet why should "outsiders" even consider the sacraments as something important for their lives? Even secular people appreciate rites of passage, entering this life, leaving childhood, entering a partnership for life, leaving life on earth, etc. For all these occasions the church offers special feasts, such as baptism, confirmation, marriage, funeral, etc. Moreover, since life is often hard and unpredictable, why not adduce the blessing of a power higher than we are, God almighty? But where does the Eucharist fit in? It is food and sustenance not just for the body, but for a journey that does not end with this life. It is "medicine for immortality." While many people will not want to admit it, they are not really content with life simply petering out. Here the benefits of Christ, salvation from the strictures of this life, and the assurance of eternal life, are a prospect that one should not reject.

PART 3

The Threefold Extension of the Church

The German American sociologist and philosopher Herbert Marcuse (1898–1979) published in 1964 a bestseller under the title *One-Dimensional Man*. Three years later the book was also translated into German and Marcuse became one of the prominent leaders of the German student revolt of the 1960s. In this book Marcuse claimed that consumerism and the modern industrial society exercise a form of social control on every aspect of culture and political life. We live in a hidden dictatorship and have become a tool in the industrial machine and a cog in the consumer machine. While this book is more than half a century old, the analysis sounds very familiar: we live to consume and our industrial society lives on the premise that we need ever new items to make our life more comfortable. The treadmill that results from our attempt to stay afloat is all too familiar. We have no time to think about the past or the future. We focus all our energy on the present simply to stay alive. We have acquired many new gadgets since we were first promised that they would save us time. But this has not come true. We have lost our vision of the future and our foundation that connects us to the past.

It is no surprise then that more and more people have no time and appreciation for the church. They live completely in the present and are absorbed with their present-day activities, whether it be at work or in their leisure time. The church appears to them as a countercultural institution that, often unknown to them, is also keenly involved in the affairs of the day. Yet its focus is much wider, extending to the past and also to the future in its utmost sense. While the church has often been in danger of losing itself in contemporary affairs, it serves as a living reminder of the roots and destiny of the present, by providing direction and encouragement for bringing about the present. Yet in so doing the church dare not become oblivious to the future, both in its ultimate and penultimate sense. If apocalyptic is the seedbed of the Christian faith, as some theologians have claimed, the church must always be mindful of the future, as a challenge toward which to strive and a restraint that reminds us that the future is a gift and not an accomplished fact.

With its three-pronged approach to the past, the present, and the future, the church offers a foundation grounded in the past and a vision for the ultimate future that is both rewarding and everlasting. And this to the one-dimensional people who are caught in the present with no real sense of either past or future.

1. THE GUARDIAN OF THE PAST

The church is conservative in the true sense of the word, preserving the past, in harmony with that what gave rise to the church. But it dare not automatically sanction everything that in the past has received approval. It must continuously discern between what should be discarded and what should be preserved. Otherwise, the church becomes as archaic as many of its critics claim it is. The reason for being a guardian of the past is not that the church has a history of nearly two thousand years. Rather, the church is the guardian of the past because its sources lie in the past and its present direction must be evaluated by the extent to which it is still true to its sources. Back to the sources was a demand of the Reformation enhanced by Renaissance scholars. Only when a firm foundation of the past is erected can we stand secure to master the present. This foundation is the Word of God as documented in the Bible.

The Bible is not a monument carved out of stone tablets, but rather reflects the growth of the tradition that was solidified in the biblical manuscripts. Consequently, the source of the church by which its truthfulness can be measured is not simply the Bible. There were external forces at work that shaped this foundational document of the Christian faith. Surprising as it may sound, we encounter different traditions there—for example, in the New Testament we have the Gospel according to Matthew and the letters of Paul, to name just two strands of the traditions. The affirmation of the Reformation insight "Scripture alone" therefore necessitates the doctrine of tradition. The content of the tradition that is to be handed on is not a doctrinal statement in terms of a peculiar tradition, but ultimately it is Jesus himself as the incarnate Word of God, giving authority to the gospel and to the authoritative Word of faith. All other traditions must be judged by the gospel of Jesus Christ and the tradition that he engendered. Without that tradition, nobody would have preserved the gospel for us. Tradition is a necessity of the Christian faith.

The necessity of tradition: God's Word comes to us only through the medium of tradition. Of course, God speaks to us today. But whatever is claimed to be the Word of God must always be measured in its truthfulness by the incarnate Word of God as it has been shown to us in Jesus Christ. Only that which is in line with the incarnate Word of God can be accepted as truly God's Word. Therefore, tradition is vital for a church that wants to adhere to God's Word. Scripture itself is the result of the handing on of tradition, as the authors freely admit (Luke 1:1–4 and John 20:30–31). Furthermore, Scripture is always encountered within a particular tradition, such as the Roman Catholic tradition, the Reformed tradition, etc. The ecumenical dialogues too have shown that even cultural traditions within the same confessional family color certain strands of the gospel tradition (e.g., the rise of liberation theology in predominantly Roman Catholic Latin America). There is a difference if a Roman Catholic appeals to Scripture or if a Lutheran appeals to it, and there is also a difference if a Roman Catholic in Italy cites Scripture or one living in Latin America. Our varying ethnic and cultural traditions necessarily influence our perception of the gospel. For instance, a liberation theologian would give more emphasis to the prophetic writings of the Old Testament, a Lutheran would focus on the Gospel of John and on Paul's Letter to the Romans, while a more traditional Roman Catholic might emphasize the Gospel according to Matthew and the Epistle of James.

Historical conditioning of our understanding of the gospel is both a promise and a danger. It is promising insofar as it shows that God's Word does not speak in opaque neutrality but is a word in and for a particular situation. The danger lies in the individualization of historical particularity, suggesting that since truth is relational it is also relative. To combat this potential misunderstanding we must remember that the historical appropriation of the gospel in a particular tradition is nourished by the fact that we are all living in a tradition that goes back to our Lord and has its roots in the Old Testament. We exist as Christians because of the handing on of the gospel testified to in Scripture, and transmitted in and by the church through the power of the Holy Spirit. Without the handing on of the gospel tradition and its living presence today, there would be no church and no Christian faith. In this respect the dictum of Cyprian is certainly correct that outside the church there is no salvation.[1]

Each theological discussion and ecumenical encounter make us painfully aware that the Christian tradition is not equally present in every Christian group and individual Christian. For the church to become one, it is certainly not necessary to agree on every minute detail concerning worship and church structure. There is not one right way to worship God and to organize the church. This should also be noted in the present discussions concerning the influence of the laity in the Roman Catholic Church. Not even the gospel tradition is equally present among us. Yet there are already different emphases in the New Testament. There is Peter next to Paul, and John next to the Synoptics. While these different emphases found their way into the New Testament, we also discover warnings there against false teachings and deviations from the truth of the gospel, evidently implying that there are traditions outside Scripture that contain distortions. To safeguard the gospel tradition against false interpretations, the canon of biblical writings evolved, and with it the creeds and the apostolic teaching office. Since the teaching office could not rely on a literary tradition except for creed and canon, a history of doctrines evolved in distinguishing right interpretations of the gospel from incorrect ones. At the same time the question again arose by what criterion one could determine genuine tradition.

The key for deciding between valid and invalid tradition became even more necessary when the Reformers claimed that the teaching office had inadequately interpreted the tradition. It is significant, however, that Martin Luther made this charge not by referring to Scripture as a whole, but by using as a hermeneutical key the Pauline insight of justification. Other Reformers used similar hermeneutical keys, such as the individual conscience under the guidance of the Holy Spirit (Enthusiasts) and the glory and the kingdom of God (Calvin). The Reformation emphasis on the Bible alone is to be understood more in a polemical sense, directed against the teaching office, than in the purist sense by eliminating all other criteria.

When we encounter the gospel contained in Scripture it is always from a particular perspective, which to some extent predetermines our understanding of the gospel. But such a discovery cannot be made as long as one is in a position of isolation or antagonistic entrenchment against all other understandings. The experience of ecumenical encounters sharpens our eyes for better perceiving our own hermeneutical key to the gospel tradition, and it makes us aware that other keys open up insights that are inaccessible from

1. Cyprian, epistle 73:21, in "Epistles of Cyprian," *ANFa* 5:384.

our own perspective. A careful analysis of different traditions will not result in the naive euphemism that all traditions are equally valid. We will notice, however, that all of them, including our own, contain particular virtues and shortcomings. We will also find that we usually have strong ecclesiastical ties to people who adhere to traditions that are similar to our own, while we have very little fellowship with those people who have traditions that are not similar to ours. Since the life of the Christian church is lived in a continuous recalling, appropriation, and transmission of the gospel tradition, listening to each other will enhance and enrich this process, while ecumenical isolation leads to increased one-sidedness and an eventual distortion of the gospel. "So the attempt must always be made to transmit the Tradition in its fullness and to remain within the community of the whole of God's people, and the temptation must be avoided of overemphasizing those elements which are especially congenial to a particular culture."[2]

Catholicity is not a possession of one particular configuration of the church even if this has been repeatedly asserted, most recently in August 2000 with the declaration *Dominus Iesus* by the Congregation for the Doctrine of the Faith of the Roman Catholic Church. It stated with reference to Vatican II: "The Church of Christ, despite the divisions which exist among Christians, continues to exist fully only in the Catholic Church, and on the other hand, that 'outside of her structure, many elements can be found of sanctification and truth,' that is, in those Churches and ecclesial communities which are not yet in full communion with the Catholic Church."[3] But similar to the wholeness of the body of Christ, catholicity is not a human possession but a gift of God's grace extended to the whole body of Christ, which demands its continuous appropriation. Contrary to Vincent of Lérins (d. ca. 445), a monk from Gaul in today's France, Catholic is not that which "has been believed everywhere, always, by all."[4] Such a notion would lead to a static concept of tradition. It does not do justice to the dynamism of the living tradition operating by the power of the Spirit throughout the church. Catholic is rather the gospel tradition that always, everywhere, and by everyone is attested to in a variety of ways. If one closes oneself off to the living tradition, assuming in exalting self-righteousness that one has the sole and full grasp of the tradition, sectarianism or even heresy arises. It was crucial that the proponents of divergent streams in the early church did not pursue their own way in splendid isolation, but that they talked to each

2. "Scripture, Tradition and Traditions," 59.

3. Congregation for the Doctrine of the Faith, *Declaration "Dominus Jesus"* (IV.16).

4. Vincent of Lérins, *Commonitory* (2.6), *NPNFa SS* 11:132.

other, attempting to maintain the wholeness of the body of Christ and its joint witness to the world (1 Cor 1:13, 12:12).

Between heresy and truth: There were three prime occasions when the church was tempted with a sectarian or heretical posture. (1) In its first centuries, in the wake of the christological controversies, the Nestorian and Monophysite churches were excluded from the mainstream of Christendom. (2) In the Middle Ages the rift between the Eastern and the Western church occurred, and (3) at the beginning of modernity the Western church disintegrated into the churches of the Reformation and the Roman Catholic Church. As a late consequence of this third schism we can point to the phenomenon of American denominationalism. To assess correctly what happened in each instance with regard to the tradition of the gospel, we must acknowledge that the church is always threatened by heresy. Heresy is not a threat from outside, like the impact of the world religions, and of secularism. Rather heresy is a danger that comes from within. It results from no longer listening to each other and, as the terms "heresy" and "sectarianism" suggest, from attacking each other and burning the bridges that connect us. Sects and heretics emerge when we neglect the common tradition and stress the differences rather than the things we share in common.

Since a heretical or sectarian group usually continues its existence within one strand of tradition by absolutizing its position, there is always an element of truth contained in any heresy. Certainly, heresy is a deviation from the truth that the church cherishes as its own tradition. But looking back at the movements that were declared heretical, we notice two characteristics: (1) Heretical movements that persist for any length of time are never completely void of truth. Even in their distorted ways they acknowledge the gospel tradition. For example, Pelagius (ca. 350/360–ca. 418/420) was certainly right with his insistence that acknowledging that we are sinners cannot serve as an excuse for not trying to lead a righteous life. (2) Heretical movements concentrate more or less exclusively on one or a few parts of the tradition that have usually been neglected by the church. While the church has been largely silent on the second coming of Christ, millennial movements have concentrated on this aspect of the Christian faith. The church will perhaps never find it possible to give as much attention to these issues as heretics do. But the rise of a heretical movement should challenge the church to reexamine its own understanding of the tradition and to decide whether the neglect was out of necessity or simply an oversight.

If the church wants to preserve the whole truth of the tradition, it dare not neglect the truth contained in the distorted statements of a heretic. Simple exclusion of heretics does not lead the church to a deeper appropriation of the truth. Exclusiveness leads to one-sidedness and impoverishment. The Reformation led not only to an antagonistic entrenchment on the side of the Roman Catholic Church, it led also—although perhaps not clearly perceived at that time—to greater orthodoxy within Catholicism. When we look at the Council of Trent, the Council did not spend its time on the veneration of saints and of relics as it would perhaps have done without the Reformation, but it focused on such important issues as justification, Scripture, and the sacraments. While this was done in perceived distinction from the Reformation, it nevertheless led back to the core of the Christian faith. As Augustine observed, a heretic must always be taken seriously, since heresies cannot "be produced through any little souls. None save great men have been the authors of heresies."[5] Heretics are not liars or dishonest people but fellow searchers for the truth who appropriate the gospel tradition in an overly slanted and therefore heterodox way.

They attitude toward a heretic should be one of dialogue, of conversation in love, and only as a last, but painful resort, one of exclusion. The church cannot accept heretical views without abandoning its own position as the guardian of the tradition. But the relationship with a heretic can never be settled once and for all. The ecumenical dialogue has taught us that views once considered divisive, through more intensive study of the common tradition and of each other's traditions, have more than once been interpreted only as different aspects of the same concern. Thus the discovery of heresy challenges the church to strive for new unity and deepening of insight. But in an age in which one dare not challenge someone else's position, can we still talk about heresy? Are not all views equally valid in our postmodern age? The criterion for right and wrong is, however, not determined by the respective age in which we live, but by the gospel tradition from which we live. According to that tradition some views are more amenable to it while others even stand in opposition to it. Whatever resists to be reconciled to the gospel tradition must therefore be determined as unacceptable or as heretical. The term "heresy" even if it may sound odd to some is still appropriate for views that are totally unacceptable when measured against the gospel tradition.

Confronted with the religious pluralism of American denominationalism, the church serves a particularly important function as the guardian of the one tradition. When we glance at the immensely diverse pluralism of American denominations, we might be tempted to regard denominations primarily as sects. Following the distinction between church and sect introduced by the German sociologist of religion Ernst Troeltsch, we

5. Augustine, *On the Psalms* 5, *NPNFa FS* 8:601, in his comments on Psalm 125.

immediately realize that denominations are sectarian only in a very limited sense. Troeltsch suggested that the church, basically conservative, accepts to a certain extent the secular order. It wants to dominate the masses and desires to cover all of humanity. The sects, on the other hand, are relatively small groups that aspire to personal inward perfection and aim for direct personal fellowship among the members of the group. They have no interest in dominating the world and are either indifferent, tolerant, or hostile toward the world, the state, and society without much desire of controlling or incorporating these forms of social life. Though sects do not seek dialogue with the other religious or secular institutions, they usually do not live completely to themselves. In pronounced opposition to the church they claim to preserve the truth of the gospel tradition that the church has neglected or suppressed.

While a sect is a kind of voluntary protest organization, it usually retains its status for only one generation. Within the next generation, a sect must institute educational and disciplinary policies. As the social status of its members improves, it must also come to terms with its relationship to the world, i.e., make the transition from indifference, isolation, or hostility to that of compromise. In other words, eventually a sect will either become extinct or assume many features of the church. As the ongoing divisions on the American denominational scene indicate, denominations are not sects, but gave rise to them. Opposing and dissenting groups have accused denominations of betraying the gospel tradition and this is the reason new splinter groups have formed. This was the case, for instance, with the formation of the North American Lutheran Church, which consists largely of former members of the Evangelical Lutheran Church of America.

The common spiritual heritage of any denomination usually centers on the Bible. Whether for the Baptist or Lutheran, Quaker or Presbyterian, Anglican or Congregational, the Bible is the center and symbol of the common Christian tradition and the highest authority to which they appeal. Each defends its idiosyncrasies by referring to this common authority, attempting to show that its denominational teaching and its way of ecclesiastical life most closely conform to the biblical pattern. As Thomas Jefferson (1743–1826) confessed: "As to tradition, if we are Protestants we reject all tradition, and rely on scripture alone, for that is the essence and common principle of all the Protestant churches."[6] This sentiment is shared by my many Protestant friends. But it does not imply, as we might assume, a joint appeal to the common tradition. On the contrary, free from the tutelage of European state churches, each denomination in America feels free to appeal

6. According to Mead, "Denominationalism," 293.

to the common tradition with the intent of justifying its own peculiar position and proving its superiority over others. Indicative of this mood is the amazing competition that has been waged between different denominations until recently. While mainline churches and many others are quite conciliatory toward other denominations even to the point of proclaiming altar and pulpit fellowship, as the ELCA and the Episcopal Church have done, this is not the case for others that are still trying to establish themselves.

While denominations preserved much of the heritage of their European parent churches, they became voluntary associations "of like-hearted and like-minded individuals, who were united on the basis of common beliefs for the purpose of accomplishing tangible and defined objectives."[7] These aims included religious objectives as well as cultural and educational forms. For instance, Norwegians gathered in the Norwegian Evangelical Lutheran Church in America, founded in 1853, to continue their own piety, speaking their own language, and preserving their own national customs especially with regard to food. Denominations initially helped to mold and shape the lives of the immigrants in the United States by keeping alive deep emotions of kinship and belonging. Yet ethnic lines are not sufficient to explain that multiplicity of denominationalism. The denominations also portrayed a kind of socioeconomic caste system that still today distinguishes the lower class denominations from the ones of the middle and upper-middle class. The denominations became "the mouthpieces of the economic and sectional groups they represented."[8] Denominations divided and emerged along the lines of geography and color of skin as well as along the lines of ethnic and religious allegiance, and along the lines of income, or even adaptation to the English language as the many First English churches or even English synods indicate. For a long time, Anglicans belonged to the upper-middle class until they were surpassed by the Presbyterians. When the ELCA was formed in 1988, next to the sixty-four geographical synods, the Slovak Zion Synod was established as the only non-geographical synod. It dates back to 1919 when Slovak immigrants founded the Slovak Evangelical Lutheran Zion Synod. But now it is no longer strictly Slovak and conducts services in many languages.

By appeal to the common biblical tradition the churches represented and perpetuated the ethics of class and nation rather than the common ethics of the gospel. But while denominations still provide a haven for those who refuse to accept the ideology of the melting pot, they have largely succumbed to the compromise between the gospel tradition and the secular

7. Mead, "Denominationalism," 291.

8. Niebuhr, *Social Sources*, 24.

world that has its own tradition of religious autonomy. Only in recent years have denominations begun to learn that their common Christian heritage requires a joint recapturing and reliance on the Christian tradition in the joint witness to the world. American Protestants are learning that one cannot naïvely reject all traditions, and at the same time attempt to retain the biblical tradition, without ending in separatist self-righteousness. We can only hope to uncover in our own denomination the common tradition that binds all Christians together as the body of Christ and present to the world a joint witness of that common heritage.

The community of saints: One might at first wonder whether the community of saints is properly located under the aspect of the church as the guardian of the past. Indeed, the community of saints has a present and a future dimension. The church is a community of people that transcends the visible boundaries of an institution and of space and time.

It is vital for the church to remember that it participates in the community of saints. This combats the false notion, often prominent in denominationalism, that the church is a gathering of like-minded people. No, the church has existed before like-minded people even gathered. The church cannot be derived from the desires of individuals. Bonhoeffer aptly reminds us that "the church does not come into being through people coming together (genetic sociology). But it is in being through the Spirit which is effective in the community."[9] It is a wrong notion that we can "attend the church of one's choice." The church is a given that we cannot choose, but through which God has chosen to accept us who have devised our own ways in our piety and in our way of life. The church is not a community on its way toward heavenly perfection, which would imply that it receives its peculiar shape from the future. The church is first of all founded on that which God has done for us. As the hymn tells us: "The church's one foundation is Jesus Christ, her Lord; she is his new creation by water and the word."[10]

Belonging to the church means that we belong to the Lord who has been active in the past, who is active in the present, and who will be active in the future. We are not the first Christians, but as a community of saints we are one with those with whom God has worked in the past. In its liturgical calendar the church rightly remembers the saints, who have participated in the visible community. The church does not adore them but it praises God for the good God has done through and with them. A church without saints is not a church in the strictest sense, because it is oblivious to

9. Bonhoeffer, *Communion of Saints*, 116.

10. *ELW* 654, stanza 1.

God's past activity. It also deprives itself of a stimulus that the community of saints exerts on our present lives. Without the living memory of "saints" such as Bonhoeffer, Augustine, and Mother Teresa our spiritual lives would be poorer.

Where saints are often not explicitly recognized as being part of the Christian community—presumably out of fear of being crypto-Roman Catholic—they are usually accepted implicitly. We preserve and use the Old Testament songbook, the Psalms, and the many hymns that have come to us through the centuries. Some of these were written by Augustine, Ambrose, Francis of Assisi, Martin Luther, Paul Gerhardt, and Charles Wesley. Paul makes clear his dependence on the saints when he calls Abraham "the ancestor of all who believe" (Rom 4:11). This is the same Paul who claimed that the Jewish law was abolished through the coming of Christ. Yet he did not feel that this meant that God had not been active long before in the forbearers of the Jews. His fervent struggle in Romans 9–11 clearly indicates that Paul was well aware that the Christian community of saints did not originate out of thin air. We stand in succession of an earlier community, the Israelites, through and in whom God worked.

New Testament research has clearly shown that we cannot sufficiently understand the roots of our faith and our tradition unless we perceive them as coming from the Israelite faith. The acceptance of the Jewish Scriptures as our Old Testament is an acknowledgment of the community of saints that comprises more than just the Christian community. It is a witness to God's larger saving activity. When the New Testament scholar Rudolf Bultmann (1884–1976) claimed that Old Testament Jewish history is a history of failure and that because of this failure it finds its fulfillment in the New Testament, he shortchanged us of this very important part of God's salvation history.

The Old Testament is very much our history, and, as Luther picturesquely claimed: "here you will find the swaddling clothes and the manger in which Christ lies, and to which the angel directs the shepherds."[11] The Old Testament is important for Christians in its own right and also because the term "New Testament" makes little sense without an Old Testament preceding it. We stand in true succession to the history the Old Testament portrays. In this way the Old Testament is part of our own history and we can say with Luther and in contrast to Bultmann that for us "the whole Old Testament has been nothing but the proper preparation and precursor to the New Testament."[12] Referring to Romans 4, Luther shows that all the

11. Luther, *Alte Testament* (1545) *Luthers Vorrede*, *WA* 8:13.6–7.

12. Luther, *Prophet Habakuk ausgelegt* (1526), *WA* 19:351.3–5.

prophets speak about the New Testament. This means it is more than just a negative backdrop against which the Christian faith looms in new light. Its people are part of the community of saints and they are in every respect our spiritual ancestors.

What does all of this mean for the disenchanted who are distant from the church? We must show them that without being rooted in the past we have no future but are stuck in the quagmire of the present. Standing on the shoulders of our forebears is much easier than treading water and never being able to really reach solid ground. Accepting the past, blemished as it may be, opens a rich treasure mine of insight and relativizes some of our anguish in the present. It is comforting to know that we are not the first Christians and that others before us had problems too. Perhaps we might even learn how to manage our own lives by learning from the successes and failures of the past.

The Christian community, while guarding the past, is also directed toward the present. From the hope that the past engenders, both as the reminder of God's activity and as an acknowledgment that this activity is still unfinished, we are summoned to inaugurate this hope in the present.

2. THE HEART OF THE PRESENT

A sociological survey might question whether the church plays a significant role in today's society. In most countries the effect is waning that the church exerts any influence on the social and political life of the community and the private life of individuals. Even where it is still effective, its impact is often minimal. Yet in most Western countries the majority of the people still claim to be Christian and in many younger nations the number of Christians is rapidly increasing. In most predominantly Christian countries, Sunday after Sunday more people turn out for worship than for any other single event, including soccer and football. Yet we do not simply record what the church is presently doing. Having traced the major steps of the church in the past, we want to ask theologically what the place of the church should have in society, and in people's lives. We do not see our primary task in describing phenomenologically what place it presently occupies. But we want to outline theologically and in practical terms what its import ought to be.

Such an undertaking is vital today in our society, because in the US at least, the majority of the people are religious but are not necessarily Christian. Even if they have a denominational affiliation they hardly differ from those who do not have one. Their professions and their income are similar to the rest of society. Most of the time their daily conduct is indistinguishable from that of other people. Given that situation it is not surprising that churches have become less and less attractive to people. In Acts 2:42 the church is described in its actual sense: "they devoted themselves to the apostles' teaching and fellowship, to the breaking of bread and the prayers." This description, however, has become the exception rather than the rule in today's society. Like everybody else, most Christians are so caught up in their daily pursuits that the churches no longer shape the lives of their members and even less of society at large. Therefore, it is important to recall what the church actually ought to be and then ask whether it would not be important for us, as individuals and society at large, to be influenced and even be shaped by what the church stands for.

Similar to the heart in a human being, the church should pump lifeblood into a cold society, it should activate complacent people to thought and action, and amid self-perpetuating routine, it should provide the impulse for a new direction in life. Among the different tasks that the church must tackle, three seem to be most important: (1) the church should be the conscience of society, (2) it should be the haven of the neglected, and (3) it should be the anticipation of the heavenly city. The indicative mood is omitted intentionally because these tasks that are essential for the future of the church are not always implemented. They still present a task which is before us.

The conscience of society: Although the worshiping community was identical with the political community in the Israelite theocracy, it was a different story in Christendom. Ever since the church first emerged, the question was debated how the church should be related to society. In the beginning it was clear that the church, as a relatively small community, had to preserve its identity to survive. Its members conducted their lives according to their own agreed-upon rules without rejecting that which they found acceptable in the rest of society. Once the church had gained majority status, in the East the notion developed that the church was the extended arm of the state with the emperor assuming the role of the *pontifex maximus*, the high priest. In the West, due to the absence of the emperor from Rome, the cradle of Latin Christianity, the church assumed many functions of the state and became the guardian of the emperor, and in many instances his opponent. The church paid a high price for its status in the West. To a large degree the Western church exchanged its spiritual role for a political one, owning land, riches, and secular power. This role was severely challenged by the Reformation. Yet the Reformers were by no means unanimous in their understanding of how to relate church and society. In the Geneva of Calvin the attempt was made to establish a theocracy, with the church becoming synonymous with the state. This idea was also propagated by the Enthusiasts (e.g., Thomas Müntzer, 1489–1525), and later by some English reformers such as Oliver Cromwell, and by the Puritans. On the Lutheran side, however, there was an insistence on the distinction between church and state, although the princes never actually granted the church a fully independent status. In the Anglican tradition we have the wedding of state and church, very much along the lines of Eastern Christendom. At the coronation of a British king or queen, the sovereign is still anointed with oil, which points to his or her sacral status as leader of the Anglican Church.

The real challenge to the relationship of church and society came during the last two hundred years with the separation of church and state in almost all countries. Now the question had to be addressed anew as to how the church should be related to a society that by and large felt it had no need for religious guidance. Through the separation of church and state the typological distinction between church and sect, set forth by Ernst Troeltsch, was no longer adequate to describe the task of the church in relation to society. It would have been utopian to assume with Troeltsch that the church is an institution that wants to include all of humanity. On the other hand, the arrangement of the sect that Troeltsch contrasts with the church is not an adequate description of the task of the church either. A sect, he feels, can only exist in confrontation with the church, and he suggests furthermore that in a few generations the sect assumes church-like features.

A more realistic possibility would be to perceive the function of today's church in analogy to that of a club. Those who still share religious feelings meet at specified times and places to cultivate their own interests. To a large extent this is the official status allowed to the church in today's China and in many Muslim countries. Any functions beyond conducting religious rites and ceremonies for its own members are severely restricted by the state. Though the voluntary nature of the church would be a tacit admission to its alleged club status, Christians assert that the church is not simply constituted by its members but by God. Further, in contrast to a club, the church encourages infant membership. And finally, the church does not seek those who already have a "religious antenna," but rather it searches for those who do not seem to care about the church and who do not feel alienated from God. The church searches for sinners and outcasts.

Another possibility would be to conceive of the church as an institution through which we receive certain benefits if we attend and contribute to it financially. For instance, we could perceive of the church in analogy to the institution of the family or of the state. We might say that we participate in the rituals of the church and support it financially and receive eternal salvation as compensation. Indeed, the church has distinct institutional features, asking for contributions and involvement of its members, electing leaders, instituting rules of conduct to assure good standing, and granting the promise of certain blessings.

Yet the church as an institution does not exist apart from the people who constitute it. (1) The church does not exist for the people, but the people themselves form the institutional church. By contrast, the American form of government, for the people, by the people, of the people, is institutionalized in the United States in such a way that the institutional government operates largely independently from the people. Even frequent elections do not change this, as we become painfully aware when different government officials are elected. (2) Any benefit derived from the church as an institution is not in response to our own participation, but, conversely, our participation in the church is in response to the promises derived from the church. Even in its darkest moments throughout history, the church never forgot completely that it could be an institution of salvation only because of what God has promised to his church, and not because of what we might bring to it.

Since the church has many institutional features, it must be an institution of a very special kind. To explain the special status, we must remember that the church's reason for existence is the fact that Christ is risen from the dead and that he is both the head of the church and the redeemer of the world. Since the risen Lord is the head of the church, we should not only expect to foreshadow the new creation and the glory of the risen Lord, but it is our mark of truthfulness to do so. In many ways the path of the church may resemble the *via dolorosa* (path of sorrows) that Jesus took on his way to Golgotha. Nevertheless, the church is called to foreshadow the glorified Christ and to announce his dominion over the whole world. Since the risen Lord is also the redeemer of the world, the church cannot be silent in the face of the secular world. It is called to announce Christ's ultimate victory over the world and to symbolize his already abiding presence within it.

As H. Richard Niebuhr pointed out in his lucid study *Christ and Culture*, the relationship between Christ and culture, or between Christ and society, can assume five positions: the church can stand against society, the church can affirm society, the church can come to stand above society, church and society can hold each other in tension, and finally the church can transform society. Niebuhr attempted to attribute to each of these types certain dominant streams in the history of the church. He sees cultural Protestantism of nineteenth-century Germany as the church's affirmation of culture, and Luther's attitude toward church and state as expressive of the tension between church and culture. But Niebuhr realizes that such typology "is always something of a construct. . . . No person or group ever conforms completely to a type. Each historical figure will show characteristics that are more reminiscent of some other family than the one by whose name he has been called, or traits will appear that seem wholly unique and individual."[13] Yet he asserts that such typology has the advantage of calling to attention the continuity and significance of the great motifs that appear and reappear in the long history of the church in wrestling with its problems.

Niebuhr admits that none of these types appears in its true form and that all of them have their advantages and shortcomings. Therefore, it seems more logical to us that they should not be separated and attributed to distinct streams if we want to outline the task of the church in today's society. To the contrary, by learning from their individual shortcomings we should take them together and carefully balance them against each other. Then we might arrive at an adequate framework within which we could describe the function of the church in today's society. We might also assume that the reason for the nonexistence of pure types is not only because they are not viable, but because they provide more of a caricature of the church than a proper description of it.

1. *The church in opposition to society*: If the church does not want to become indistinguishable from the rest of society it must first of all stand in opposition to society. This does not mean that the church is opposed to everything that goes on in society. Yet from the very beginning there was a fundamental tension between the church and the world and simultaneously, one of intense relevance. For instance, the Son of Man came into the world to save it; the Christian dies to the sinful world to rise as a new creature; the church is ruled by the prince of this world, who is already judged. Each of these assertions reflect the immense opposition of church and society. Yet the church does not abandon society. To fulfill its task the church must be itself, true to its own calling, not of the world but in the world. Furthermore, since the world is God's creation and God also rules the world, the church can affirm in this world whatever it finds acceptable and what is not contrary to the gospel.

The church must be an institution, insisting strongly on the right continuity with its origins. Amid the situation of unrest and instability it provides a haven of rest and stability, the tranquil eye at the center of a stormy world. While the world emphasizes rapid change in every respect, the church provides a strong sense of corporate identity. It knows what it stands for, it knows its Lord and what he has in store. It is not swayed by steadily varying trends and fads. As a beacon of heavenly guidance the church cherishes the gospel tradition and the administration of the sacraments. In other words,

13. Niebuhr, *Christ and Culture*, 43–44.

the church has what the world cannot give, an ultimate reference point for life and living, and the living presence of the power of the resurrection that protects it from ultimate destruction. The church lives by the standard of grace and forgiveness that entitles it to ever new beginnings. It does not live by the law of achievement and the selective pressure that is derived from our finite creation, which therefore bears the sting of death itself.

Tempting as it may be, the church's otherness cannot lead it to isolation and withdrawal from the world. It is significant that the stepping stones of the church from Jerusalem into the Roman Empire were not the secluded desert sites of Pella and Qumran, but the bustling cities of Ephesus, Corinth, and Rome. Steering its own course, the church ventured into a foreign world, challenging what it found and calling this same world to a higher and more durable allegiance. Opposition to the world is always characterized by a momentum for mission.

It is not mere accident that in the United States at present the membership of the mainline churches is rapidly eroding, while conservative churches are at least holding their own. The reason is simple: "*Religious organizations are stronger to the degree that they impose significant costs in terms of sacrifice and even stigma upon their members.*"[14] In terms of real costs and benefits the more mainline churches lower the value of belonging to the church, the more this eventually results in widespread defection from it. They shy away from proclaiming that the world is corrupted by sin, that the world endangers our humanity, that earthly treasures are eaten up by moth and rust, and therefore the world needs to be saved. They forget to remind their members not to love the world and the things that are of the world. They ought to be strangers and pilgrims in this world. But there is also time for positively engaging the world. The biblical witnesses show us that Christ came into the world to save it and not to condemn it. As God has sent me, so do I send you, Jesus reminds us according to the Johannine witness. Similarly, we hear Paul say that God was in Christ reconciling the world to himself. Therefore, Luther could claim "A mighty fortress is our God, a bulwark never failing." In the same vein we sing today: "Onward Christian soldiers, marching as to war."[15] The opposition to the world is opposition to the belief in self-righteousness, in humanity's inherent natural goodness and moral perfectibility.

By exposing the world as corrupt, as being under the dominion of the seductive anti-Godly powers, the church cannot confine itself to redeeming

14. So the sociologists Finke and Stark, *Churching of America*, 238.

15. *Lutheran Book of Worship*, 509, stanza 1. This hymn is no longer contained in *Evangelical Lutheran Worship* perhaps since it may sound too much like a battle hymn. Yet the battle that must be fought is against the "foe," the devil.

individual souls. The church dare not neglect the individual and the spiritual side of its message. But its effectiveness is severely hampered if it is not brought to naught, unless it also addresses itself to the bodily and material dimensions. This means that the church's opposition to society and its subsequent redemptive onslaught must be directed to the whole of society, both to body and spirit, both to corporate structures and individual human beings. Yet any missionary approach to society would be futile or, at most would result in an exchange of respective positions, unless the church were convinced that it comes to stand above society. After all this is said, we must also conduct serious self-examination: To what extent dare the churches and its members really be countercultural? Are we distinguishable from the rest of society or do we blend in nicely? Do we really lift high the cross as a hymn says or do we pursue the values of the world? The list of questions could easily be extended. But the point is clear: If we are not different, why should people join us? They would only receive what they could get somewhere else. Churches everywhere will be losing members if they try to follow the prevailing trends in society, laudable as they may be. For example, if such issues as sexual and racial equality became their main credo. Then the churches would be perceived as having nothing special to offer. They would be perceived as pursuing some kind of civil religion, instead of proclaiming the gospel of Jesus Christ. It must always be clear that the churches stand for something that the world cannot give, the redemptive gospel of Jesus the Christ.

2. *The church in its stand above society*: At the height of the Middle Ages Pope Innocent III (1161–1216) asserted that the relationship between church and state compared to that between sun and moon, i.e., that the moon receives its splendor from the sun. Though we might find such a statement ill-fitting for a church that imitates the servant role of its Lord, there is some truth contained in this assessment of the relationship between church and society. Without the influence of the church—or a comparable religious organization—society does not gain a complete understanding of humanity. For instance, in a society in which the church does not have freedom to announce the gospel, usually human rights are violated too. The philosopher of law and former judge at the Federal Constitutional Court of Germany Ernst-Wolfgang Böckenförde (1930–2019) rightly reminded us: "The liberal, secularized state lives from presuppositions which the state itself cannot guarantee."[16] These presuppositions are largely provided by the Judeo-Christian tradition and to some extent also by Hellenism. When

16. Böckenförde, *Staat, Gesellschaft, Freiheit*, 60.

they are attenuated more and more the state itself may be in trouble as we become painfully aware that the radical fringes are becoming ever more dominant in our democracy.

Defending the human within the society, the church does not rival the task of the state. When in its socialization process the state assumes many of the traditional functions of the church, such as the care for the poor, the sick, and the elderly, and the education of the young, the church will not be edged out of its decisive role in the world. Other neglected areas will demand its attention, such as the humanization of technology, the relationship of labor and management, and the sensitizing of affluent societies to the widening gulf between North and South on the globe and in our own country. When the state claims new areas of responsibility, the church is not pushed from one corner into another. Rather the opposite is true. Through its involvement in areas neglected by society it examines and sharpens society's understanding of humanity. It makes society aware of what it neglects and encourages society to accord justice and equal rights to everyone.

In the process of adequately defending that which is human in society, the church needs and will demand a somewhat preferred or exceptional position in society. Most countries recognize this by providing certain privileges for the church, such as subsidy for operating expenses, the privilege of collecting church tax from its members, exemption from real estate tax, etc. While these benefits may vary considerably from country to country, it is fair to say that "the churches have as their primary expectation from the state a freedom to practice and propagate their faith. The state on the other hand has as its primary expectation the formation by the churches of virtuous and patriotic citizens."[17]

Often the idea is advanced that in fulfilling its function as the conscience of society, the church does not expect to receive anything from the state nor does it give anything away. Similarly, the sentiment is strong that the state as the guardian of the worldly order acts mostly in its own sphere without expecting any help from the church. In being the guardian of the worldly order, the state realizes that this world order is not simply given but must be continuously shaped and maintained. Such order, however, cannot be safeguarded without the implicit or explicit consent of society. Especially in this regard the government has a fundamental expectation of the church, namely that it shapes virtuous and patriotic citizens who maintain this order, be it in respect to paying taxes, in keeping speed limits to reduce traffic casualties, or in other respects that safeguard the peaceful order of living

17. So Drinan, *Religion, the Courts, and Public Policy*, 219. Though Drinan calls this an oversimplified generalization, it presents a fairly correct summary.

together. It is interesting that Thomas Jefferson, who was instrumental in getting the separation of church and state included in the US Constitution, asserted that a person "has no natural right in opposition to his social duties."[18] This means that Christians too have social duties that, as we might add, are informed by their Christian ethics of love.

But how can the church educate Christians to function as virtuous and patriotic citizens if the influence of religion never reaches beyond the private life of a Christian? Moreover, how can society expect ultimate sanctioning of any virtue of patriotism if the church is excluded from the public sector? A totally secular state that by its definition eliminates (metaphysical) ultimacy from its public horizon relativizes itself in the values it espouses so much that in the long run it is doomed to failure. For instance, what would be the bond that binds public servants to their duty?

The only alternative is a state ideology, as it is advanced in the frequent singing of the national anthem and the pledge of allegiance to the flag. But the ideas of freedom, liberty, and concern for the well-being of the community that are commonly associated with such state ideologies, are by no means secular insights. Historically they are grounded in deep religious commitments, which means for us in the West as well as in many younger nations, the Judeo-Christian tradition. We can refer here to Martin Luther, who stated that each person has various professions, such as mother, teacher, citizen, or church member. In each of these professions we fulfill the various obligations as a service not just to others but ultimately to God. Service to God is therefore service to the neighbor and vice versa. When Friedrich Engels (1820–95), the collaborator with Karl Marx, conceded that the most revolutionary insights of Marxism, the concern for the oppressed and the outcast, the anticipation of the kingdom, and the equality of all people show a similarity to those of the early Christian tradition, he sensed a commonality of Christian concerns and that of a good and benevolent secular government. We could even say that these concerns stem directly from the gospel tradition. Whenever and wherever they were separated from the liberating power of the gospel tradition they became truncated and, in many instances, their application led to renewed bondage and enslavement instead of freedom and greater equality.

Society cannot disassociate or even emancipate itself from the church, unless it wants eventually to abrogate its task of maintaining secular order and upholding virtue and patriotism. That most of our societies, influenced by the West, are still functioning relatively well is not the result of the separation of church and state or due to the fact that the societies are secular.

18. Jefferson, "Letter to the Danbury Baptist Association in Connecticut."

The reason is rather that there are still so many Western, and this means Judeo-Christian, convictions present in our societies that help to form a bond of unity and advance self-respect and mutual concern. It is not without significance that in the US the Supreme Court ruled in 1952 "that the nation's 'institutions presuppose a Supreme Being' and that government recognition of God does not constitute the establishment of a state church as the Constitution's authors intended to prohibit."[19] It was evidently felt that the recognition of God is necessary for society. Yet the more these convictions become obliterated and attenuated, the more it becomes necessary for the church to act as the guardian of society, to function as the state's transcendental reminder of the eternal value and responsibility of each human being. However, any attempt by the church to rise above our sinful society, to act as a beacon and reminder of a common metaphysical obligation, will arouse the suspicion of some people. They will question whether such a position is too presumptuous or even unnecessary. Therefore, the tension between church and society will continue.

3. *Church and society in tension*: As long as the church exists it will live in tension with society. Even in the United States, a country that prides itself on its clear separation of state and church, the state is always in danger of becoming a church, with an official faith or ideology called civil religion, with the White House serving as the focal point of that ideology. Is it really by mere accident that in the United States most state capitol buildings and the national capitol building are so similar to St. Peter's Basilica in Rome, the heart of the Roman Catholic Church? Is it only by accident that occasionally some US presidents have asked pastors to conduct worship services in the White House, with invited guests as worshipers? Former President Trump even stood in front of a church across from the White House waving a Bible to make a point. Clearly the temptation for the state to become a church is tempting. And more than once in history the church has attempted to legislate its own rules of conduct for everyone.

To avoid the twin dangers of clerical domination or of a civil religion, some theologians introduced the distinctions between the two kingdoms of God, the kingdom to the left (the world) and the kingdom to the right (the church). Picking up the biblical notion of a distinction between the world and the kingdom of God, Augustine outlined the progress of the city of God over the city of the world, intending to show the spiritual superiority of the former. While such a view left no doubt as to the abiding necessity of the

19. https://en.wikipedia.org/wiki/Separation_of_church_and_state_in_the_United_States.

church for society, it also furthered a clerical domination over the world instead of holding it in check. It was not until Luther that a doctrine of the two kingdoms evolved that avoided the inherent danger in Augustine's system without abolishing the tension between the church and the state.

It is unfortunate that H. Richard Niebuhr labels as dualistic the tension between church and culture that results from the doctrine of the two kingdoms. Though Niebuhr immediately qualifies his typological assessment, it certainly colors his description and evaluation as to the relationship between church and society.[20] Niebuhr, however, recognized that Luther does not compartmentalize the world into church and state, but that he strictly distinguishes between the kingdom on the left, the earthly kingdom, and the kingdom on the right, the heavenly kingdom. We also agree with Niebuhr that, though Luther's approach brought about valuable social change, it was basically conservative, more apt to preserve the world than willing to change it.

Unlike Augustine, Luther did not identify the kingdom of God with the kingdom on the right nor the kingdom of the devil, with the kingdom on the left. Though Luther distinguishes between the kingdom of Christ and the kingdom of the world, the latter means for him the totality of all orders of God, the orders of nature as well as civil justice. The line of scrimmage between God and the anti-Godly powers goes through both kingdoms and Satan attempts to turn both into an anti-Godly chaos. Their purpose as bulwarks of God against the destructive assaults of the devil testifies to the inner unity of both kingdoms. Luther writes:

> For God has established two kinds of government among men. The one is spiritual; it has no sword, but it has the word, by means of which men are to become good and righteous, so that with this righteousness they may attain eternal life. He administers this righteousness through the word, which he has committed to the preachers. The other kind is worldly government, which works through the sword so that those who do not want to be good and righteous to eternal life may be forced to become good and righteous in the eyes of the world. He administers this righteousness through the sword.[21]

This passage from 1526, which we quoted earlier in a slightly different context, shows clearly that the same God stands behind both kingdoms and is actively present in them, but in different ways. While God works in both kingdoms according to his goodness and love, one kingdom is concerned

20. For this and the following cf. Niebuhr, *Christ and Culture*, 149–50 and 171–72.

21. Luther, *Whether Soldiers, Too, Can Be Saved* (1526), *LW* 46:99–100.

with faith and eternal salvation, the other with outward peace and prevention of evil. The secular kingdom serves the earthly life and is temporal like our life on earth, while the spiritual kingdom serves for eternal life, the actual goal of God's work. Luther observes very properly that even Christians cannot escape the secular kingdom and its distinctions: "We are all included in them; indeed, we were born into them even before we became Christians. Therefore we must also remain in them as long as we are on earth, but only according to our outward life and our physical existence."[22] We are citizens of the secular kingdom according to our secular needs, while we are citizens of the spiritual kingdom according to our spiritual existence. This shows that all of their differences notwithstanding there is an organic interdependence between the two kingdoms.

This interdependence becomes especially evident when Luther observes that the spiritual kingdom needs peace and order in this world—the result of the secular kingdom—so that Word and sacrament can be effectively administered. Another point where this interdependence is found is in the inclusive character of the secular kingdom. The secular or temporal kingdom does not just comprise authority, government, and the orders of nature, but all means of earthly sustenance of life, such as matrimony, family, property, the economy, and all professions. These human enterprises are executed according to the law, or what is synonymous for Luther, according to the sword. But how does one know about the law if one is not a Christian? Luther recognizes that the rules and regulations in this world are not given by Christ, but they are given by God in the natural law.

While the knowledge of God's will is often distorted and obliterated in this world, Luther was convinced that the law of the country sufficiently answers the question of what a father, a mother, a prince, or a judge must do in a particular situation. Of course, these laws are historically conditioned and changeable. Luther demands that we must use reason to investigate the expression of the natural law they ought to represent. But he is rather optimistic about the value of the positive law of the country. He is convinced that there is always a hidden order behind the world's obvious order, or disorder. In the long run, no power can exist without God's hidden order. We see, Luther contends, that according to this hidden order God allows one state to grow and thrive, but he also dissolves it.

The natural order is expressed, for instance, in the Magnificat. Mary sings that God "has brought down the powerful from their thrones, and lifted up the lowly; he has filled the hungry with good things, and sent

22. Luther, *Sermon on the Mount* (1530/2), *LW* 21:109, in his comment on Matthew 5:38–42.

the rich empty away" (Luke 2:52–53). The rational order of the world is God's order without his actual presence. But how can we penetrate to the natural law and find out whether these orders are still God's orders and in accordance with the natural law? Luther points here to the golden rule and responds: "For nature teaches—as does love—that I should do as I will be done by."[23] Luther refers to the same maxim that was used more than two centuries later by the philosopher Immanuel Kant in his *Groundwork of the Metaphysics of Morals*. Luther mentions nature and love in one breath. He is convinced that though the secular kingdom is governed by laws and coercion, this does not exclude love. This is especially important for Christians, since they, being led by love, must by necessity live in the secular kingdom that is governed by coercion.

Luther encourages Christians to assume secular office. He says if there is need of judges, lords, and princes, and if you think you are qualified for it, you should apply for such offices. Otherwise the necessary authority is held in contempt and becomes weakened. Whereas he admonishes neither to exert power too freely nor too sparsely, he concedes: "To err in this direction, however, and punish too little is more tolerable, for it is always better to let a scoundrel live than to put a godly man to death."[24] How far Luther is from the idea of a power-centered secular order can be seen by his advice that Christians in secular positions should imitate Christ. Since Christ, as supreme prince, came and served without seeking his own power and honor, so Christians in authority shall not look out for their own but serve those under them so that they will be protected and defended.

While Luther's distinction between the two kingdoms certainly provides no panacea of how to relate church and society, it makes one point unmistakably clear: no sphere of our life can be excluded from Christ's lordship. His lordship, extending over all of life, proceeds in different forms and with different methods. If the distinction becomes blurred between the different forms and methods according to which the two kingdoms conduct their affairs, either clerical triumphalism or secular utopianism results. The church must remind society under whose dominion society stands and under whose ultimate authority it conducts its business. Conversely society serves as a reminder for the church that this world, though searching and longing for wholeness and redemption, is still broken.

Luther realistically discerned that the same forces of darkness are at work in both church and society. In the church the lust for power, the execution of injustice, and the disregard for love are present to threaten the very

23. Luther, *On Temporal Authority*, *LW* 45:128.

24. Luther, *On Temporal Authority*, *LW* 45:104–105.

credibility of the gospel. We notice this painfully in the present discussions in the Roman Catholic Church with its pyramidal power structure. The church is always called to repentance not only for the sins of society, but also for its own sins. As a community of people the church cannot escape the necessity for law and order. Its structures cannot be maintained with love alone, but must be upheld with authority in the name of love. However, the necessity for an order in the church of different layers and the call to obedience that this order implies dare not be mixed with or misunderstood as the call to obey the gospel tradition. Even in its own house the church must distinguish between the kingdom on the left and the kingdom on the right. If it fails to do so, it ends up peaching law in the name of the gospel. Let me illustrate this with an incident that occurred in one of my seminar classes in a theological seminary. One of the assignments in the seminar consisted of writing a paper. One of the students refused to write the required paper with the excuse that he had never before written a seminar paper. When I told him that without a paper there would not be a passing grade for him, he responded: "Is there no grace in this class?" My answer was: "No, since there are rules which must be obeyed by everyone." We cannot mix rules (the law) with grace (the gospel).

That Christ is not only the Lord of the life of a Christian, but the Lord of the whole world, has been rediscovered by many who do not necessarily claim the name of Luther in their heritage. For instance, the *Chicago Declaration of Evangelicals* states: "We affirm that God lays total claim upon the lives of his people. We cannot, therefore, separate our lives in Christ from the situation in which God has placed us."[25] This sentiment is compounded by the growing number of people who having set their heart primarily on social causes now realize that the gains do not compare to the time, capital, and energy that they have invested. Therefore, there is an increased readiness to accept "a balanced biblical concern for both social restructuring and individual conversion." This insight gains new vigor when "conservatives" discover to what extent governments who espouse law and order are morally corrupt. Thus evangelism and social concern not only are considered as very important, but we increasingly realize that they are inseparable. The theologian and social activist Ronald Sider (1939–2022) addressed the issue very appropriately when he claimed:

25. For this and the next two quotes see Sider, ed., "Declaration of Evangelical Concern," (front cover), *Chicago Declaration of Evangelicals*; and Sider, ed., "An Historical Moment for Biblical Social Concern," *Chicago Declaration of Evangelicals*, 17 and 30, text in brackets added by the author.

> Evangelistic proclamation is fully biblical only when it calls for repentance from all types of sin [i.e., not just private ones] and urges a biblical discipleship in which all relationships, both personal and societal, are transformed. And prophetic social criticism is fully biblical only when it announces both that participation in structural evil is as a damnable sin against God Almighty and also that divine forgiveness is bestowed on those who repent and turn from all their sins.

Sider created Evangelicals for Social Action, now called Christians for Social Action (CSA), as a network to fulfill those commitments made in the *Chicago Declaration*. CSA is a "think-and-do" tank that helps Christian communities cultivate a faith-fueled commitment to justice. For five decades, Sider and the organization he founded have been synonymous with faithful engagement in the spheres of education, politics, and the church, addressing both global and domestic issues, building broad coalitions, and engaging in courageous civil dialogue with people across the theological and political spectrums.[26] In 2005 the Sider Center was established at Eastern University, a Christian university in Philadelphia, with a Sider Chair in Theology, Holistic Ministry, and Public Policy, where the CSA has now found its home.

But evangelical Christians are by no means unanimous on how to address the public square. This is shown by Sherwood Wirt (1911–2008), who was affiliated with the Billy Graham Association, and who comes at the issue of relating church and society from a slightly different angle. Acknowledging that social problems exist wherever humans exist, he is still hesitant to address social issues on a large scale. He distinguishes appropriately between evangelism and social action, defining evangelism as "presenting Christ to men in the power of the Holy Spirit," while social action is seen as "an effort to apply Christ in finding solutions to human problems."[27] But he wonders whether one really can or should convert power structures, since it is always individuals who make up these structures. It might be much better to address the individuals within the structures so that the structures would change with them. Wirt also questions whether the church should act as a pressure group and engage in political lobbying. Yet he recognizes that the church has a biblical mandate to be alert to its social responsibility. But corporate church pronouncements on social matters "should deal with the

26. https://christiansforsocialaction.org/about-us/history/.

27. Wirt, *Social Conscience*, 129.

heart of the moral issue and where possible should the couched in general rather than specific terms."[28]

As Sherwood Wirt paradigmatically demonstrates, there is still a frequent tendency within the church to shy away from specific corporate pronouncements concerning significant issues in society. The reason for this hesitancy is not a lack of courage—evangelism requires courage too—but a wrong understanding of society, namely that it is seen as the enemy of the church, instead of as an additional element of God's presence in the world. To overcome this inadequacy, the church must affirm society and dialogue with it.

4. *The church's affirmation of society*: Immanuel Kant's *Religion within the Limits of Reason Alone* (1793/94), Friedrich Schleiermacher's *On Religion. Speeches to Its Cultured Despisers* (1799), and finally Adolf von Harnack's famous literary exchange with Karl Barth of 1923, had convinced many that the affirmation of society by theology and the churches had gone too far. It became labeled Culture-Protestantism and therefore received an unsavory reputation. We certainly cannot advocate that God is synonymous with humanity's own possibilities. But Harnack was rightly worried when he asked Karl Barth:

> If religious experience is contrary to or disparate from all other experience, how can the necessity of a radical flight from the world be avoided . . .? If God and world (life in God and worldly life) are absolute contrasts, how are we to understand the close connection, even equating, of love for God and love for our neighbor which constitutes the heart of the gospel? . . . If God and the world (life in God and worldly life) are absolute contrasts, how can we lead people to God, that is, to what is good?[29]

Barth's answer was not very comforting when he asserted that "the faith which is awakened by God will never be able fully to avoid the necessity of a more or less 'radical' protest against *this* world, inasmuch as it is a hope for that which is promised but unseen."[30]

Barth's attitude of a protesting disassociation from the world was well taken in confrontation was the Nazi tyranny of the 1930s and forties. But if Barth had remembered Luther's insight that a tyrant is against God's will and will be toppled by another tyrant, his unqualified acceptance of Stalinist Communism would have been more discerning. Furthermore, if we claim

28. Wirt, *Social Conscience*, 134.

29. Harnack, "Fifteen Questions," 165.

30. Barth, "Fifteen Answers," 168 (answer 4).

the lordship of God as christocentrically as does Barth, how can we convincingly assert that God is also present and active in the whole world and not just in the church? If we were to follow Barth, the church could not even meaningfully criticize society, since society would have no God-given antenna to understand this criticism and respond with positive action. But what positive force could be present in the world that would allow for such response unless it were God himself to whom all people witness (Rom 1:19)? Knowing about human sinfulness, the church cannot assume that God's presence in the world is self-evident to everyone. The church must therefore act as the conscience of society, acting in solidarity with it, and at the same time sharpening society's own conscience for the demands of God.

It is very unlikely that in secular society the church will get a hearing, except among its own members, if it cannot appeal to insights that are accessible to everyone in the church and in society. Thus we must look for a common ethical platform, and set common ethical goals for Christians and non-Christians in society. Such "Christian humanism" will take seriously that all of humanity, not only that part which associates with the church, is created and sustained by God.

But where do we perceive such common ground? Today a metaphysically grounded natural law has fallen into disrepute. Yet Luther's emphasis on the common knowledge of the natural law, in his attempt to relate church and society, may contain more insight than we are willing to attribute to him. For instance, the Swiss Reformed theologian Emil Brunner (1889–1966) warned long ago that if there is nothing universally valid and no justice beyond ourselves that meets all of us as an undeniable demand, then there is no actual justice, only organized power plays.[31] The alarming frequency with which totalitarian systems have emerged during the last one hundred years should make us wonder whether our own humanity is a sufficient foundation to safeguard the survival of human existence. Even during the reign of absolutism the kings and princes understood that they enjoyed their rule by the grace of God. But today's dictators exercise their rule in their own name. They no longer feel that they must justify their actions to anyone else. The individual human being has become their own ultimate measure for right and wrong.

But we should also remember Charles Darwin's assertion that human moral and mental faculties differ in degree rather than in kind from the capacities of animals. If there is indeed a moral continuity between animals and humans, there should be even more reason to assume such continuity between one human being and another. Perhaps the reason why we tend

31. Cf. the eloquent argument in Brunner, *Justice and the Social Order*, 8.

to deny the basic unity of human morality lies in our sinful estrangement from each other. We are so far apart from each other that we tend to forget our common destiny. Ethnological research has adduced more and more evidence that indeed there are some basic norms of human behavior. The biologist Arnold W. Ravin (1921–81) expressed this very appropriately when he said:

> Every culture has a concept of murder, that is a specification of conditions under which homicide is unjustifiable. Every culture has a taboo upon incest and usually other regulations upon sexual behavior. Similarly, all cultures hold untruth to be abhorrent, at least under most conditions. Finally, all have a notion of reciprocal obligations between parents and their children. These universal or near universal ethics . . . indicate some profound and fundamental needs in all men to behave within certain limits or ethical boundaries.[32]

This tells us that by nature the behavior of society is not as free and unspecified as we might initially assume. To be a human being means to act according to certain norms that enable us to live together and further our own species. The explicit forms that these norms assume, however, depend upon the environment in which the social behavior takes place.

These insights and conclusions give new significance to the traditional theology of orders. The moral norms are at least in principle accessible to everyone. They are goal-oriented, intended to preserve the species rather than to constitute it. It might be good to follow the suggestion of the Lutheran theologian Walter Künneth (1901–97) and perceive moral norms as orders of preservation and not just orders of creation. If we regard them as orders of creation only, they appear too static, disallowing for any changes. Künneth, however, maintains that creation must be perceived under the aspect of God's conserving activity.[33] This is even more necessary, since we know God's creation only in its fallen condition, under the aspect of preservation. According to Künneth the orders of preservation counteract the tendencies of the destructive anti-Godly powers. They are a sign that God does not want to destroy the world but instead conserves it for Christ's sake and toward Christ. The orders of preservation have an eschatological character, for they urge on toward the end-time fulfillment in the new creation. To ensure their function for preservation we should at least periodically ask

32. See Ravin, "Science, Values, and Human Evolution," 151. For a more extensive discussion cf. Schwarz, *Human Being*, 51–62.

33. Cf. for the following Künneth, *Politik zwischen Damon und Gott*, 139–40.

whether they still fulfill this function or whether they need to be adapted to the present situation.

Since these orders are no longer evident in their original divine creational intention, they assume the character of a law and an obligation. They enable and facilitate the living together of people. They express a mutual obligation and therefore have the basically diaconal character. Yet they are also susceptible to sinful distortion and can be misused to perpetuate injustice and inequality. Therefore, it is necessary never to divorce them from God as the originator and grantor of these orders. This does not mean, however, that we should go as far as Karl Barth does when he claims that through its sinful existence humanity is in such a depravity that it cannot know about these fundamental moral laws. Barth insists that these orders cannot be found anywhere; they are disclosed to us only through Jesus Christ and God's Word. But such an exclusively Christocentric approach to these orders—whether we accept their foundation in Christ or not—obscures the fact that the acknowledgment of certain moral norms is a necessary condition for human existence as such.

Atheists can recognize these norms of moral behavior as partly inborn and partly handed on by tradition. In the light of God's self-disclosure in Jesus Christ, however, Christians perceive in these norms God's preserving activity. They realize that through the evolving moral process God is present in the human community, preserving it against self-destruction and against the destructive and seductive tendencies of the anti-Godly powers. Luther expressed this very picturesquely when he said: "If [God] would withdraw his protective hand you would become blind, or an adulterer and murderer like David, you would fall and break your leg and drown."[34]

Through God's self-disclosure in Jesus Christ we are reminded of God's presence in society, and of society's transitory character. Society will find its fulfillment and completion in the eschatological new creation, when God's orders will be unimpaired and self-evident and when God will dwell in the midst of his people. It is shortsighted and a neglect of our responsibility as people of God if we simply sit back and wait for that eschatological goal of perfection to arrive. Once we have discovered our common meeting point and affirmed God's preserving presence in society, we should witness to God's presence in the midst of his fallen world. This means that we attempt to transform the world so that it may bear more resemblance to the new creation toward which it is designed.

34. Luther, *Predigten des Jahres 1531*, *WA* 34/2:237.3–4, in a sermon on the eve of the festival of St. Michael's.

5. *The task to transform society*: The abiding presence of the anti-Godly destructive powers in this world makes the task of the church to transform society a continuous and perennial one. Any millennial or utopian ideas that advocate an evolutionary convergence of church and society neglect the reality and radicality of evil in this world and forget the eschatological proviso that limits our human endeavors. Yet shy of establishing the kingdom of God, which by its very nature is an end-time event, the church would betray its own reason for being if it did not press on to transform society.

The transformation process, however, must go in two directions. There is a need for a continuous transformation of that part of society that is the church, so that it may become a better example of the new community and the beacon of hope in the face of oppression and injustice. There is also a continuous need for a transformation of that part of society that is outside the church. The truth that God is active in the world must come to ever clearer expression. Sinful humanity and the structures it designed to perpetuate its sinfulness must be converted to become expressive of the will of the Lord. The process of such conversion foreshadows God's eschatological goal of salvation envisioned for all people. This pressing on for the advancement of humanity would include on the social level: economic justice in the face of exploitation of people by other people, human dignity in the face of political oppression of human beings by other human beings, human solidarity in the face of alienation of one person from another, and hope in the face of despair in one's personal life.

Some rightly ask whether the theologies of liberation, revolution, hope, and even of rebellion are not just transitory fads that seek to ride on the bandwagon of global social upheavals that marked the collapse of the European colonial powers. Though there may be some truth to this, the attempt of the church to transform the world is as old as the church itself. While the church has compromised this missionary goal many times, Friedrich Engels made a significant observation when he said: "In the popular risings of the Christian West . . . the religious disguise is only a flag and a mask for attacks on an economic order which is becoming antiquated. This is finally overthrown, a new one arises and the world progresses."[35] Engels recognized that in the name of the Judeo-Christian tradition actual societal change takes place, whereas in other societies reform movements "are clothed in religion but they have their source in economic causes; and yet, even when they are victorious, they allow the old economic conditions to persist untouched."

35. For this quotation and the following see Engels, "On the History of Early Christianity," 276, in a footnote by Engels.

We must now ask what allows for and engenders this transformation of society in the "Christian West." What was it that drew millions of people to emigrate to the "New World" and what stimulated them to turn it into a beacon of hope for many others living under oppression and poverty? What was it that had lured at least one-third of the world's population to embrace Marxist doctrines, a teaching that served as a sign of freedom from domination and slavery in many younger nations? Though economic reasons may have acted as a powerful stimulus, they fail to explain the whole picture, because often the affluent intellectuals of a nation had been especially attracted to Marxist doctrines.

Of course, we could say that the endeavor to transform society results from the peculiarly human phenomenon of pressing on to ever new horizons, of being open to the world and searching for constantly new experiences. Again this answer fails to account for the fact that primarily the "Christian West" served as the starting point for societal transformations. Perhaps the religious component cannot just be understood with Engels as a disguise, but as the propelling and driving force for the creation of a new society. The Judeo-Christian hope for a new world order and for a new humanity served as a stimulus for the Marxist vision of a "socialized humanity."[36] The Judeo-Christian faith also stood behind the assertion in *The Declaration of Independence* "that all men are created equal, that they are endowed by their Creator with certain inalienable rights, that among these are life, liberty, and the pursuit of happiness."

But we recognize at the same time that the Marxist vision had been tarnished by countless acts of new oppression. In the course of its enactment, which finally failed, millions of people lost their lives. *The Declaration of Independence* also significantly qualified the insight of equality within the human family when it called the American Indians "merciless savages" who attack the white immigrants. Regardless of these frequent lapses the search for a responsible world society continues. This search involves not just rudiments of the Judeo-Christian tradition as in the Marxist vision and in *The Declaration of Independence,* but Christians themselves of many nationalities and confessions are active in this search. Inspired by the hope that is within them they are willing to give an accounting for it (1 Pet 3:15) and contribute through a common effort to a deeper unity and deeper insight.

36. Cf. Marx, "Theses on Feuerbach," thesis 10, 64, where he talks about a new society as a "*human* society, or socialized humanity." Cf. also the important study of Cohn, *Pursuit of the Millennium*, in which he convincingly shows that many modern totalitarian movements, such as Marxism and Leninism, have their roots in medieval millennial movements.

For Christians humanity is not a fact that can be taken for granted, but a process constantly being created and re-creating itself.

The Christian vision of a new world order gains constantly new hope and refinement through its connection with Jesus Christ as the originator and source of the hope for a new humanity. Consequently, it is distinguished from all ideologies and movements it engendered, through its intensity and clarity. The living dialogue of summons and response between Christ and his followers ensures that the hope for a new humanity, though not without a material basis, is different from what can be expected through genetic input and environmental conditioning alone. It will result in a truly human creation of a loving process. This dialogue will also assure that we are not taking the future in our own hands by replacing the old tyrannies of oppression with new tyrannies of liberation.

We must caution here that the abolition of laws and orders of oppression does not necessarily imply freedom and justice. History has shown that, for instance, the transformation of the Soviet Union into democratic countries has often not yielded the desired results, but the emerging new power structures have again become instruments of oppression in the "new democracies." The church must be discerning and cautious in its inclination to support any and every so-called revolution. Not only can it come under the control of extremists but a revolution can never be an end in itself, or be identified with ushering in the kingdom. "Revolution should not be regarded as a normal remedy, as a beneficial panacea, but as a last desperate operation and it carries with it certain serious risks."[37] This was also the conviction of Eugen Gerstenmaier (1906–86)—who became president of the Federal Republic of Germany 1954–69—and others of the so-called *Kreisauer Kreis* who plotted the failed attack on Hitler of July 20, 1944. When they saw no other (peaceful) possibility they finally executed an attack on Hitler's life.

Once the careful and deliberate conclusion is reached that the evil and risks of a revolution outweigh by far the injustice and cruelty of the present system, one should always keep in mind that "there is no basis in the New Testament for identifying the Kingdom with a new social order and there is no basis in our experience for doing so either."[38] At the most, we can attain a partial embodiment of the kingdom of God in society. This means that revolutions, whether peaceful or not, fall shy of their goal, to bring about true justice, and therefore stand under the judgment of God who calls them to repentance and renewed transformation. Consequently God "has chosen

37. Davies, *Christians, Politics and Violent Revolutions*, 112.

38. So rightly Bennett, *Christians and the State*, 203, who concedes, however, that the kingdom can be partially embodied in a society.

to create human beings as makers of their own history with full freedom inherent in the individual and collective destinies."[39] We must understand ourselves as the hands and arms of God, molding ourselves and others and being molded into a foretaste of the eschatological kingdom.

The representatives of liberation theology rightly remind us that, as ambassadors of God's redemptive news, we are accountable to the global human family and must become living witnesses to the coming of the kingdom. If we take seriously God's covenant extended to us in Christ, the eschatological vision of a renewed humanity is not just otherworldly. Paul's insight reinforces this when he claims: "And all of us, with unveiled faces, seeing the glory of the Lord as though reflected in a mirror, are being transformed into the same image from one degree of glory to another" (2 Cor 3:18).

We can argue that the prospect of sanctification, the progressive transformation into God's true representatives, is too costly. If this were our response we would not exert any inspiring and corrective influence on the global human family. We would rather tacitly condone the present turmoil, violence, and oppression. Any vision of a new humanity, whether utopian or ideological, would be superior to such a negative stand and offer at least a semblance of hope. On the other hand, we can participate in God's covenant community and become beacons of hope for a new humanity. Such a venture, however, will not be convenient. As the frequent imperatives in the Pauline letters indicate, it will mean a continuous battle against our sinful desire to join the mainstream of society. We will also become offensive to those who want to perpetuate traditional patterns of oppression, injustice, and exploitation, and who mistakenly look for Christians to uphold the status quo. All of us know the so-called seven last words of a church: "We've never done it any other way." No, we must be creative in searching for new ways to become beacons of hope for the new creation. By pressing on in patient hope for signs of the new creation we will take seriously our charge to be the conscience of society. We will make people more sensitive to each other's needs and we will become living witnesses of the good news of God's new creation.

The haven of the neglected: If the church assumes the role of the conscience in society, it cannot do this in triumphalist fashion without betraying its own objectives. The church must rather assume a servant role, working on the fringes of society on behalf of those who are neglected and outcast. The church is certainly never free of arrogance and self-aggrandizement, especially when it speaks out against social inequality in a faraway country, or

39. Goulet, *New Moral Order*, 130.

supports the politically oppressed and economically exploited in a distant land or in a different economic system. The actual reason for such involvement should usually be an expression of global solidarity in the attempt to eliminate unnecessary pain and hurt.

In an age in which millions of people travel to different countries every year and in which global communication has become nearly instantaneous, no situation of any magnitude remains hidden before the eyes of the world community. But the speck in the brother's eye should never deserve priority over the log in one's own eye (Matt 7:3) lest our concern be turned into hypocrisy. The church's most convincing stand for the disinherited in a different societal context must be accompanied by a similar attitude on the home front. The church also must realize that siding with those without material and political power is not something that most people desire. But by so doing the church follows the example of its Lord of whom Scripture says he "came not to be served but to serve, and to give his life as a ransom for many" (Matt 20:28). The Gospel of John even reminds us that "no one has greater love than this, to lay down one's life for one's friends" (John 15:13).

The notion of the servant church was vigorously expressed in the Vatican II statement "On the Church in the Modern World." Since this pastoral constitution was published, the concept of the church as servant has been restated in many other official documents of the churches. This emphasis on the imitation of Christ as one who lays down his life for others was advocated earlier in this century by Dietrich Bonhoeffer in his *Letters and Papers from Prison*. Bonhoeffer wrote:

> The Church is the Church only when it exists for others. To make a start, it should give away all its property to those in need. The clergy must live solely on the freewill offerings of their congregations, or possibly engage in some secular calling. The Church must share in the secular problems of ordinary human life, not dominating, but helping and serving. It must tell men of every calling what it means to live in Christ, and to exist for others. In particular, our Church will have to take the field against the vices of *hubris*, power-worship, envy and humbug, as the roots of all evil. It will have to speak of moderation, purity, trust, loyalty, constancy, patience, discipline, humility, contentment, and modesty.[40]

Bonhoeffer gains these insights from the example that Jesus set and with which Paul confronts us when he mentions the cross as the decisive event in Jesus' life.

40. Bonhoeffer, *Letters and Papers from Prison*, 211.

Others have picked up this emphasis. For instance, Harvey Cox (b. 1929) claimed: "The church's task in the secular city is to be the *diakonos* of the city, the servant who bends himself to struggle for its wholeness and health."[41] Two years before Harvey Cox, the social ethicist Gibson Winter (1917–2002) entitled a whole chapter of a book "The Servant Church in a Secularized World" and stated: "In the servant Church, the ministry is servanthood within the world. Ministry is discerning the promise of the saving history in the historical decisions of public responsibility; ministry is also discerning the truly human in the spheres of personal association and family life."[42]

While the servant role portrayed by Cox and Winter in the 1960s was a rather confident one, convinced that this social involvement would lead to a brighter future, just a decade later the German political theologian Dorothee Sölle (1929–2003) came back to Bonhoeffer's original observation, which showed more genuine suffering and self-giving. She says for instance, that "we can change the social conditions under which people experienced suffering." But there is also "brutalization, insensibility, mutilation and injury that no longer can be reversed."[43] Sölle discovered correctly that "the difficulty and the future task of a political theology consists in speaking appropriately of the gospel. . . . What is involved is giving credibility to the possibility of liberation from oppressive structures; what is involved is the inducement model for becoming truly human."[44] This is still true today. While we cannot give up on the gospel's vision of a new heaven and a new earth, our present situation has not become brighter. We realize more and more the depth and complexity of injustice and suffering and the limited resources that the church has to alleviate them. Even the giving away of the church's riches would not go far in the face of worldwide hunger, just to mention one calamity. Since 2014, the number of people affected by hunger has been slowly on the rise and comprised in 2021 roughly 700 million people.

But the awareness that our own resources and efforts will not noticeably change the human predicament cannot serve as an excuse for conducting business as usual. Bonhoeffer was certainly right when he reminded us that we should not underestimate the importance of examples. The greatest handicap for the church is usually not its limited resources but its own posture. The power struggle within many church bureaucracies, the want of thrift and exemplary lifestyle of both leaders and followers, and the

41. Cox, *Secular City*, 116.

42. Winter, *New Creation as Metropolis*, 59.

43. Sölle, *Suffering*, 178.

44. Sölle, *Political Theology*, 106.

discrepancy between what we preach and what we do are greater liabilities than the lack of skill or of workers. When the spirit of self-giving love prevails it can often be the leaven that makes change and renewal both possible and endurable.

We should remember that the church has always seen the servant role as a characteristic ingredient of being in the world. Following the example of its Lord, it has been willing to serve even to the point of self-sacrifice (Mark 10:45). The church knows that service to the least in this world is service to its Lord, and we are reminded: "As you did it to one of the least of these who are members of my family, you did it to me" (Matt 25:40). In a similar vein Paul encourages us when he said: "Do not use your freedom as an opportunity for self-indulgence, but through love become slaves to one another" (Gal 5:13). From the very beginning the church realized that service includes those who are in need within the church as well as those on the outside. While Paul took up the collection for the suffering Christians in Jerusalem, it was especially in the first centuries of the Christian faith a "trademark" of Christians to care for the less fortunate. The Christian apologist Lactantius (250–317) admonished the Christians saying that God teaches us never to do evil and always to do good. This means for him "to give assistance to the depressed and those laboring, to furnish food for those who have it not."[45] Similarly, Bishop Ambrose of Milan (ca. 340–397) asserted: "Your service will glow the brighter if the oppression of a powerful man, which some widow or orphan cannot withstand, is checked by the assistance of the Church, and if ye show that the command of the Lord has more weight with you than the favor of the rich."[46]

Being a servant does not mean simply giving from one's surplus; it also means standing up for the underprivileged and taking the risk of becoming one of them. In other words, servanthood is solidarity with those who are suffering. The servant character pertains to the individual who does duties of charity, as well as to the whole church. If one is elected to public office one's conduct must still be measured with the same criteria. It is significant that the public servant call of the Christians was emphasized very early in the history of the church. As soon as the Christian faith had become the majority religion, the Council of Arles (AD 314) stated that since the Christian faith has now become a recognized religion, the bishop in the area in which a governor resides should watch over him and assist the governor with the advice that he might commit no injustice in an office that included the *jus gladii* [the law of the sword: the right to absolve from, or condemn a person

45. Lactantius, *The Divine Institutes* 6.10, *FaCh* 49:418.

46. Ambrose, *De officiis* 2.29, *NPNFa SS* 10:66.

to death].[47] If he violated Christian principles and did not heed the advice of his bishop, he was to be excluded from the congregation. The same was true for municipal authorities. Living a Christian life means doing what is right, even if it excludes that which is popular. The German theologian Gerhard Uhlhorn (1826–1901) summed up well the servant function of the early church:

> It was when misery became greater and greater in the perishing world, when the arm of the state was more and more paralyzed, when the authorities no longer offered assistance to the poor and the oppressed, nay, themselves took part in oppressing and exhausting them, that the church became on a grand scale the refuge of all the oppressed and suffering.[48]

The servant role of the church did not go unnoticed in the world. Often worldly authorities took advantage of the church's servant role, installing bishops to fulfill temporal functions and endowing them with lands and valuables as compensation. Consequently, the church often and involuntarily exchanged its servant role for one of domination and support of the oppressors. We remember that the Reformation was due in part to the church's having become primarily the pursuer of worldly goals. Yet the servant role never died out completely. As the examples of Savonarola (1452–1498) and St. Francis of Assisi (1181/2–1226) show, it was continued at least in some circles, such as in certain (reform) monasteries. Today the servant role has again assumed a very significant function. Modern economic industrialization has brought undreamed of blessings for many, but in its wake have emerged new forms of injustice and widespread poverty. Thus we have witnessed the rise of the church's social mission, exemplified by people like Friedrich Bodelschwingh the Elder (1831–1910) in Bethel, Germany, Johann Hinrich Wichern (1808–81) in Hamburg, Germany, and Walter Rauschenbusch (1861–1918) in New York City. Today there are attempts to give a technological world a more human face and more the resemblance of human solidarity and care for each other through programs such as the Church World Service, Caritas, Miserior, and Bread for the World.

Anticipation of the heavenly city: Confronted with the immense problems of today and the limited resources that the church has, one is tempted to conclude that the church's servant role will not significantly alter the face of this world. At first glance this might be true. But we must remember that the lowliness of Jesus and his shameful cross do not stand for defeat.

47. Hefele, *History of the Councils*, 1:188, in his comments on canon 7.

48. Uhlhorn, *Christian Charity in the Ancient Church*, 362.

Quite the opposite! Our Lord could not be contained by cross and tomb. The symbols of apparent defeat were turned into signs of triumph over the powers of destruction. Where Christians are living out their allegiance to the Lord, the cross of Christ takes on new meaning. It becomes the rallying point for the oppressed and the powerless and a sign of inspiration that in this sign we will win over all adversity and be able to participate in the new heavenly community. In the face of a torn and divided world, in the face of the rift between East and West and South and North, the church must anticipate proleptically this new community on a local and also on a global scale. When we talk about proleptic anticipation, three potential misunderstandings must be averted:

(1) Anticipation of the heavenly city does not mean that we attempt to institute now what is promised to us in the eschatological, i.e., heavenly reality. As Dietrich Bonhoeffer in his seminal book *Life Together* pointed out:

> So between the death of Christ and the Last Day it is only by a gracious anticipation of the last things that Christians are privileged to live in visible fellowship with other Christians. It is by the grace of God that a congregation is permitted to gather physically in this world to share God's Word and sacrament.[49]

The church is only an interim institution between Pentecost and parousia, waiting and hoping for replacement by the heavenly community of all the saints. The utopian attempt to bring about in totality that toward which the church now moves would destroy the condition that makes such an existence possible. It is, for instance, one of the strange paradoxes of Marxism that it lived and strove for the anticipation of the heavenly community in a Marxist classless society. By refusing, however, to admit that its attempts and programs were only provisional, Marxism destroyed that which engendered and encouraged its hopes, the God-provided eschatological perfection. Moreover, since perfection was to be attained in this world, Marxism just as any other utopian system behaved intolerantly and dictatorially to attain its desired goal and thereby diminished even more the ideal vision for which it allegedly stood. Today the so-called green party in Germany is often called a prohibition party since it strives to attain its environmental goals with many legal prohibitions. But people will always find ways to circumvent legalism.

(2) Anticipation of the heavenly city is a divine gift and not a human accomplishment. Community is not something we accomplish, but something that is given and that we discover. In our anticipatory endeavors we do not attempt to fulfill a dream or a utopian vision, but we live according

49. Bonhoeffer, *Life Together*, 18.

to the presence of God through his Spirit. Whenever the church loses its spiritual dimension it is reduced to the status of a club in which its members seek to pursue their own interests. The theocentric structure of the Christian community reminds us of God, our ultimate allegiance and authority. Our dreams and visions will be destroyed by the cross of Christ, the living reminder that we live under the realities of this world but are not sustained by them.

There have been many visionary Christian communities: the controversial Oneida Community, founded near Oneida, New York in 1848; the Franciscans spiritualists under Joachim of Fiore (1135–1202); and the Enthusiasts during the Reformation period under Thomas Müntzer. Though assuming they lived from the power of the Spirit, they lived according to their own hopes and dreams, neglecting the reality of the cross. After the initial excitement had waned, their attempts were doomed to failure. Bonhoeffer rightly reminds us that "God hates visionary dreaming; it makes the dreamer proud and pretentious."[50] Living under the new life means for the Christian community to live under the word of forgiveness, the source of new life, and under God's Word that is extended to us through others. Since the extension of the forgiving and encouraging Word of God is always mediated through the community in which we live, we must mention a third misunderstanding.

(3) Anticipation of the heavenly city is not a purely spiritual reality. While the world aches for transformation and healing, God is not a distant observer but an abiding presence at the margins, in the soil, in chaos and quiet places, in pleasure and pain. Emulating our Lord, we dare not restrict the anticipation of the heavenly city to the spiritual, lest we encourage the strange notion that the Christian community does not transform lives and conditions, but only spirits. Bonhoeffer rightly observes that "a purely spiritual relationship is not only dangerous but also an altogether abnormal thing."[51] There must also be a physical interaction between members of the spiritual community of which we are part. Process thought has perhaps best captured this notion when it talks about the close interaction between God and the world. For instance, according to Alfred North Whitehead (1861–1947) there exists a reciprocal relationship between God and the world. "What is done in the world is transformed into a reality in heaven, and the reality in heaven passes back into the world."[52] Similarly, Paul depicts with the image of the body of Christ an intense interaction between the Lord and

50. Bonhoeffer, *Life Together*, 27.

51. Bonhoeffer, *Life Together*, 38.

52. Whitehead, *Process and Reality*, 532.

his church. The body of Christ is mirrored in the Christian community and its individual members who make up this body.

Throughout the centuries the anticipation of the heavenly city has perhaps come to life best in the monastic ideal. Monastic groups were usually started to strengthen people's spiritual life. They thereby disciplined their daily lives and transformed the surroundings in which they lived, working through education, buildings and art, and community projects of charity. Similarly, the Protestant counterparts such as the Oxford Group of Frank Buchman (1878–1961), which he developed in 1938 into the Moral Re-Armament, an international moral and spiritual movement, or the Herrnhut Brethren of Count Nikolaus von Zinzendorf, later known as the Moravian Church, had a profound impact not only on their own adherents but on the communities in which they lived and worked. Of course, the same is expected of the local worshiping community. The Christian faith is not only a Sunday morning affair. It lays claim on the total lives of the members of the local congregation and should exert an impact on the community in which a congregation is located. As anticipation of the heavenly city the church on the local level must become a visible reality, a beacon of hope and a bastion of the new humanity within a fallen and hurting world. Yet the vision of the church is always larger than the local church. As the ecumenist J. Robert Nelson (1920–2004) rightly pointed out, "The primary task of the church in history is to be the bearer of the reconciling work in every generation."[53] To make credible such reconciling message and action at least two criteria must be met:

(1) The church would contradict its message as a beacon of hope if it were torn by strife and rivalry. The church needs to give witness to the unity to which it points. This does not mean that suddenly all diversity and plurality should disappear either in favor of the relativistic concept of truth or in favor of a monolithic authoritarian faith structure. Even when the church looked like a uniform edifice, as for instance in the Middle Ages, the diversity of its theological production bore witness to a considerable plurality. Since the gospel comes to us always through other Christians, we must realize that we do not own the truth and the gospel. It opens itself to us only if we listen to it as it is offered to us. We also notice that there are other Christians who are not always from our own tradition. We must acknowledge that our grasp of the gospel tradition, accurate as it may be, does not have an original claim on the whole truth, but grasps it only from a certain perspective. It is in constant need of correction and upbuilding, lest it become exclusive and distorted. Unity means realizing and making manifest

53. Nelson, "Signs of Mankind's Solidarity," 14.

our interdependence as heirs of the kingdom, celebrating the unity we seek, and amalgamating the pieces thereof that we have already discovered. With its many bilateral talks, the ecumenical movement is a serious first step in this direction. It shows that our respective insights gain new clarity and correction from jointly listening to the gospel tradition.

(2) Our credibility as bearers of the message of reconciliation only holds up if we venture beyond the local situation. Friedrich Nietzsche rightly reminded us that as Christians we should not just express love toward our neighbors, but toward those who are most distant from us. As bearers of the message of Christ we cannot stop at our own city walls, we must go beyond our local communities to the ends of the earth. The mission of the church goes hand in hand with discovering the church's unity, since only a reunited Christian church can become the symbol and instrument of the unity of humanity. The pursuit of Christian unity and the concern for human solidarity are closely related among different churches, and come most eloquently to the surface in the World Council of Churches.

Foreshadowing the heavenly city that is not torn by rivalry, strife, and injustice, the church must seek to manifest the criteria of the new humanity in its global structure. Through its global witness, the church can serve as a powerful stimulus to induce signs of the eschaton among the whole of humanity. Without the church's presence, life in the twenty-first century will grow colder and more merciless. Serving as the conscience of society, as the haven of the neglected, and as the anticipation of the heavenly city, the church is the symbol of human solidarity, expressing in its internal relationship and in its outward actions God's love for the world, God's cherishing of each human being, and God's desire that none be lost. The church is a manifestation and reminder of God's love amid a world in turmoil. The reason for the church's functioning in this direction cannot be derived from the dedication of its members, though that should not be underestimated. The reason for the church being the heart of the present can also not be delineated from its strong ties to the past, though they serve as a strong reminder to live up to the ideals of its founder, Jesus of Nazareth.

The reason for the church to continue its task in the face of all defeat and misery can only come from a power that at least in principle is stronger than all its distortions, injustice, and self-centeredness. This power has shown that it can and will destroy all darkness, nay, it has destroyed it already. The power of the church is not its own, but that of its Lord. As Paul asserted, Christ has shown in his resurrection that the ultimate victory is his. Since we have such a Lord, Paul can admonish us: "Be steadfast, immovable, always abounding in the work of the Lord, knowing that in the Lord your labor is not in vain" (1 Cor 15:58). With such confidence the church cannot just be the heart of the present. It must gladly become the reminder of the future, of the new world to come.

3. THE REMINDER OF THE FUTURE

The reminder of the future in an ultimate sense is perhaps part of the church's proclamation that has been most neglected. It even took Jürgen Moltmann (b. 1926), premier theologian of a theology of hope, roughly thirty years after his seminal book *Theology of Hope* (1967) to write a Christian eschatology.[54] While the church never neglected the proclamation of Christ's death and resurrection, it often left the so-called last things to fundamentalistic and sectarian quarters. But the death and resurrection of Jesus Christ is not restricted to the present. Far the opposite, it is the foundation of the future and that in a penultimate and ultimate sense. Leaving Jesus not in the tomb but raising him to new life, God showed that there is new life and a new creation beyond death. Especially in a society that is focused on the present and the temporary and thereby shuns everything ultimate, the church must proclaim that there is a future beyond space and time in God's new creation. With this claim it relativizes the obsession with the present. Christians can relax, because their future is already being provided by God. This shows again that the church does not fit into a world that assumes that the course of its history is predictable, being determined by humanity's own efforts and the available resources. The church knows and confesses that "if we in our own strength confide, our striving turns to losing."[55] In a secular and self-relying culture, the church must not only be essentially countercultural, it must also give witness to a future provided by God and not by humanity.

The symbol of the future: The involvement of the church in the affairs of the world, in the struggle for justice, human rights, and the provision of life's necessities serves a dual purpose: (1) The church indeed wants to serve those who are in need. (2) Being aware that all of its efforts are at best patchwork, Band-Aids on the wounds of a hurting world, the church points with its actions to a world that will no longer be torn apart. Similar to the miracles of our Lord having not only the function of helping people in need, but being signs of a new creation, the church in its actions is a symbol of the future.

The eschatological symbol of the new creation becomes visible not just in social involvement, but in every activity of the church. Each absolution is a reminder of the love of God that one day will find its completion. Each

54. Moltmann, *Coming of God*.

55. *ELW* 505, stanza 2.

Eucharist is a reminder of the celestial banquet. The twofold phrase in the words of the institution of the Lord's Supper, "This do in remembrance of me," does not just imply that *we* should remember Christ's sacrifice. It also means that *God* should remember the sacrifice of his Son and speed up the coming and completion of the kingdom. At every celebration of the Eucharist the church proclaims the beginning of the time of salvation and waits for the inception of the consummation. The gathered community is reminded to celebrate the Eucharist until he comes, again a vivid pointer toward the eschatological consummation.

In the context of the Lord's Supper, we must also remember the Aramaic term *maranatha* spoken of in 1 Corinthians 16:22, Didache 10:6, and perhaps in translated form in Revelation 22:20. Though it cannot be clearly determined whether the term means "our Lord is present" or "Our Lord, come," it is clear that this formula had a common liturgical usage. If *maranatha* means "our Lord is present" then it is a phrase that asserts the Lord's presence in the Eucharist and also presses for the final public disclosure of his presence. If, however, it can be translated "Our Lord, come," then we again encounter the eschatological waiting and longing of the community for his coming in glory.

The Christian community must understand itself as the symbol of the future that has already begun. This is also emphasized in the Lord's Prayer. As a constituent part of the communion liturgy, the Lord's Prayer belonged, in the early church, to that part of the service in which only those who were baptized were permitted to participate. The your-petitions, "hallowed be your name," "your kingdom come," and "your will be done," are in content closely related to the expectant cry, "Our Lord, come." They are seeking the point at which God's profaned and misused name will be glorified and the reign of his kingdom be revealed. In a world enslaved by evil, distress, and conflict, the Christian community looks forward to the revelation of God's glory. These petitions are filled with confidence and are not just wishful thinking. In the face of an evil world surrounding and encroaching upon the church, the faithful take seriously God's promise and address God with utmost confidence as "Our Father." Since God's Son taught the disciples this prayer they are absolutely certain that God will redeem his promises. As God spoke according to Ezekiel: "I will sanctify my great name, which has been profaned among the nations, and which you have profaned among them; and the nations shall know that I am the Lord, says the Lord God, when through you I display my holiness before their eyes" (Ezek 36:23). Quite often, however, when the pastor encourages a congregation to pray "as our Lord has taught us" the prayer is diminished to a sentimental remembrance without the vigorous hope that it actually contains.

The other phrases in the Lord's Prayer witness also to the yearning for and expectation of the eschaton. For instance, in the petitions for bread and forgiveness, the church asks that God might grant today, in this place, the bread of life and the blotting out of sins. The praying church becomes a beacon of hope in the darkness of this world. Amid failure, apostasy, and denial, God's kingly rule over the lives God's people is being realized. Though still a symbol of the future, the bread of life and God's endless mercy are present already, indicators of his almighty glory in the coming of the kingdom.

When we briefly look at baptism we immediately perceive that the prevalent practice of infant baptism would be utterly ridiculous if we regarded baptism simply as incorporation into the visible, institutional church. The notion of dying and rising with Christ, and of being incorporated into his body, envisions more than just institutional membership. It also means more than being converted to Christ and becoming a confessing Christian, as adult baptism usually implies. When Paul mentions that we should walk in the newness of life since we have become a new creation, he admits two things: (1) We are still in a state of transition, from this eon to the future eon. While this eon cannot hold us completely, the world still ensnares us. Luther was right when he called for drowning of the old Adam through daily repentance. (2) We must recognize that the existence of a Christian is dynamic and not static. Together with the whole creation we are yearning and longing for the revelation of the sons of God and the manifestation of the kingdom.

Dying and rising with Christ makes sense only when it means breaking out of the natural cycle of birth and death from which the image is borrowed. There must be a time when death will no longer score a victory and we can forever walk in the newness of life. Similarly, becoming part of the body of Christ only makes sense when at one point our sinful alienation and spatio-temporal separation from Christ is overcome. We must be able to celebrate with him the proverbial celestial banquet and enjoy him forever. In other words, baptism remains an empty shell unless it is verified through the coming of the kingdom. But baptism is also a sign and symbol of that future verification and is administered in hope and trust. The same is true for the Eucharist. It is intrinsically eschatological, foreshadowing and hoping for the eschatological realization.

It has become clear that in its actions, in its liturgical celebrations, and in its prayer life, the church must be a symbol of the future, in part foreshadowing of things to come, and in part patiently but intensely hoping and trusting for their ultimate verification. Yet the church would be a strange community if it thought it could bring about these things by its own power. The power and encouragement for both anticipation and expectation is derived from the experience of Christ. Through the presence of Christ and the power of the Spirit, the church realizes that the life and destiny of Jesus the Christ are the prime examples of its own life and destiny. It knows beyond doubt that ultimately all history will serve to make his kingdom triumph. We can be confident that God "will vindicate his people, and have compassion on his servants" (Ps 135:14), so that this hope which God inspired will not be in vain.

The whole people of God: Intrinsic to the Christian hope is a common destiny for all humanity. It expresses itself in the hope for the unity of the whole church and for the unity of all people under the dominion of God. Friedrich Schleiermacher (1768–1834) certainly had a point when he argued that "there are great difficulties in thinking that the finite issue of redemption is such that some thereby obtain the highest bliss, while others (on the ordinary view, indeed, the majority of the human race) are lost in irrevocable misery."[56] The church cannot stand in judgment of the unbelievers, but must be the vivid and living reminder that God wants all people to be saved. But the church would rob itself of its reason for being if it asserted with Schleiermacher that "through the power of redemption there will one day be a universal restoration of all souls." Only God can decide the ultimate fate of everyone and not the church.

The church's reason for being is to represent Christ to the world and to bring it the gospel. It is dangerous to assume that we have to revise our hopes of converting the world to Christ, with the argument that it is no longer plausible to believe that the church will score big victories on secular or religious fronts. If success were our criterion for engagement we would also give up the hope of making this world a better place to live. Yet despite continuous setbacks, those who have given up converting the world in the traditional sense often continue their crusade with ever-increasing vigor to make our world more human. They emulate the world by focusing on this life only.

A church that rallies around the crucified and risen Lord cannot make success or plausibility its prime criterion. It cannot even make its work easier or its failures less painful by attributing to all "good" and "faithful" non-Christian believers the honorary title of anonymous Christians. If the church wants to be the reminder of the future, it dare not leave humanity as it is, in its antagonism and self-destruction. The faithful proclamation of the gospel tradition must be a challenge to every status quo, whether it be Muslim or Buddhist, socialist or capitalist.

56. For this and the following quote see Schleiermacher, *Christian Faith*, 2:722 (par. 163, appendix).

The acknowledgment and proclamation of Christ as Lord of the whole world will not simply bring Christ to the world, it must also ask how Christ is "present and operative in the faith of the individual non-Christian."[57] Since Christ is present and operative in and through his Spirit in non-Christian believers and their religions, we can affirm what is good and wholesome in them. Conversely, we should expect that they also recognize good and wholesome features in the gospel tradition. It would be utopian, however, to demand in every religious dialogue that commonality triumphs over diversity and contradictions. Yet a dialogue might foster understanding and fellowship and unity among people of different religions. They might begin to understand that all people form a single community, springing from God as their origin and moving toward God as their goal. There is a positive point of contact, however hidden, in every religious expression, something worthy of cultivation, augmentation, and expansion. But we dare not close our eyes to that which is wrong and misapprehended, which needs supplanting and conversion.

Since the church is never identical with Christ, it also stands under the affirmation and judgment, as do non-Christian believers. Only the Lord and his gospel are the criteria for discovering what is good and true and what is in error and misconceived. The dialogue with all people brings us closer together, since it places all of us under that judging and liberating word of our Lord. Though we hope that his words will make a difference in this world, creating increasing solidarity among all people, we are not sure that all people will eventually listen to him. Our most sincere proclamation of the gospel tradition in word and deed, for the soul and the body, and through words of grace and acts of mercy, can never assume that a universal homecoming of all people will result. The realization of our common destiny as the whole people of God can only be a most daring eschatological hope and the content of fervent prayers. By sharing Christ even at the most remote places on earth, we are reminded that in one way or another, whether with everyone's approval or without it, our Lord will one day be acknowledged as the Lord so that "God may be all in all" (1 Cor 15:28).

It would be totally irresponsible if the church would bring the gospel to non-Christians, calling for solidarity and jointly listening to the Lord of the world, without being utterly disturbed about its own divided house. The division into different churches and denominations is not just the fault of others. Every Christian is responsible for this disunion. While the church must be Greek to the Greeks and American to the Americans, its necessary

57. Rahner, *Foundations of Christian Faith*, 315, still seems to underestimate the necessity for proclaiming Christ to non-Christians.

culturalization and diversity does not justify the present divisiveness. Immense progress towards representing the whole people of God has been made by the World Council of Churches, the various world federations of confessional families, the national councils, and the many bilateral dialogs. But institutional inertia and egotistic pride are still the two greatest obstacles to actual unity. Movements toward unity, such as the Consultation on Church Union in the United States (COCU), progress much more slowly than originally envisioned and with less tangible results. It was inaugurated in 1962 and resulted in the formation in 2002 of Churches Uniting in Christ (CUIC) as its successor organization, consisting of ten denominations. Overcoming racism has been a focal point of CUIC since its inception. But this issue has also been a major dividing factor between and among churches. Whether its goal of unity among the participating denominations can be achieved remains to be seen. Regardless of the internal strife within and among denominations, we must honestly ask whether race and sex are the high points of the Christian faith or whether they should not be treated in a more subdued manner so that the gospel can shine through more clearly and perhaps even bring solutions to these vexing issues.

Looking on from the outside, the unchurched part of the population frequently does not distinguish between different denominations. For them, churches are simply lumped together. And indeed, the unchurched have a point in not distinguishing, because we too discover more and more how much we actually share in common with other denominations. The division into different denominations and churches seems, in many cases at least, anachronistic and therefore sinful. In the last fifty years approximately sixty church unions have taken place, resulting in churches such as The Church of South India and the United Church of Christ in the United States. Today in at least thirty countries negotiations toward church union are being conducted.

The Fifth Assembly of the World Council of Churches in Nairobi (1975) once again instructed its member churches to "provide opportunities for a careful study and evaluation of the concept of conciliar fellowship as a way of describing the unity of the Church."[58] Conciliarity is not the same as the medieval call for conciliarism, which meant the shift of power from a central authority (the pope) to that of councils. Conciliarity is also not the result of reconciled diversity. Rather conciliarity means that the churches no longer exclude and fight each other, but instead realize each other's validity while they preserve at the same time their own integrity and structure. Conciliarity recognizes the fact that the church always needs assemblies to represent it. As history shows, councils are convened by churches that

58. "Recommendations of Section 2: What Unity Requires," in *Breaking Barriers*, 69.

enjoy a unity of faith and that faith expresses itself prominently in eucharistic fellowship. The frequent assemblies of churches that do not enjoy full eucharistic fellowship are not councils in the strictest sense of the word. But they can decisively advance unity and in fact have done so. We could even say that the ecumenical movement is working toward a time when a truly ecumenical council can become a reality. Conciliarity therefore does not exclude organic union, nor does it merely encourage organic church union but instead requires it.

The vision of organic union should not be misunderstood as moving toward a centralized superstructure. Such a structure would neither do justice to the local necessities nor would it be an effective instrument in witnessing to the world. Conciliarity is not reserved for a superstructure but belongs to all levels, the congregational, national, regional, and worldwide. The reason why union must be expressed on every level is grounded in the concept that at each point at which the church exists the whole church comes to expression. Knowing the local or regional church means knowing the whole church, and knowing the worldwide church means knowing its local manifestations. There is an intrinsic connection between the local and the universal life of the church. For instance, if the local church is not mission minded, the mission mindedness of the church headquarters does not compensate for this lack of vision. On the other hand, if the church as a synod or convention is hopelessly entrenched in parochialism, the local congregation can only venture so far without alienating itself too much from the rest of the church.

Olav Fykse Tveit, general secretary of the World Council of Churches from 2010 to 2020, writes in his Foreword to the Faith and Order Paper *The Church: Towards a Common Vision*: "There is a certain and reasonable impatience among many to see more movement in the reception of ecumenical dialogues and agreements. . . . There are tendencies toward fragmentation and more attention to what is uniting the few rather than the many."[59] Indeed church unity is far from being an accomplished fact. Already the Salamanca Consultation (1973) of the Faith and Order Commission put our dilemma, our task, and our hopes very succinctly: "*Jesus Christ founded one church. Today we live in diverse churches divided from one another. Yet our vision of the future is that we shall once again live as brothers and sisters in one undivided church.*"[60] A divided church is an offense

59. World Council of Churches, *Church,* Faith and Order Paper No. 214, v. This paper was twenty years in the making and is a sequel to the Faith and Order Paper No. 73 of 1975 (*One Baptism, One Eucharist and a Mutually Recognized Ministry*).

60. Report of the Salamanca Consultation, "The Unity of the Church—Next Steps," 293.

to its Lord, an offense to the gospel, and an impediment to mission. Divided Christendom is a reminder of our sinfulness and of the tasks still ahead of us. But it also reminds us of the eschatological future when our human divisiveness can no longer intrude on the manifestation of the whole people of God. Therefore intermediate steps toward union, such as involvement in joint mission projects, shared worship, public declaration of our common intention on all levels, common theological education, training of laity, Christian education and literature, and joint evaluation of priorities and use of funds, are not only a sign of repentance of our sins of the past but also a sign of overcoming them. They are indications that the power of the Spirit is at work in his people and that the people are willing to anticipate something of the great celestial council when all will share the same table and the same food.

Even at the risk of being redundant we must again mention here that the mission of the whole people of God includes church and synagogue, Jew and gentile. Jürgen Moltmann claims emphatically that "Israel is Christianity's original, enduring and final partner in history. . . . The church of Christ can only understand its historical consciousness of its own nature in accordance with the kingdom and messianically (that is, in specifically liberating terms) if it grasps its relationship to Israel, to the Old Testament, and to the divine future."[61] We stand on the shoulders of our Jewish forebears and our central hope is foreshadowed in the Old Testament messianic predictions.

It should also make us wonder why people without a homeland for nearly two thousand years, a people who suffered the most systematic persecution ever carried out, a people dispersed throughout the world, why such a people did not abandon its faith in God. Of course, the Jewish population whether in Israel or in other countries is as diverse as the Christian population in the West. But when we look at the synagogues being rebuilt in Germany or at the observance of the sabbath in Israel, religion is still deeply rooted in the Jewish population. In many ways the Jewish people are surely an enigma but also a source of inspiration and hope. God may lead the people through valleys of shadow and death, but God does not abandon them. God sustains, calls, and nourishes them. The Jewish people can rejoice that for the first time in two thousand years they can live in their homeland and are not forced to live in an alien land. But this blessing to the Jews brings with it also a curse to those people who have been driven out of Palestine. Redemption for all nations still lies in the future.

The Jewish people are not just a symbol that God will not abandon his promises, they are a symbol of insight. As the sculpture on medieval

61. Moltmann, *Church in the Power of the Spirit*, 135.

churches of the blindfolded synagogue indicates, Jews may have been tolerated, but Christians have never accepted them as equals. Yet Jews consider us and all other peoples as equals. They perceive all of humanity as the descendants of one father and the creatures of one Creator and still maintain a vision of one humanity under the reign of God at the end of time. In the face of its own adverse history, Israel has not given up this hope for all people. The Jewish people have even "recognized access to God and saving virtue outside of Judaism, since its own covenant with God bound the covenant community only."[62] The church, therefore, must take the great commission seriously and go into all the world, proclaim the good news, and baptize those who are still without a covenant relationship with God.

Instead of aiming at victories for our Lord, we should acknowledge that the victory has already been won and that his love is greater than our accomplishments. The hope kept alive among Jewish people serves as a timely reminder that the wholeness of God's people does not depend on our actions, though it can be considerably enhanced by them. The oneness of the human family rests on God's promises, which will not return empty.

"*And God will dwell in their midst*": A theology of glory is not the proper topic to conclude a study on the future of the church. Even the Roman Catholic Church, with which the notion of a theology of glory has often been associated, is rediscovering the role of servanthood and suffering. But persecution and suffering are not necessarily the signs of the true church either. There is suffering and pain among believers and unbelievers, among Christians and non-Christians, as we witness for instance with the persecution of the Rohingya Muslims and the Christians in Myanmar. But if the church is a historical agency "through which God is remaking the human world,"[63] and if it is the living organism that connects the historical acts of God through which God overcame our sinfulness with future acts of the establishment of the new Jerusalem, then it would be anachronistic to contemplate only suffering and pain. Even servants need moments of festivity and celebration to make their servanthood livable and meaningful. We can see this very vividly with the African American spirituals, which were not just work songs but also gospel songs.

Festivity and celebration are not moments of rest in a troubled world, but the point from which we look forward to the eternal Sabbath, a time of pure joy and rejoicing. In remembering Christ as both crucified and resurrected, we faithfully celebrate our liberation and freedom as children of

62. Greenberg, "Mankind, Israel and the Nations in the Hebraic Heritage," 37.

63. So rightly Kaufman, *Systematic Theology*, 482.

God, though knowing that we are still entangled in a troubled world. The church would betray its own source of strength and hope if it would see its function exhausted in rendering assistance to a troubled world. The church must also serve as a beacon of hope, demonstrating the Christ-won freedom in its own life and manifesting its rejoicing in that freedom. A theology of glory need not be a betrayal of the gospel tradition if it means glorying in what God has done in and through the church, what God is doing, and what God will do. Anticipation of the heavenly glory, both in remembering God's past acts and in looking forward and hoping for the eschatological perfection, is as important for the church as realizing that it still lives in a valley of death and injustice.

Especially in worship, proclamation, and ecclesiastical arts, the church must express something of the anticipated glory. As Moltmann reminds us: Worship is a messianic feast "of the assembled community, which proclaims the gospel, responds to the liberation experienced, baptizes with the token of the new beginning and, at the table of the Lord, anticipates the fellowship of God's kingdom."[64] It is a misunderstood sense of the servant role when the church opts only for multipurpose buildings and folding chairs. Certainly, the lush carpeting of the sanctuary can stand in the way of spreading the gospel and serving the world. Yet a world characterized by efficiency and the increase of the capital of its investors needs to be reminded that we do not live by bread alone. A God who produces so much splendor in nature deserves praise and adoration through all the media. His eschatological perfection though depicted with restraint is never painted in drab and efficient colors, but with the vivid and splendid images of pearly gates and celestial choirs. The last judgment painted by Michelangelo (1475–1564) in the Sistine Chapel in Rome, the majestic oratorios of the Messiah by George Frederick Handel (1685–1759), the choral preludes by Johann Sebastian Bach (1685–1750), and the spires of the Cathedral Notre-Dame (begun 1194) in Chartres, France, are just a few examples of praise to God for his past actions and his future promises. The church that no longer uses art as a form of remembering and anticipating God's promises has a truncated understanding of the magnitude of the gospel tradition. It also underestimates the expected response to God with our whole being. If we refrain from giving glory to God with all our senses and all means of expression, we fail to recognize that participation in this glory is more than verbal or literary assent. It is not insignificant that music and the visual arts draw many people to churches that otherwise rarely attend church services. The arts in the service of the church should not be neglected when we talk about mission.

64. Moltmann, *Church in the Power of the Spirit*, 261.

It is significant that in the wake of liturgical experimentation and renewal the Roman Catholic Church has moved away from a one-sided display of splendor, rediscovering the necessity for proclamation, while many Protestant denominations have detected that worship is more than listening to a sermon and singing a few hymns. It is dramatizing God's saving acts in Christ and the celebration of the future glory of all the saints. Liturgical gowns, processions, chanted liturgy, hymns of praise, and even occasionally incense, remind us that we do not just celebrate God with our ears, but with our whole being and with all our senses. This does not imply a return to the Latin liturgy that hardly anybody understands or rehearsing in each hymn the whole salvation history. To the contrary, a contemporary liturgy could be a good entry point for the people for whom a traditional liturgy still sounds antiquated. Similarly, in proclamation we should strive for a balanced expression of the whole gospel tradition, that gives adequate focus to Christ's death and resurrection and no longer dwells almost exclusively on the cross. We remember with sorrow that our world did not accept its Lord and rejected him through the cross. But we must also triumph in the glory of the resurrected One and the promise that his resurrection contains. There is also emerging a more inclusive understanding of the gospel tradition that includes the Hebrew Scriptures as part of this tradition that should be proclaimed in sermons as our Old Testament. We remember with thanksgiving that God has acted in this world throughout the centuries, even before the incarnation of our Lord, and that God continues to act in this world. We expect and hope that God will complete his actions so that God will finally dwell in the midst of his people.

As mentioned earlier, it is unfortunate that the expectation of the heavenly future has never been a strong point of the church. Sectarian groups always had to remind the church of the necessity and centrality of this part of the gospel from which we derive our power and vision. Theology recaptured in the last century the significance of an eschatological perspective. By the same token it still remains for the so-called last things to be rediscovered. Perhaps the church rightly feels that it is a rather threatening vision that the seer of the book of Revelation expresses:

> I saw no temple in the city, for its temple is the Lord God the Almighty and the Lamb. And the city has no need of sun or moon to shine on it, for the glory of God is its light, and its lamp is the Lamb. The nations will walk by its light, and the kings of the earth will bring their glory into it. Its gates will never be shut by day—and there will be no night there. (Rev 21:22–25)

In the midst of a cruel, unjust, and divided earth, such eschatological harmony among people and nations seems unreal. We might also feel that we are too solidly grounded in our own achievements on this earth to abandon it in favor of God's complete dominion in a heavenly city. Staunch church members and ecclesiastical administrators may feel uneasy over the vision of a city in which the presence of God will replace all temples. How dearly do we love our church structures and ecclesiastical empires that we erect and safeguard?

Indeed, the vision shared by the book of Revelation sounds unreal. It is something out of a different world that threatens the status quo and our self-established security. But was not the same already true for the coming of the Lord? Does not the Gospel of Matthew tell us that Herod slaughtered all the innocent infants in Bethlehem because he felt the birth of the Messiah threatened his security? God's saving activity always threatens our security. Yet how reliable is our security? We seem to stagger from one crisis to another. The Great Depression, World War II, the Korean War, the numerous Middle East crises, the Vietnam War, the energy crisis, climate change, and the COVID-19 pandemic are just a few reminders that our security is more a wishful dream than a reality. Perhaps the psalmist was much more realistic in assessing our situation when he said that our years contain "but toil and trouble; they are soon gone, and we fly away" (Ps 90:10).

As we discover more and more the fleeting of time and our dwindling natural resources, the vision of eschatological perfection gains new credibility and urgency. The church does a disservice to its members and to a world in trouble when it neglects announcing the eschatological future that God will dwell in the midst of God's people. Yet such a message proclaimed with vigor and confident hope must not induce the relinquishing of our responsibility. It must not be used as a heavenly escape valve, contrary to what Karl Marx predicted. As the Swiss Roman Catholic missiologist Walbert Bühlmann (1916–2007) recognized:

> The orientation towards God as absolute future does not remove our responsibility for this world but makes it more radical. He who knows that God will one day wipe away all tears will not resign himself to letting the tortured go on suffering. . . . Either hope with anticipatory realization now in this world created and loved by God, or no hope at all![65]

Our hope encourages us to take the parable of the faithful steward seriously, because we know that our Lord and the Lord of all the world is coming. Only when we become oblivious to the coming of our Lord will we

65. Bühlmann, *Coming of the Third Church*, 397–8.

be tempted to shed our responsibility and set ourselves up as masters and oppressors (Luke 12:45), even in the name of freedom and liberation. A church that remains faithful to its calling of announcing the glad news that God will dwell in our midst, will in turn instill hope, courage, and a sense of direction in a confused world. It will remain and become a beacon and a rallying point for the future. While it is a stumbling block for some, it is a firm foundation for many. The church is a symbol of God's promise that the gates of hell shall not prevail.

Having described the church in this threefold way, extending to the past, standing firm in the present, and reaching out toward the ultimate future, we have painted an ideal picture. At present these three ways are largely obliterated with the attempt to be relevant in today's society. To attain this goal, language, means of communication, and concepts are being overhauled and brought in line with what society presumably wants and finds acceptable. Yet so far even the best attempts have brought hardly any success. The church is still pursuing the path of irrelevance and decline. So, what future is there for the church?

PART 4

Epilogue: Has the Church a Future?

In Europe and North America, the churches do not seem to have a future at least in their present form. As we noted in the beginning, memberships are dwindling. If denominations are still growing, it is usually through a shift of membership from one denomination to another. But the unchurched population remains largely untouched and its number is steadily increasing. Forty-eight percent of the millennials (born between 1984–2002) can be called post-Christian in their beliefs, thinking, and worldview. As the older generation, which has been more churchly, is gradually dying, this is an alarming signal for the churches. Moreover, the cases of sexual misconduct, primarily in the Roman Catholic Church, but also among evangelical Protestants, have hurt public esteem of the churches. The majority of the population no longer regards the churches as exemplars of conduct but rather of misconduct. Once one has lost trust, whether on a congregational level or in the general public, it is very difficult to reestablish that trust. Then there is the hierarchical system still overtly advocated in the Roman Catholic Church and in a more subtle way in many Protestant denominations. This discourages the active participation of the laity. The church is perceived as a stumbling block to necessary changes and people leave the church out of despair.

The churches are in a crisis. There are two possibilities of how to react to a crisis. One could simply ignore it and continue to do business as usual. Most likely the crisis will not go away but become deeper with the possibility that it could engulf the church and drive it to insignificance. The other possibility is to ask what is needed to master the crisis. This is the time for decisions in which we can show what possibilities we have for the future. If we look at the world for hints on how to master the future, we are usually told that we must be successful. Yet when we look at the Bible as our source of inspiration and guidance, we do not find success as a criterion to prepare for the future. Neither Jesus nor any of the apostles were successful by earthly standards. Jesus pursued his mission in unwavering steadfastness. The same can be said for the apostles once they were endowed at Pentecost with God's Holy Spirit. Most revealing is the reply of Peter and John when they were told by the Jewish authorities to refrain from proclaiming that "in Jesus there is the resurrection of the dead." They responded: "We cannot keep from speaking about what we have seen and heard" (Acts 4:20). It would have been much easier for Peter and John to be silent about Jesus and to join the Jewish majority. Yet they stuck to their mission and remained faithful to their calling. Exactly this is the first point in our current crisis, being faithful.

1. NOT SUCCESSFUL BUT FAITHFUL

It would be wrong to imply that the churches do not try as hard as possible to master the present crisis. Indeed, most denominations try hard and want to be faithful to their calling. Yet it is the word "calling" that is at the root of many of the problems. What is the calling of the church? Is it to change the world? Should our priority be to sensitize people to climate change? Is it to change society? Should our priority be to advocate inclusivity and diversity? Is it to change its structures? Should our priority be to fight patriarchy in its various forms? The answer is: "None of the above." While these issues may indeed be worthy of consideration and engagement by the churches, they dare not become our prime concern. As long as we focus our attention on things or persons in this world, we have missed our calling, even with our best intentions, and we become indistinguishable from secular groups and movements. Our number one calling is to the point to Jesus of Nazareth and to what God has done in and through him. Nobody else but Christians and their churches proclaim the gospel. This is their mark of identification.

The conviction that God had raised Jesus from the dead was the turning point for the apostles. They realized that the mission of Jesus had not ended in failure and that death was not the end. We must come back to our roots and rediscover the success story of the Christian faith. As far as we know, with the possible exception of John, all the apostles died as martyrs. Yet the Christian faith continued to spread to the ends of the then-known world.

What made the Christian faith so contagious? Our present situation is not radically different from the situation at the beginning of the Christian faith. We live in an age of pluralism in terms of worldviews, lifestyles, and religions, to name just a few convictions. As the storming of the Capitol in Washington, DC in the wake of the 2020 elections showed, many people have a deep-seated distrust of institutions and the feeling that we must take the future into our own hands. As a consequence, individuals joined together to storm the Capitol. This means that even in an age of pluralism individuals need community to make their convictions heard. Fortunately, we could say, these people were driven back and peace was at least temporarily restored. Trying to realize your convictions whether jointly or as an individual is usually met with very limited success. Therefore, there is much frustration and resignation. The same was true in antiquity. The general mood was one of resignation and people lived according to the motto quoted by Paul: "Let us eat and drink, for tomorrow we die" (1 Cor 15:32). A similar sentiment is portrayed by the Stoic idea of the eternal recurrence of the same, and by the "wheel of time" in Hinduism and Buddhism. There is nothing new under the sun, just another configuration of the same. Yet the Christian faith portrays a linear hope that knows of fulfillment beyond space and time.

The Christian faith broke through the latent or overt pessimism of antiquity and of the Eastern religions. It had something different to offer, the trust in a personal God and the assurance that through Jesus Christ this God has given us the hope in an eternal, everlasting life of which this life is only a faint semblance. Since God was understood by Jesus as a loving Father, this newfound hope was carried by Christians to their own kind and also to others. In a self-centered environment such hope was truly countercultural and attractive for many who yearned for fulfillment and peace. The diaconal support system of the church made an especially deep impression and won many people for the Christian faith. Emperor Julian the Apostate (331–363), who intended to revert the Roman Empire back to the old religions, wanted to imitate this work of Christian love but did so in vain. He wrote to Arsacius, the high priest of Galatia: "While even the impious Galileans [i.e., the Christians] provide not only for those of their own party who are in want, but also for those who hold with us, it would indeed be disgraceful if we were to allow our own people to suffer from poverty."[1] But this support for which the emperor called did not come forth from the Roman religion. The Christians, however, who initially only supported their own members, helped non-Christians too if they were in need.

1. Quoted in Sozomen, *Ecclesiastical History* (V:16), *NPNFa SS* 2:338.

Being only a small group in a corner of the huge Roman empire, Christianity spread amazingly fast from one corner to the other. Why should such a success not be possible for us today? As long as the churches are faithful and are focused on their mission to lead people into a growing relationship with God through Jesus Christ, we need not to be afraid of the future.

2. POINTERS TOWARD A VIABLE CHURCH

The church is inherently communal. What we can do together by far surpasses that which we can do alone. Therefore, there will always be an organized church of some form. We need each other for encouragement, correction, and direction. The church also provides an important form of companionship and fellowship and a place for conversation for many members who otherwise live in isolation.

Consumer Christians ask what they can get out of the church and if their needs are not met, they often withdraw. Though we should carefully listen to people's needs and expectations, we cannot cater to everybody's wishes. While some will enjoy what we do as a congregation, others will be disappointed. Since Christians ought to proclaim Christ in word and deed, we should never follow the expectations of the people or of society. We must be decidedly countercultural, offering that which is not of this world but that which the world needs. We should be careful not to focus primarily on ourselves and our viewpoints. Our prime focus is on Jesus and the world that he redeemed. Just like Jesus, we must be focused on other people and not primarily on ourselves. We must treat them with kindness and compassion in everyday life and attend to their spiritual well-being. Of course, we still have to make decisions in our congregations about music, worship times, involvement in social justice, and attending to physical needs. But as Bonhoeffer reminded us, we must be a church for others and not for ourselves. I remember one couple in our congregation whose prime interest in giving was to donate for benevolence. The care and love for others was one of the key factors for the rapid expansion of the first century church. This means that the church has to equip people to live out their faith in the world. Not withdrawal from the world but engagement in the world is the key factor for which the church must prepare its members. But for this engagement in the world the members must also be given some time free from church activities.

In the wake of the COVID-19 pandemic discussion arose around the online church. The online churches might be the church for some who do not have any other access to the church, such as homebound people. But in the long run human relationships require physical presence. Therefore, the online church can serve as a supplement in time of crisis but not as a substitute for communal worship. While online relationships are real relationships, they are not the greatest relationships people can have. Online churches have the potential to become a massive front door for the curious, the unconvinced, and for those who want to know what Christianity is all about. Churches' online presence can become the first home for people, which eventually may lead to a personal encounter with Christ and ultimately to the gathered church.

Let me finish this epilogue with seven pointers toward a viable church (most of these assertions are phrased in the indicative mood, since they should naturally ensue from our Christian existence and are not be understood as a new law):

(1) *The Christian church engenders a passion for Christ*: Without apology Christians love Christ. They live a faith which moves their hearts. Faith is more than a worldview, it is an orientation toward Christ as the leader of our lives. This relieves us from seeking meaning in this life alone, because this life is a preparation for the life to come. Since we have this all-powerful guide for our lives, we need not be afraid of the future. Whatever may come, Christ will be on our side.

"Christ alone" was Martin Luther's conviction. There are no other authorities that could be joined to Christ. He demands our exclusive allegiance. Jesus enjoined us: "Who acknowledges me before others, I also will acknowledge before my Father in heaven; but whoever denies me before others, I will also deny before my Father in heaven" (Matt 10:32–33).

(2) *The Christian church engenders a love for the Bible and for prayer*: Especially for Lutherans "Scripture alone" should be a natural. Often, however, the Bible is the most unread book on our bookshelves. It seems amazing when we read that most people today consider the Ten Commandments to be very important. But the majority of people cannot even recite all of the Ten Commandments. The question is, how can they order their lives according to these divine precepts when they do not even know what they are? Daily Bible reading in an informative, critical, and still dedicated way, must be learned in the church. For this we should conduct Bible studies and have prayer groups. We should pray for our congregation, for society, for the church at large, and for the world. Again, this must be learned in the church because quite often an active prayer life no longer takes place in families. The Christian church is also a singing church, even if our voices are not trained. Our gatherings should always start with singing a hymn. A songbook can also be a prayer book, as the book of Psalms reminds us.

(3) *The Christian church engenders a movement for mission*: Christians witness Jesus Christ to the world in their private and public lives. I have often been surprised when former students told me how important this or that remark of mine was in their lives. We are usually unaware of the impact of our words and actions. Especially as Lutherans we talk about the priesthood of all believers. But do we as Christians invite everyone to faith in Jesus Christ or at least to visit our congregation? I remember a woman working in a department store. After she found out that I was a Lutheran she insisted that I visit her congregation because her pastor and her congregation were just great. I did not visit since I was fine with the congregation to which I was attached. A few weeks later I happened to meet her again in that store and again she told me that I should surely visit her congregation and I did attend the following Sunday, simply to be kind to her. She was there and introduced me to different members. This is evangelism. But those we lose in numbers we can only win back one by one. Once people have dropped out denominational reaffiliation is not all that common. Yet there is still the possibility of winning some unaffiliated "nones" back to the church. "What stands out for most of these converts is that they eventually took up religious affiliation and involvement upon the invitation of a trusted friend, some of whom were converts themselves."[2] In other words, we must first win their confidence and only then is there a chance that we might win them back. Building up trust and having patience are important ingredients for doing mission. This has also been the case in doing foreign mission. For instance, it took "thirteen long years of missionary toil" until Lutheran missionaries in Papua New Guinea could baptize the first local people in 1899.[3] But due to the labors of the missionaries Lutherans are now a large contingent of the population in this country. Mission can pay off.

There is something else that is right next to evangelism and that is diaconal work. Word and deed, evangelism and diaconal actions, belong together. Christians should "testify about how their Christian faith makes a difference in the world."[4] In everything we say and do we are called to live out our Christian vocation. No congregation exists for long without spreading the gospel in word and deed through its individual members. It is through this that the creativity of the communal life of a congregation is shown.

(4) *The Christian church engenders a movement that has a responsibility for the world*: It is the task of every Christian to cultivate God's creation and

2. Thiessen and Wilkins-Laflamme, *None of the Above*, 53.

3. Wagner and Reiner, eds., *Lutheran Church in Papua New Guinea*, 41.

4. Nessan, "Tear down Magical Walls," 6:9.

to be a good steward of this creation. This includes protecting life in every form and standing up for the weak and the needy and respecting the dignity of every person. This is the case for medical ethics as much as for rescuing people who are fleeing for their lives from their regions or even from their countries. But it also includes stewardship of the earth. Are we wasting nonrenewable resources at home and in our congregation or are we really conscious of our obligation to care for the earth?

(5) *The Christian church engenders a distinction between ideologies and the Christian faith*: Throughout the centuries the Christian faith has been misused to propagate ideologies, for instance by the so-called German Christians promoting the Nazi ideology, i.e., national socialism, in the 1930s. Yet Christians know the difference between the world and Jesus Christ. The world is ruled by God through politics and sometimes even by ideologies. Yet the Christian faith is supported by the gospel. The Christian knows that ideologies come and go and politics change. The gospel, however, stays until Christ comes again. Therefore, ideologies and politics always take second place for Christians as things that strictly belong to this world and are subject to God's judgment.

(6) *The Christian church engenders space for education and science*: Since God created us with hearts and minds, we do not shy away from education and science but embrace them as God's gifts. At the same time, we are aware of our responsibility that education and science furthers the human good and does not endanger it. There is no reason to reject scientific claims and findings as long as they make us better understand the world in which we live. Creationism and scientism are ideologies that have nothing to do with our Christian faith. This also applies to modern medicine. If God provides for us through human ingenuity an effective vaccine to fight COVID-19 there is no reason for Christians to reject it, as if it were something slyly disseminated by the devil.

(7) *The Christian church engenders the feeling for aesthetics, style, and appropriateness for our time*: While Christians are good stewards of the gifts that are entrusted to them, too much thrift is not appropriate for any congregation and also not for the individual life of a Christian. Our church services, music, and congregational edifices should be attractive for a diversity of people and mirror the beauty of God's creation. They should also bear witness to our love for others.

Will these seven points help us to reach people in our postmodern time and lead them to become members of our congregational lives? If we simply look at what we do, we certainly will fail. If we look at Jesus as our guidepost and source of inspiration it might be slightly different. It depends on whether we become sojourners among our contemporaries in such a way that they feel we really have something to offer. Even today people are yearning for relationships that endure. In pointing to God in Christ we can offer them this kind of relationship. We have been given this potential in the great promise of God's grace. When we rediscover God in Christ as the center of our ecclesial existence and as the center of our personal lives, the future of the church need not look so bleak.

Bibliography

Aland, Kurt. *Did the Early Church Baptize Infants?* Translated with an introduction by G. R. Beasley-Murray. Preface by John Frederick Jansen. London: SCM, 1961; reprint Eugene, OR: Wipf & Stock, 2004.

Albright, William Foxwell. *Yahweh and the Gods of Canaan: A Historical Analysis of Two Contrasting Faiths*. Garden City, NY: Doubleday Anchor, 1969.

Badham, Paul, and Linda Badham. "Death and Immortality in the Religions of the World: An Editorial Survey." In *Death and Immortality in the Religions of the World*, edited by Paul and Linda Badham, 1–8. New York: Paragon, 1987.

Baillie, John. *The Belief in Progress*. New York: Scribner's, 1951.

The Barmen Declaration. https://www.ekd.de/en/The-Barmen-Declaration-303.htm.

Barth, Karl. *CD*, vol. 2/2: *The Doctrine of God*. Ed. G. W. Bromiley and T. F. Torrance. Edinburgh: T. & T. Clark, 1957.

———. "Fifteen Answers to Professor von Harnack." In *The Beginning of Dialectic Theology*, edited by James M. Robinson, translated by K. R. Crim and L. D. Grazia, 167–70. Richmond, VA: John Knox, 1962.

———. "Gospel and Law." In *God, Grace and Gospel. Scottish Journal of Theology* Occasional Paper no. 8. Translated by J. S. McNab, 1–28. Edinburgh: Oliver and Boyd, 1958.

———. *The Teaching of the Church Regarding Baptism*. Translated by E. A. Payne. London: SCM, 1948.

———. "The Word of God and the Task of the Ministry." 1922. In *The Word of God and the Word of Man*, translated by Douglas Horton, 183–217. New York: Harper Torchbooks, 1957.

Barth, Karl, and Eduard Thurneysen. *Die große Barmherzigkeit*. Munich: Christian Kaiser, 1935.

Beckwith, Roger. "The Age of Admission to the Lord's Supper." *Westminster Theological Journal* 38 (Winter 1976) 123–51.

Bennett, John C. *Christians and the State*. New York: Charles Scribner's, 1958.

Benz, Ernst. *Evolution and Christian Hope: Man's Concept of the Future from the Early Fathers to Teilhard de Chardin*. Translated by Heinz G. Frank. Garden City, NY: Doubleday Anchor, 1968.

Bingener, Reinhard. ". . .Jüngere sind gegenüber der Kirche oft gleichgültig." In *Frankfurter Allgemeine Zeitung*, July 14, 2021. https://www.faz.net/redaktion/reinhard-bingener-11104253.html?offset=14#authorPagination.

Böckenförde, Ernst-Wolfgang. *Staat, Gesellschaft, Freiheit*. Frankfurt a. M.: Suhrkamp, 1976.

Bonhoeffer, Dietrich. *The Communion of Saints: A Dogmatic Inquiry into the Sociology of the Church*. Translated by R. G. Smith. New York: Harper, 1963.

———. *The Cost of Discipleship*. Rev. ed. Translated by Reginald H. Fuller. London: SCM, 1959.

———. *Letters and Papers from Prison*. Rev. ed. Edited by Eberhard Bethge; translated by R. Fuller. New York: Macmillan, 1967.

———. *Life Together*. Translated by John W. Doberstein. New York: Harper, 1954.

Brand, Eugene L. "Baptism and Communion of Infants: A Lutheran View." *Worship* 50 (January 1976) 29.

Breaking Barriers, Nairobi 1975: The Official Report of the Fifth Assembly of the World Council of Churches, Nairobi, 23 November–10 December, 1975. Edited by David M. Patton. Grand Rapids: Eerdmans, 1976.

Brenan, Megan. "40% of Americans Believe in Creationism." July 26, 2019. https://news.gallup.com/poll/261680/americans-believe-creationism.aspx.

Brunner, Emil. *Justice and the Social Order*. Translated by M. Hottinger. New York: Harper, 1945.

Bühlmann, Walbert. *The Coming of the Third Church: An Analysis of the Present and the Future of the Church*. Translated by Ralph Woodhall and A. N. Other. Maryknoll, NY: Orbis, 1977.

Calvin, John. *Institutes of the Christian Religion*. Vol. 20 of *The Library of Christian Classics*. Edited by John T. McNeill. Translated by F. L. Battles. Philadelphia: Westminster, 1960.

Code of Canon Law. https://www.vatican.va/archive/cod-iuris-canonici/eng/documents/cic_lib2 cann204-207_en.html.

Cohn, Norman. *The Pursuit of the Millennium: Revolutionary Millenarians and Mystical Anarchists in the Middle Ages*. Rev. and expanded ed. New York: Oxford University Press, 1970.

Collingwood, R. G. *The Idea of History*. London: Oxford University Press, 1967.

Congregation for the Doctrine of the Faith. *Declaration "Dominus Iesus." On the Unicity and Salvific Universitality of Jesus Christ and the Church*. http://www.vatican.va/roman_curia/congregations/cfaith/documents/rc_con_cfaith_doc_20000806_dominus-iesus_en.html.

Conzelmann, Hans. *1 Corinthians: A Commentary on the First Epistle to the Corinthians*. Translated by James W. Leitch. Bibliography and references by James W. Dunkly. Edited by George W. MacRae. Philadelphia: Fortress, 1975.

Cox, Harvey. *The Secular City: Secularization and Urbanization in Theological Perspective*. Rev. ed. New York: Macmillan, 1968.

Cyprian. *De Lapsis and De Ecclesiae Catholicae Unitate*. Text and translation by M. Bévenot. Oxford: Clarendon, 1971.

Davies, J. G. *Christians, Politics and Violent Revolutions*. Maryknoll, NY: Orbis, 1976.

Descartes, René. *Discourse Concerning the Method*. In *René Descartes: The Essential Writings*, translated with an introduction and concordance by John J. Blom, 101–66. New York: Harper Torchbooks, 1977.

Drinan, Robert F. *Religion, the Courts, and Public Policy*. New York: McGraw-Hill, 1963.

Engels, Friedrich. "On the History of Early Christianity." In *On Religion*, by Karl Marx and Friedrich Engels; introduction by Reinhold Niebuhr, 275–302. New York: Schocken, 1964.

Die Eucharistie: Das Sagorsker Gespräch über das hl. Abendmahl zwischen Vertretern der Evangelischen Kirche in Deutschland und der Russischen Orthodoxen Kirche. Edited by Kirchliche Aussenamt der Evangelischen Kirche in Deutschland. Bielefeld: Luther-Verlag, 1974.

Eusebius. *The Church History.* A new translation with commentary by Paul L. Maier. Grand Rapids: Kregel, 1999.

Fahmy, Dalia. "Key Findings about Americans' Belief in God." April 25, 2018. https://www.pewresearch.org/fact-tank/2018/04/25/key-findings-about-americans-belief-in-god/.

Finke, Roger, and Rodney Stark. *The Churching of America, 1776–1990: Winners and Losers in Our Religious Economy.* New Brunswick, NJ: Rutgers University Press, 1992.

Fransen, Piet. "Orders and Ordination." In *Sacramentum Mundi.* Vol 4. New York: Herder and Herder, 1968–1970.

Fretheim, Terence E. *The Book of Genesis.* The New Interpreter's Bible, vol. 4. Nashville: Abingdon, 1994.

Gilkey, Langdon. *Reaping the Whirlwind. A Christian Interpretation of History.* New York: Seabury, 1976.

———. *Religion and the Scientific Future: Reflections on Myth, Science, and Theology.* New York: Harper & Row, 1970.

———. "A Retrospective Glance at My Work." In *The Whirlwind in Culture. Frontiers in Theology*, edited by Donald W. Musser and Joseph L. Price, 1–35. Bloomington, IN: Meyer-Stone, 1988.

Goethe, Johann Wolfgang von. *Faust*, Parts 1 and 2. Translated by G. M. Priest. Vol. 47 of *Great Books of the Western World*, edited by Robert M. Hutchins. Chicago: Encyclopaedia Britannica, 1952.

Goulet, Dennis. *A New Moral Order: Studies in Development Ethics and Liberation Theology.* Foreword by Paulo Freire. Maryknoll, NY: Orbis, 1974.

Green, Robert W., ed. *Protestantism and Capitalism: The Weber Thesis and Its Critics.* 2nd ed. Boston: Heath, 1973.

Greenberg, Moshe. "Mankind, Israel and the Nations in the Hebraic Heritage." In *No Man Is Alien: Essays on the Unity of Mankind*, edited by J. Robert Nelson, 15–40. Leiden: Brill, 1971.

Gritsch, Eric W. "Infant Communion. Old Bone in New Contention." *Lutheran Forum* 13 (Lent 1979).

Gros, Jeffrey, Thomas F. Best, and Lorelei F. Fuchs, eds. *Growth in Agreement III: International Dialogue Texts and Agreed Statements, 1998–2005.* Grand Rapids: Eerdmans, 2007.

Harnack, Adolf. "Fifteen Questions to Those among the Theologians Who Are Contemptuous of the Scientific Theology." In *The Beginning of Dialectic Theology*, edited by James M. Robinson, translated by K. R. Crim and L. D. Grazia, 165–66. Richmond, VA: John Knox, 1962.

Harrod, Andrew E. "Always Declining: The Evangelical Lutheran Church in America's Stillborn Quarter Century of Existence." *Juicy Ecumenism*, August 14, 2013.

https://juicyecumenism.com/2013/08/14/always-declining-the-evangelical-lutheran-church-in-americas-stillborn-quarter-century-of-existence/.

Hefele, Karl. *History of the Councils: From the Original Documents*. Vol. 1. Translated and edited by William R. Clark. Edinburgh: T. & T. Clark, 1894.

The Heidelberg Catechism. https://www.crcna.org/welcome/beliefs/confessions/heidelberg-catechism.

Herodotus. *The History of Herodotus*. Translated by George Rawlinson. Edited by Manuel Komroff. New York: Tudor, 1932.

Hitler, Adolf. "Der Staatsmann entscheidet nicht über Glaubens- und Bekenntnisfragen." In *Der nationalsozialistische Staat und die religiösen Bekenntnisse*, 3rd ed., by Gotthilf Herrmann, 9. Zwickau: Johannes Herrmann, 1934.

Höllinger, Franz. "Die Erfahrung der Präsenz des Göttlichen: Religiöse Kultur in Brasilien, den USA und Westeuropa." In *Woran glaubt die Welt? Analysen und Kommentare zum Religionsmonitor 2008*, edited by Bertelsmann Stiftung, 453–80. Gütersloh: Bertelsmann Stiftung, 2009.

Hodgson, Robert, Jr. "Holiness (NT)." *ABD* 3:249–54.

Huber, Wolfgang. "evangelisch.de." June 12, 2020. https://www.evangelisch.de/inhalte/171290/12-06-2020/huber-kirche-ist-nicht-systemrelevant-sondern-existenzrelevant.

Jefferson, Thomas. "Letter to the Danbury Baptist Association in Connecticut." January 1, 1802. https://founders.archives.gov/documents/Jefferson/01-36-02-0152-0006.

Jeremias, Joachim. *Infant Baptism in the First Four Centuries*. Translated by David Cairns. London: SCM, 1960; reprint: Eugene, OR: Wipf & Stock, 2004.

———. *The Origins of Infant Baptism: A Further Study in Reply to Kurt Aland*. Translated by Dorothea M. Barton. London: SCM, 1962; reprint: Eugene, OR: Wipf and Stock, 2004.

Joas, Hans. "Religion heute. Die USA als Trendsetter für Europa?" In *Religionsmonitor 2008*, edited by Bertelsmann Stiftung, 179–85. 2nd ed. Gütersloh: Bertelsmann Stiftung, 2008.

John Paul II. "General Audience." September 29, 1999. https://www.vatican.va/content/john-paul-ii/en/audiences/1999/documents/hf_jp-ii_aud_29091999.html.

Johnson, Elizabeth A. *Friends of God and Prophets*. New York: Continuum, 1999.

Kant, Immanuel. "What Is Enlightenment?" In *The Philosophy of Kant: Immanuel Kant's Moral and Political Writings*, edited with an introduction by Carl J. Friedrich, 132–39. New York: Random House, 1949.

Kasper, Walter. "Law and Gospel." In *Sacramentum Mundi* vol. 3. New York: Herder and Herder, 1968–1970.

Kaufhold, Martin. "Heutige Probleme in der Kirche wurzeln im Mittelalter." *Allgäuer Zeitung*, February 22, 2021. https://www.allgaeuer-zeitung.de/bayern/historiker-heutige-probleme-in-der-kirche-wurzeln-im-mittelalter_arid-271360.

Kaufman, Gordon D. *Systematic Theology: A Historicist Perspective*. New York: Charles Scribner's, 1968.

Keating, Karl. "What Does the Expression 'Ex Opere Operato' Mean?" https://www.catholic.com/qa/what-does-the-expression-ex-opere-operato-mean.

Künneth, Walter. *Politik zwischen Damon und Gott: Eine christliche Ethik des Politischen*. Berlin: Lutherisches Verlagshaus, 1954.

Lessing, Gotthold Ephraim. *The Education of the Human Race*. In *Lessing's Theological Writings*, selected and translated with an introductory essay by Henry Chadwick, 82–98. London: Adam & Charles Black, 1956.

The Leuenberg Concord. Translated by John Drickamer. In *The Springfielder* 35 (March 1972) 241–49.

Lewis, A. J. *Zinzendorf. The Ecumenical Pioneer. A Study in the Moravian Contribution to Christian Mission and Unity*. Philadelphia: Westminster, 1962.

Löwith, Karl. *Meaning in History: The Theological Implications of the Philosophy of History*. Chicago: University of Chicago Press, 1949.

Lutheran Book of Worship. Minneapolis: Augsburg, 1978.

Lutheran Congregations in Mission for Christ. https://en.wikipedia.org/wiki/Lutheran_Congregations_in_Mission_for_Christ.

Marx, Karl. "Theses on Feuerbach." In *On Religion*, by Karl Marx and Friedrich Engels; introduction by Reinhold Niebuhr, 62–64. New York: Schocken, 1964.

Mead, Sidney E. "Denominationalism: The Shape of Protestantism in America." *Church History* 23 (December 1954) 291–320.

Moltmann, Jürgen. *The Church in the Power of the Spirit: A Contribution to Messianic Ecclesiology*. Translated by Margaret Kohl. New York: Harper & Row, 1977.

———. *The Coming of God: Christian Eschatology*. Translated by Margaret Kohl. Minneapolis: Fortress, 1996.

Nelson, J. Robert. "Signs of Mankind's Solidarity." In *No Man Is Alien: Essays on the Unity of Mankind*, edited by J. Robert Nelson, 1–14. Leiden: Brill, 1971.

Nessan, Craig L. "Tear down Magical Walls." *Living Lutheran*, June/July 2021. https://www.livinglutheran.org/2021/07/my-take-tear-down-magical-walls/.

Niebuhr, H. Richard. *Christ and Culture*. New York: Colophon, 1975.

———*The Kingdom of God in America*. New York: Harper Torchbooks, 1959.

———. *The Meaning of Revelation*. New York: Macmillan, 1967.

———. *Radical Monotheism and Western Culture: With Supplementary Essays*. Foreword James M. Gustafson. Louisville: Westminster John Knox, 1993.

———. *The Social Sources of Denominationalism*. New York: P. Smith, 1987.

———. *Theology, History, and Culture: Major Unpublished Writings*. Edited by William Stacy Johnson. Foreword by Richard R. Niebuhr. New Haven: Yale University Press, 1996.

Niebuhr, Reinhold. *Beyond Tragedy: Essays on the Christian Interpretation of History*. New York: Charles Scribner's, 1946.

Nietzsche, Friedrich. *The Birth of Tragedy* Or: *Hellenism and Pessimism*. In *The Birth of Tragedy and The Case of Wagner*, translated with a commentary by Walter Kaufmann, 3–146. New York: Random House Vintage, 1967.

Pannenberg, Wolfhart. "Das Abendmahl—Sakrament der Einheit." In *Ethik und Ekklesiologie*, 286–92. Göttingen: Vandenhoeck & Ruprecht, 1977.

Pew Research Center. "Members of the Evangelical Lutheran Church in America (ELCA)." https://www.pewforum.org/religious-landscape-study/religious-denomination/evangelical-lutheran-church-in-america-elca/.

———. "Religion and the Unaffiliated." October 9, 2012. https://www.pewforum.org/2012/10/09/nones-on-the-rise-religion/.

Pollack, Detlef. "Wer einmal austritt, kommt nicht wieder." *Publik-Forum*, March 26, 2021. https://www.publik-forum.de/Religion-Kirchen/wer-einmal-austritt-kommt-nicht-wieder.

Pollack, Detlef, and Olaf Müller. *Religionsmonitor. Verstehen was verbindet. Religiosität und Zusammenhalt in Deutschland.* Gütersloh: Bertelsmann Stiftung, 2013.

The Porvoo Communion. http://porvoocommunion.evlutkirkko.fi/porvoo_communion/statement/the-statement-in-english/.

Rad, Gerhard von. "The Theological Problem of the Old Testament Doctrine of Creation." In *The Problem of the Hexateuch and Other Essays,* translated by E. W. Trueman Dicken, 131–43. Edinburgh: Oliver & Boyd, 1966.

Radziszewski, Nicole. "The Shrinking Church." *The Living Lutheran*, January 7, 2013. https://www.livinglutheran.org/2013/01/shrinking-church/.

Rahner, Karl. "Christianity and the Non-Christian Religions." In *Theological Investigations*, vol. 5: *Later Writings*, translated by K. H. Kruger, 115–34. Baltimore: Helicon, 1966.

———. *Foundations of Christian Faith: An Introduction to the Idea of Christianity.* Translated by William V. Dych. New York: Seabury, 1978.

———. "The Word and the Eucharist." In *Theological Investigations*, vol. 4: *More Recent Writings*, translated by K. Smyth, 253–86. Baltimore: Helicon, 1966.

Ravin, Arnold R. "Science, Values, and Human Evolution." *Zygon* 11 (June 1976) 138–54.

Remmers, Johannes. "Apostolic Succession: An Attribute of the Whole Church." Translated by J. Drury. *Concilium*, vol. 34: *Apostolic Succession. Rethinking a Barrier to Unity*, edited by Hans Küng, 36–51. New York: Paulist, 1968.

Report of the Salamanca Consultation. "The Unity of the Church—Next Steps." Reprinted in *Ecumenical Review* 26 (April 1974) 131–43.

Sampley, J. Paul. *The First Letter to the Corinthians.* New Interpreter's Bible 10. Nashville: Abingdon, 2002.

Scanlon, Regis. "Is Christ 'Really' Among Us Today?" https://www.catholicculture.org/culture/library/view.cfm?recnum=7081.

Schleiermacher, Friedrich. *The Christian Faith.* Edited by H. R. Mackintosh and J. S. Stewart. Introduction by Richard R. Niebuhr. New York: Harper Torchbooks, 1963.

Schulte, Raphael. "Sacraments." In *Sacramentum Mundi* vol. 5. New York: Herder and Herder, 1968–1970.

Schwarz, Hans. *The Human Being.* Grand Rapids: Eerdmans, 2013.

"Scripture, Tradition and Traditions." In *The Fourth World Conference on Faith and Order, Montréal 1963*, edited by P. C. Rodger and Lukas Vischer, 50–60. New York: Association, 1964.

Shell Jugendstudie 2020. https://www.shell.de/ueber-uns/shell-jugendstudie.html.

Sider, Ronald, ed. *The Chicago Declaration of Evangelicals.* Carol Stream, IL: Creation House, 1974.

Siebert, Ludwig. "Die Kirche ist unpolitisch!" In *Der nationalsozialistische Staat und die religiösen Bekenntnisse,* 3rd ed., by Gotthilf Herrmann, 15. Zwickau: Johannes Herrmann, 1934.

Sölle, Dorothee. *Political Theology.* Translated with an introduction by J. Shelley. Philadelphia: Fortress, 1974.

———. *Suffering.* Translated by E. R. Kallin. Philadelphia: Fortress, 1975.

Thiessen, Joel, and Sarah Wilkins-Laflamme. *None of the Above: Nonreligious Identity in the US and Canada.* New York: New York University Press, 2020.

Tillich, Paul. *Systematic Theology*. Vol. 1: *Reason and Revelation. Being and God.* Chicago: University of Chicago Press, 1951.

Toynbee, Arnold J. *Civilization on Trial*. London: Oxford University Press, 1946.

Troeltsch, Ernst. *Protestantism and Progress: A Historical Study of the Relation of Protestantism to the Modern World.* Translated by W. Montgomery. Boston: Beacon, 1958.

Uhlhorn, Gerhard. *Christian Charity in the Ancient Church*. New York: Scribner's, 1883.

Unterburger, Klaus. "Das System könnte in 20 Jahren implodieren." *Mittelbayerische Zeitung*, February 23, 2021. https://www.mittelbayerische.de/region/regensburg-stadt-nachrichten/katholische-kirche-geraet-in-schieflage-21179-art1981635.html.

Wagner, Herwig, and Hermann Reiner, eds. *The Lutheran Church in Papua New Guinea: The First Hundred Years 1886–1986*. Adelaide: Lutheran Publishing, 1986.

Weber, Max. *The Protestant Ethic and the Spirit of Capitalism.* Translated by T. Parsons. Foreword by R. H. Tawney. London: Allen & Unwin, 1948.

Whitehead, Alfred North. *Process and Reality: An Essay in Cosmology*. New York: Macmillan, 1929.

Winter, Gibson. *The New Creation as Metropolis*. New York: Macmillan, 1963.

Wirt, Sherwood E. *The Social Conscience of the Evangelical*. New York: Harper, 1968.

World Council of Churches. *The Church: Towards a Common Vision*. Faith and Order Paper No. 214. Geneva: World Council of Churches, 2013.

———. *One Baptism, One Eucharist, and a Mutually Recognized Ministry*. Three Agreed Statements. Faith and Order Paper No. 73. Geneva: World Council of Churches, 1975.

Zscheile, Dwight. "Will the ELCA Be Gone in Thirty Years?" In *the faith + leader*, September 2019. https://faithlead.luthersem.edu/decline/.

Index of Names

Index of Subjects

Made in the USA
Las Vegas, NV
01 February 2024

85183774R00121